Twayne's New Critical Introductions to Shakespeare

Twayne's New Critical
Introductions to Shakespeare

A MIDSUMMER NIGHT'S DREAM

James L. Calderwood

TWAYNE PUBLISHERS · NEW YORK
An imprint of Macmillan Publishing Co.

Published in the United States by Twayne Publishers,
imprint of Macmillan Publishing Co.,
866 Third Avenue, New York, NY 10022

Published simultaneously in Great Britain by
Harvester Wheatsheaf
Campus 400, Maylands Avenue, Hemel Hempstead, Herts

Twayne's New Critical Introductions to Shakespeare, no. 14

Library of Congress Cataloging-in-Publication Data

Calderwood, James L.
    A midsummer night's dream / James Calderwood.
      p.   cm. — (Twayne's new critical introductions to Shakespeare
: no. 14)
    Includes bibliographical references and index.
    ISBN 0–8057–8733–X (cloth). — ISBN 0–8058–8734–8 (pbk.)
I. Title.   II. Series.
PR2827.C34   1992
822.3′3—dc20   92–22796
                                           CIP

Titles in the Series

GENERAL EDITOR: GRAHAM BRADSHAW

Jane Adamson	*Troilus and Cressida*
James L. Calderwood	*A Midsummer Night's Dream*
Maurice Charney	*Titus Andronicus*
Harriett Hawkins	*Measure for Measure*
Alexander Leggatt	*King Lear*
Michael Long	*Macbeth*
John Lyon	*The Merchant of Venice*
A. D. Nuttall	*Timon of Athens*
Adrian Poole	*Coriolanus*
Wilbur Sanders	*The Winter's Tale*
Vivian Thomas	*Julius Caesar*
J. P. Ward	*As You Like It*
Cedric Watts	*Hamlet*
Cedric Watts	*Romeo and Juliet*
R. S. White	*The Merry Wives of Windsor*
Sheldon P. Zitner	*All's Well That Ends Well*

Contents

General Editor's Preface   xi

Acknowledgements   xiii

A Midsummer Night's Dream: A Note on the Text   xiv

A Midsummer Night's Dream: The Stage History and Critical
    Reception   xx

1. The Law of the Father   1

2. Desire, the Eyes and the Gaze   23

3. The Anamorphic Gaze and Theseus' Dream   48

4. Liminality: Puck's Door   72

5. Names and Translators   97

6. Walls, Partitions and Performances   117

7. Making Amends: Puck's Epilogue   146

Notes   159

References   202

Index   221

For Cleo, the fairest dame that lives, that loves, that likes, that looks with cheer.

General Editor's Preface

The *New Critical Introductions to Shakespeare* series will include studies of all Shakespeare's plays, together with two volumes on the non-dramatic verse, and is designed to offer a challenge to all students of Shakespeare.

Each volume will be brief enough to read in an evening, but long enough to avoid those constraints which are inevitable in articles and short essays. Each contributor will develop a sustained critical reading of the play in question, which addresses those difficulties and critical disagreements which each play has generated.

Different plays present different problems, different challenges and excitements. In isolating these, each volume will present a preliminary survey of the play's stage history and critical reception. The volumes then provide a more extended discussion of these matters in the main text, and of matters relating to genre, textual problems and the use of source material, or to historical and theoretical issues. But here, rather than setting a row of dragons at the gate, we have assumed that 'background' should figure only as it emerges into a critical foreground; part of the critical endeavour is to establish, and sift, those issues which seem most pressing.

So, for example, when Shakespeare determined that *his* Othello and Desdemona should have no time to live together, or that Cordelia dies while Hermione survives, his deliberate departures from his source material have a critical significance which is often blurred, when discussed in the context of lengthily detailed surveys of 'the sources'. Alternatively, plays like *The Merchant of Venice* or *Measure for Measure* show Shakespeare welding together different 'stories' from quite different sources, so that their relation to each other becomes a matter for critical debate. And Shakespeare's dramatic practice poses different critical questions when we ask − or if we ask: few do − why particular characters in a poetic drama speak only in verse or only in prose; or when we try to engage with those recent, dauntingly specialised and controversial textual studies which set out to establish the evidence for authorial revisions or joint authorship. We all read *King Lear* and *Macbeth*, but we are not all textual critics; nor are textual critics always able to show where their arguments have critical consequences which concern us all.

Just as we are not all textual critics, we are not all linguists, cultural anthropologists, psychoanalysts or New Historicists. The diversity of contemporary approaches to Shakespeare is unprecedented, enriching, bewildering. One aim of this series is to represent what is illuminating in this diversity. As the hastiest glance through the list of contributors will confirm, the series does not attempt to 'reread' Shakespeare by placing an ideological grid over the text and reporting on whatever shows through. Nor would the series' contributors always agree with each other's arguments, or premisses; but each has been invited to develop a sustained critical argument which will also provide its own critical and historical context − by taking account of those issues which have perplexed or divided audiences, readers, and critics past and present.

Graham Bradshaw

Acknowledgements

My thanks to Graham Bradshaw both for originally suggesting that I do one of the texts in the *New Critical Introductions to Shakespeare* series and for subsequently performing the duties of General Editor with graceful efficiency. I am especially indebted to Michael Clark, good colleague and close friend, for his patient willingness to expound upon psychoanalytic notions of such bottomless profundity that man would be but a patched fool if he would offer to say what they were.

An abbreviated version of Chapter 3 was printed in the *Shakespeare Quarterly* in 1991 as '*A Midsummer Night's Dream*: Anamorphism and Theseus's Dream', *SQ*, 42 (4): 409–30.

The text referred to throughout is that of David Bevington in his *The Complete Works of Shakespeare*, 3rd edition (1980). Citations of the sort '(Pepys 1970: 208)' or '(Stone 1965: 150)' refer to texts listed under 'References' at the end of the book. Comments, essays and asides either too peripheral or, more often, too indecent for the text proper nevertheless survive in semi-repressed form as endnotes – to which, I need hardly add, the wise reader may well wish to repair first and remain longest.

A Note on the Text

There are three early printed versions of *A Midsummer Night's Dream* – two quartos and the First Folio text. The First Quarto (Q1) was published by Thomas Fisher in 1600. The title page of the Second Quarto (Q2) says it was printed in 1600 by James Roberts, but in fact it was printed in 1619 by William Jaggard, who later printed the collected edition of Shakespeare's work, the First Folio of 1623, in which the third text of the play appears. Q1 seems to have been typeset from Shakespeare's 'foul paper' copy – that is, from the original script before it was revised into a final 'fair copy' draft and given to the company's prompter to annotate and copy into the prompt-book for use in the theatre. Printing from 'foul papers' sounds like a dubious project. In this case, however, foul papers are less foul than the term implies, because instead of transcribing and polishing them into a fair copy, as most playwrights did, Shakespeare habitually made corrections on them. Thus a text printed from these foul papers, as Q1 was, is actually quite reliable. Even so, there are a number of unmarked exits and, more important, entrances, as well as some inconsistencies in speech tags, especially regarding Puck, who is sometimes 'Puck' and sometimes 'Robin' or 'Rob' – the kinds of confusions to be expected in a text printed from the author's papers.

With the exception of five leaves, Q2 merely reprints Q1 (with additional stage directions based presumably on the prompt-book copy). And since the First Folio text reprints Q2 (adding still further stage directions but also further errors), editors usually regard Q1 as the most authoritative of the three. (It is the basis for the text I have used, edited by David Bevington and appearing in *The Complete Works of Shakespeare*, 3rd edition (1980).) I should add, however, that there is one significant difference between Q1 and the Folio. In the former, Hermia's father, Egeus, does not appear in the final scene; in the latter, he not only appears but is given lines assigned to Philostrate in Q1. As critics have recently noted (Hodgdon 1986; McGuire 1989), whether Egeus is present or absent here crucially affects an interpretation of the play, his absence in Q1 implying his refusal to acknowledge Hermia's wedding and his alienation from Athenian society, his presence in the Folio leaving room for various inferences ranging from an Egeus fully acceptant of the marriage to one too embittered even to speak to his daughter.

DATE

As with most of Shakespeare's plays, determining just when *A Midsummer Night's Dream* was written and first performed is something of an exercise in divination. For one thing, because 'writing' cannot be limited to the time when words are actually put down on paper, the date of any text is impossible to establish precisely. But even in the familiar sense of the word, the writing of *A Midsummer Night's Dream* is hard to date. Although the text of the play was not entered on the Stationer's Register – the official record of London booksellers and printers – until 8 October 1600, it's generally agreed that Shakespeare wrote the play and his company the Chamberlain's Men, staged it sometime between 1594 and 1596. A date earlier than 7 September 1598 is dictated by the registration on that day of Francis Meres' *Palladis Tamia, Wit's Treasury*, in which *A Midsummer Night's Dream* is listed as one of twelve plays by Shakespeare worthy of comparison to the classics; and a date later than 30 August 1594 is suggested in part because of the relevance to the play of the baptismal feast held on that day for Prince Henry, son of King James IV of Scotland (later James I of England). An account of the feast published in *A True Reportarie* in October 1594 mentions a chariot drawn into the presence of King James by a Moor:

> This chariot should have been drawne in by a lyon, but because his presence might have brought some feare to the nearest, or that the sights of the lights and the torches might have commoved his tameness, it was thought meete than the Moor should supply that room. (Brooks 1979: xxxiv)

Bringing a lion into a baptismal feast in Scotland evidently generated as much anxiety as bringing one 'among the ladies' during a performance of *Pyramus and Thisbe* in Athens. Of course the mere fact that a lion is called for in the plot of *Pyramus and Thisbe* may have been sufficient to inspire Shakespeare's foolery about the trials of theatrical realism, but, as Harold F. Brooks argues, knowing about the Scottish lion incident (if indeed he did) may well have contributed to his inspiration (Brooks 1979: xxxv; however, see Franke 1979: 285). If so, then the date of the play would be between mid-1594 and mid-1598. This period can be narrowed to 1595 or 1596 if, as is often assumed, the play were originally designed as entertainment for an aristocratic wedding (cf. Olson 1957; Siegel 1953). The leading candidates for this occasion are the wedding of William Stanley, Earl of Derby, to Elizabeth Vere, daughter of the Earl of Oxford, on 26 January 1595; that of Henry Percy, Earl of Northumberland, to Lady Dorothea Devereux, younger sister of the Earl of Essex, on 1 May 1595; and that of Thomas Berkeley and Elizabeth Carey on 19 February 1596. The last seems highly plausible in view of the fact that the bride was the granddaughter of Henry Carey, 1st Lord Hunsdon, who from 1585 had held the powerful post of Queen's Lord Chamberlain and from 1594 had been the patron of Shakespeare's company (Savage 1961; May 1984). What more likely than that the Lord Chamberlain's Men should be asked to provide a play to celebrate the wedding of the Lord Chamberlain's granddaughter?

On the other hand, John Draper (1972) makes a persuasive argument in favour of the Percy–Devereux wedding based on the theory that the right wedding would take place on 1 May in keeping with Theseus' remark on discovering the sleeping lovers, 'No doubt they rose up early to observe / The rite of May' (iv.i.131–2). Draper had earlier settled on 1 May 1595 as the likeliest date for the play's first performance, since that was the time when the new moon appeared in the sky along with Venus as the morning star (to which Oberon refers twice and Puck once (iii.ii.61, 107, 380)). Professor Draper puts Peter Quince in nearly total eclipse as a coordinator of calendars and celestial events:

A computation based on the transit of Venus across the sun on December 7, 1631 N.S. [New Style, i.e., by the Gregorian calendar], shows that the planet was in superior conjunction on March 1, 1595, and remained west of the sun until inferior conjunction on December 18. Its greatest western elongation – i.e., its greatest angular distance from the sun and therefore greatest prominence in the sky – was May 12 N.S., which would be May 2 according to the Julian calendar then used in England. Thus in 1595, it was a bright and very obvious morning star from the latter part of April into June; and further computation shows that this is the only year between 1592 and 1598 in which Venus was clearly visible at this season as a morning star [Draper 1938: 267]. . . . all these dates agree in showing an astronomical new moon on April 29, 1595 O.S.; and the thin crescent might be dimly visible on the following evening and more clearly on May first. On the years immediately preceding and following, moreover, no new moon fell near to May Day (Draper 1972: 268).

Hence the possibility that the Percy–Devereux wedding on 1 May 1595 was the occasion for which Shakespeare first wrote his play (Draper 1972; see also J. N. Brown 1980).

Not, whatever the case, that Shakespeare wrote *A Midsummer Night's Dream* to be performed on only one private occasion. Not even he could afford to be that prodigal with his scripts, and certainly no commercial acting company would have wanted him to be. Thus although the play is perfectly suited for private performance in a mansion before a noble wedding party, nothing in it is incompatible, assuming certain modifications, with an appearance on the public stage, which is no doubt where Francis Meres saw it sometime between 1596 and 1598.

SOURCES

The plot of *A Midsummer Night's Dream* is Shakespeare's own invention, but its components derive from several sources. Thomas North's translation (1579) of Amyot's French translation (1559) of Plutarch's *Lives of the Noble Grecians and Romans* provided him with the 'courtship' and wedding of Theseus and Hippolyta. Their transformation into 'Duke' Theseus and Queen Hippolyta derives from Shakespeare's reading of Chaucer's *The Knight's Tale* – 'Ther was a duc that highte Theseus'. There was also a Chaucerian wood, highte wood, into which on a May morning Duc Theseus rides to hunt deer 'With hunte and horn and houndes hym beside' (*Knight's Tale*, 1673–8), very much like the wood Theseus enters, apparently on 1 May, to the sound of the hunting horn and the harmonious baying of hounds. Again, in both texts two almost indistinguishable young men are rivals for the hand of a young woman. The resolution of this rivalry in *The Knight's Tale*, which features a trial by combat governed by Saturn, is comically paralleled in *A Midsummer Night's Dream*, where the woodsy trial by combat of Lysander and Demetrius is benevolently aborted by Puck and Oberon in the interests of love (Champion 1970: 47–59; Brooks 1979: lxxvii–lxxx; Thompson 1978; Donaldson 1985: 30–49; Mowat 1989: 338–41).

Of course Shakespeare complicates and squares off the love relationships by adding a second woman in *A Midsummer Night's Dream*, as he had
done previously in *A Comedy of Errors* and *Two Gentlemen of Verona*. The
latter play (and Montemayor's *Diana*, on which it is based) also includes the
kind of cross-courtship and recovery that occurs in *A Midsummer Night's
Dream* when one of the young men shifts his attentions to the other's lady
love and then comes to his senses. A nearer but less influential source may
have been John Lyly's play *Gallathea* (1584–8), which also features lovers
and a choice between virgin death and flight into a forest visited by
quarrelling deities and apprentice artisans. In the forest confusion
abounds, helped along by a mischievous spirit, and a transformation of one
of the lovers by the gods precipitates a happy return to the outside world
and everyone's participation in a wedding feast (Scragg 1982).

Shakespeare's assification of Bottom was probably inspired by Apuleius'
The Golden Ass, which because of its abstruse Latin he probably read in the
translation of William Adlington in 1566 (Tobin 1984). It relates the
adventures of a young man transformed into an ass, and one chapter in
particular recounts how a high-bred lady, albeit not a fairy queen, fell in
love with the bestial hero and insisted on bedding him. Again, in *The
Discoverie of Witchcraft* (1584) Reginald Scot scoffingly tells of a man
supposed to have been bewitched into the shape of an ass and laments
that St Augustine retailed and evidently believed similar stories of men
converted into horses and the like. Bottom's itchy ears may derive from the
familiar story (told by Ovid among others) of how Apollo bestowed ass's
ears on the presumptuous King Midas for calling Pan a better musician
than he. On the other hand, Shakespeare may have got the idea from
observing that donkeys like to have their ears scratched.

Reginald Scot also mentions Puck or Robin Goodfellow, but dismissively, as one of a host of fantastic beasts, spirits and bogeymen
employed by adults to frighten children but hardly to be credited by the
informed. Puck may come from the folk imagination, but Oberon very
likely comes, in name at least, from a French romance called *Huon de
Burdeux* (translated by Lord Berners around 1540), or perhaps from
Spenser's *The Faerie Queene*, II.i.8 (1590), or Greene's play *James IV* (1591),
in all of which he is a fairy king or elfin father. Titania's name appears in
Ovid's *Metamorphoses*, in reference to both Diana and Circe; and, as that
would suggest, Shakespeare's fairies may be to some extent a transforma-
tion of Ovid's pagan gods and goddesses, as was the case in medieval
romances like *Sir Orfeo* or in Chaucer's *Merchant's Tale* (Martindale and
Martindale 1990: 72). The rest of the fairy lore probably comes from
William and Mary Shakespeare, various aunts and uncles and local
Warwickshire sages, and even perhaps from a few nocturnal boyish

ventures into Arden Forest when, 'imagining some fear', how easy is the wind in the leaves supposed a flight of fairies.

The story of *Pyramus and Thisbe* Shakespeare took primarily from Ovid's *Metamorphoses* (Book IV), though there were other versions of the tale in Chaucer's *The Legend of Good Women* and various Elizabethan poems, most notably in Thomas Mouffet's *The Silkewormes and their Flies*. The latter, a poem full of hilarious *double entendres* by a poet with an incorrigibly single *entendre* mind, may have caught Shakespeare's eye as a wonderful source of parody (Muir 1954; but see Duncan-Jones 1981). Or, as E. Talbot Donaldson has argued (1985: 7–18), he may have taken some cues from Chaucer's *Tale of Sir Thopas*, itself a parody of the Middle English romance. As *Sir Thopas* mocks the worst features of romance, so the dramatic form and style in which Shakespeare casts his tale mock those of popular English plays of the 1570s and 1580s – ranting plays like *Horestes* and *Cambises*, 'tragical comedies' like *Damon and Pythias* and *Appius and Virginia*, and Heywood's 1561 translation of Seneca's *Hercules Furens* (Young 1966: 34–42). At the same time, the fears and foibles of Peter Quince's company of players had a far nearer source in Shakespeare's own theatrical experience coupled with a playful imagination.

As for non-dramatic sources: the drift of the young lovers from Athens out to the wood and back again seems associated with the festive pattern of 'going a-Maying' in rural Elizabethan England (Barber 1959: 3–35; Young 1966: 16–24). On the eve of May Day (1 May), but also at other times of the year – Midsummer's Eve and Whitsuntide, for example (Vlasopolos 1978) – villagers went into the forests to gather garlands and boughs and to bring back a maypole to dance around. These festivities are often held to derive from archaic fertility rituals. A related influence seems to have been the fond pageants, shows and tableaux presented at places like Kenilworth in 1575 and Elvetham in 1591 to entertain Queen Elizabeth during her progresses. For these, as for *A Midsummer Night's Dream*, Ovid's *Metamorphoses* furnished an abundance of chases through forests, battles with centaurs and especially occasions on which a Diana–Elizabeth figure could still the rude waters with an imperious glance, silence roaring beasts with a wave of her wand or glide about in 'maiden meditation' as Cupid's darts flew everywhere but into her impenetrably chaste heart (II.i.148–74).

Such tricks hath Shakespeare's strong imagination that all of these influences, literary and non-literary, come together like the lovers' stories of the night and grow to something of remarkably great constancy. Or do they? How, in fact, should we interpret Shakespeare's story of the night? If we look at the critical reception of the play, as I shall do in the following section, the answer to that question would seem to be 'variously'.

The Stage History and Critical Reception

Introductions to a play usually include a section on its 'stage history' and another on its 'critical history'. But this is a rather arbitrary division, inasmuch as each production is itself an act of criticism, expressed, to be sure, in the language of the theatre instead of the study. Theatrical language is, however, notoriously evanescent, and hence, to those of us who were not present, what was said and done on stage is normally available only in the language of the study after all. One such study belonged to Samuel Pepys, a frequent playgoer, in whose diary the Shakespearian performances he witnessed shrivelled into laconic recordings of pleasure or, more often, of displeasure. All that remains of a performance of *A Midsummer Night's Dream* at the King's Theatre on the night of 29 September 1662, for instance, is the following entry, the earliest known criticism of the play:

> [Went] to the King's Theatre, where we saw *Midsummers nights dreame*, which I have never seen before, nor shall ever again, for it is the most insipid ridiculous play that ever I saw in my life. I saw, I confess, some good dancing and some handsome women, which was all my pleasure. (Pepys 1970: 208)

Actually, this is not the earliest known criticism of the play. That honour would fall to a performance at the court of King James on New Year's night

1604, billed as *A Play of Robin Goodfellow*. If this was indeed *A Midsummer Night's Dream*, the modified title indicates where the appeal of the play was thought to lie. If it was not Shakespeare's play, then this is the first of several cannibalisations, the others being *The Comedy of Pyramus and Thisbe* (pre-1624) and an interregnum droll called *The Merry Conceits of Bottom the Weaver* (1646). All of this extraction and independent performing of parts of *A Midsummer Night's Dream* suggests that the antics of the fairies and the workmen were regarded as amusing but that audiences had difficulty grasping the play as a coherent whole.

But let me skip back to Pepys, whose distaste for the play may have been owing to the fact that stagings of it have so often taken their cue from the presence of fairies and presented it as a fairyland fantasia of song and dance. In 1692, for instance, Thomas Betterton transformed it with the aid of Purcell's music into an opera called *The Fairy Queen*, first of a series of operatic and mock-operatic stagings throughout the eighteenth century. By 1816, when Hazlitt saw *A Midsummer Night's Dream*, or at least something that went by that title, the play itself had disappeared beneath the cosmetic splendour of scenic and musical effects. 'The spirit was evaporated', he complained:

> the genius was fled; but the spectacle was fine: it was that which saved the play. Oh, ye scene-shifters, ye scene-painters, ye machinists and dress-makers, ye manufacturers of moon and stars that give no light, ye musical composers, ye men in the orchestra, fiddlers and trumpeters and players on the double drum and loud bassoon, rejoice! This is your triumph; it is not ours. (Sālgādo 1975: 117).

This sounds suspiciously as though Hazlitt were addressing Peter Quince's company of, if not 'machinists', mechanicals. For certainly the spirit and genius of *their* play, the 'tedious brief scene of young Pyramus / And his love Thisby', evaporates as the gimmickry of theatrical presentation condenses into a self-proclaiming Wall that blocks all vision and a talkative Moon that truly gives no light.

In Berlin a few years later, in 1827, the poet Ludwig Tieck continued the musical emphasis in a revival of the play for which Mendelssohn wrote his famous overture. Earlier, in 1755, David Garrick had subtracted the workmen and staged what he called *The Fairies*; and later, in 1911, Beerbohm Tree added live rabbits to the cast, along with other scenic marvels, to fashion an extravaganza that proved highly successful commercially. In 1914, Harley Granville-Barker got ninety-nine performances out of a production that featured fairies with gilded faces and golden thigh-pieces, having either arisen from Atlantis or descended from Venus. Until the 1970s, productions of the play continued to oscillate between the poles of masque and ballet, occasionally prompting a somewhat 'anti-poetic' reaction, especially in the late 1950s and 1960s, in which the buffoonery of the mechanicals was given full comic scope (Stratford, Conn. 1958, 1960; New York Shakespeare Festival 1961).

After a long run as a lightsome affair of music and dance ending on a high note of happiness, the play began to take on a different aspect around the turn of the twentieth century. Its darker implications were cited as early as 1904 by G. K. Chesterton, who felt that the reappearance of the fairies at the end of the festivities should blur the audience's sense of reality (Chesterton 1904: 14), and were intensified in 1932 by G. Wilson Knight, who claimed to see in the play 'a gnomish, fearsome, *Macbeth*-like quality . . . just touching nightmare' (Knight 1932: 69). But the most influential argument along these lines has been that of the Polish critic Jan Kott, who, taking a cue from illustrations featuring Bottom and Titania by the late eighteenth-century painter Henry Fuseli, finds brutality and eroticism beneath the veneer of romantic love. Thus Titania's drug-induced infatuation with Bottom becomes for Kott a rapacious but liberating desire for animal love, mirrored less obviously by the other lovers as they 'enter the dark sphere of animal love-making' (Kott 1964: 218).

Kott's interpretation of the play directly influenced Peter Brook, whose 1970 Royal Shakespeare Company production did its best to break with all prior productions by featuring not only an ithyphallic Bottom in fairyland but also Oberon and Puck aloft on trapezes, rock musicians on catwalks, and lovers on ladders – a production almost as preoccupied with the machinery of staging as the one that caused Hazlitt to cry, 'This is your triumph; it is not ours' to the scene-shifters and extravaganza-makers of his day. Brook's production served as a fulcrum in the shift towards a 'director's theatre' that, depending on your perspective, either liberated the stage from the tyranny of the author and the text or arrogantly substituted the tyranny of the director for the authority of the author and did to the text what Brook all but depicted Bottom doing to Titania. Either way, since 1970, directors like Robin Phillips, John Barton, Ron Daniels and Elijah Moshinsky have demonstrated great ingenuity and considerable licence in translating the play into modern theatrical parlance.

Meanwhile, in the period roughly from the mid-century to 1980, criticism of the play took its cue from Hippolyta's remark about the stories of the night growing to 'something of great constancy' (the title of David Young's excellent study of 1966), and sought through a focus on imagery, theme and genre to resolve the play's various 'worlds' into some kind of unity (e.g. Goddard 1951; Zitner 1960; Zimbardo 1972). Unity, however, is not easily come by in a play whose characters divide into fairies, lovers, mechanicals and royalty and whose action splits geographically between palace and wood and metaphysically between nature and supernature. Perhaps that is why critics, taking as a keynote the *concordia discors* of Theseus' hounds at the end of Act 4, habitually characterise the play in terms of harmony, a concept that allows for the discreteness of individual notes while acknowledging their fusion as an emergent higher whole.

Even so, the fairies present difficulties (as one would expect with a mischief-maker like Puck among them), if only because they remain invisible to all humans except Bottom, to whom in a sense they are also invisible. But this very invisibility may inspire grand visions. Unwilling to accept Theseus' dismissal of 'fairy toys', many critics discern in the fairies suggestions of a cryptic otherness denied to reason and not entirely accessible to the imagination. If they do not represent the mysteries of nature (Sewell 1960), then they serve as instruments of neoplatonic love (Vyvyan, 1961), as reminders that 'this world of sense in which we live is but the surface of a vaster unseen world by which the actions of men are affected or overruled' (Goddard 1951: 74), as a recollection of the heaven available to us in prelapsarian times (Bryant 1964), or perhaps as metaphors for the workings of the mind (Freedman 1991). Searching for a unity of meaning behind these various views, one might claim to find it in the imagination, whose role in putting the play together is alleged a bit breathily by Harold Goddard:

> There are the fairies. There are the lovers. There are the rustics. There is the court. What metaphysical as well as social gulfs divide them! But Imagination bridges them all. Imagination makes them all one. (Goddard 1951: 77)

However, whether imagination really does make them all one has been at issue ever since those early productions featuring the fairies but not the workmen, or the workmen but not the fairies, or Pyramus and Thisbe without, perhaps, either. Even the old 'new critics', to whom formal unity was sometimes as dear as the 'One' to Renaissance neoplatonists, conceded a complicating doubleness to the play. For Stephen Fender (1968), the contrasting responses to fairyland of Bottom, the lovers and Theseus forecast a general sense of irresolution and puzzlement with which the play leaves its audience (Fender 1968: 59–60). R. Chris Hassel (1970) finds the paradox of human fineness and failure reflected in an Epilogue that balances, or teeters, on a tightrope between the imagined and the real; and Ronald F. Miller emphasises the mysterious and tantalising effects brought about by Shakespeare's pluralistic presentation of fairyland as simultaneously desirable and incredible (R. F. Miller 1975: 267–8).

Much of this doubleness of effect issues from Shakespeare's theatrical self-consciousness. J. Dennis Huston maintains that despite other virtues, 'none of the mature comedies manages the dramatic medium as spectacularly as *A Midsummer Night's Dream*, and none so obviously affirms, demonstrates and celebrates the dramatist's play-making powers as this' (Huston 1981: 121). Even Barber's classic study of 1959 spoke of how Shakespeare's sophisticated play on the ambiguities of theatre muddies the pure illusions that Hazlitt, Lamb and other romantic critics desired to see on stage but could find only when reading the play in their study (Barber 1959: 140–1). Instead of providing access to other-worldly visions, the imagination (or the lack of it, as in *Pyramus and Thisbe*) provides metadramatic observations on theatrical art itself, usually in ways that extend theatricality into the offstage world of social behaviour and shed light inward on the theatre of the mind (Dent 1964; Young 1966; Edwards 1968; Iser 1961; Homan 1969; Carroll 1985; Marshall 1982; Rhoads 1985).

Since around 1980, criticism of the play has come to reflect new developments in critical theory. Freudian criticism had been around for some while, of course (Gui 1952–3, Holland 1960; Faber 1972), but not until the essays collected in *Representing Shakespeare* did the work of Jacques Lacan, D. W. Winnicott, Erik H. Erikson and other psychoanalysts become influential (Holland 1980; Marshall 1982; MacCary 1985; Freedman 1991). During the same period, cultural materialists (Krieger 1979; Evans 1986; Schneider 1987), 'new historicists' (Montrose 1983; Leinwand 1986; Tennenhouse 1986; Patterson 1989) and feminists (Garner 1981; Montrose 1983) have by and large shifted the critical focus away from the formal or aesthetic features of the play, seeking to evaluate it in light of and as contributing to Elizabethan ideological, political and social structures. Yet the light cast by these studies remains subject to the indeterminacy principle: wave-like, the play 'panders to an aristocratic ideology by wreaking comic punishment on all those who defy the prince's legislation of desire' (Freedman 1991: 155), yet, particle-like, it explores and even criticises the uses and abuses of power in Elizabethan society (Leinwand 1986: 30). What is generally agreed on, however, is that the happy ending once so roundly applauded is subtly but severely compromised, whether by the play's 'collaboration with the state ideology' (Freedman 1991: 155), by the 'unreconciled hostility' of the workmen (Schneider 1987: 205) or by an 'ironic prognosis for the new marriages' (Montrose 1983: 44).[1]

Of course, when critics are as sensitively attuned as we are today to 'political bias' (race, gender, species, nation, ethnicity, religion, etc.), it is questionable whether the happy ending of any Shakespearian comedy can survive scrutiny.[2] This can be a mixed blessing, or a mixed curse, depending on your viewpoint. For C. S. Lewis, it was a mixed curse brought about by our readiness to judge the past by standards we take to be superior when in fact they are often merely different, usually in degree, sometimes almost in kind:

> A modern, ordered to profess or recant a religious belief under pain of death, knows that he is being tempted and that the government which so tempts him is a government of villains. But this background was lacking when the period of religious revolution began. No man claimed for himself or allowed to another the right of believing as he chose. All parties inherited from the Middle Ages the assumption that Christian man could live only in a theocratic polity which had both the right and the duty of enforcing true religion by persecution. Those who resisted its authority did so not because they thought it had no right to impose doctrines but because they thought it was imposing the wrong ones. (C. S. Lewis 1954: 39)

In a similar vein (but in a passage I can no longer locate), Northrop Frye rebukes modern readers for an anachronistic tendency to accuse Shakespeare of being anti-democratic when in fact he is simply pre-democratic. Surely a good deal depends on the context of comparison: set him beside Terry Eagleton and Shakespeare is a misogynist, but next to Rabelais, he is a proto-feminist.

A major danger in writing 'politically conscious' criticism of *A Midsummer Night's Dream* is that the critic may discover in himself a capacity to ferret out sins that borders on genius but that also belies the spirit of comedy and militates Malvolio-like against life's cakes and ale. The genre Shakespeare worked in when writing *A Midsummer Night's Dream* – a blend of Graeco-Roman 'New Comedy' and native English festive forms filtered through Lyly and seasoned with Ovid – defined its happy ending as social reconciliation and provided little encouragement for the kind of satiric subversiveness of so-called Old Comedy. C. L. Barber first drew attention to the influence on Shakespearian comedy of festive traditions featuring a saturnalian movement through holiday release to clarification and social communion (Barber 1959: 8). This ritual movement – described by anthropologists like Van Gennep and Victor Turner and, in its carnivalesque form, by Mikhail Bakhtin – has been seen by later critics to underlie the three-part structure of *A Midsummer Night's Dream* and to permit the expression of social criticism within a condoned and containing form (Berry 1984; Bristol 1985; Kott 1987; Patterson 1989). The carnivalesque is represented by the workmen and especially by their performance of *Pyramus and Thisbe.*[3] However, the sexual *double entendres* (T. Clayton

1974; F. W. Clayton 1979; Franke 1979) and social and generic subversions of the workmen and their play are, as Michael D. Bristol says, 'social critique by inadvertency' (1985: 178). It is not as if the play ends with the workmen smouldering with social and political resentment, though it may end with the audience sympathetically re-evaluating those 'whose energies the social system relies on' even while it laughs at their foolery (Patterson 1989: 69).

As that implies, any attempt to issue definitive pronouncements about *A Midsummer Night's Dream* risks being baffled by an elusive doubleness and ambivalence that leave us feeling, as Puck's Epilogue implies we should feel, much like the lovers and Bottom looking back on their mysterious experiences in the wood. 'Methinks I see these things with parted eye', Hermia murmurs, and many a playgoer has nodded agreement. 'The real meaning of *A Midsummer Night's Dream*', Stephen Fender claims, 'is that no one "meaning" can be extracted from the puzzles with which a fiction presents its audience' (1968: 64). Thus with Puck in the Epilogue standing flush before us while he invites us to dissolve him and the entire play into a dream, we are given a final warning about the hermeneutical hazards of this duck-rabbity dreamwork, and we can hardly help hearing in his words an echo of Bottom's caveat that 'Man is but an ass, if he go about to expound this dream of mine' – a remark hardly calculated to inspire hubris in anyone about to disburden himself of a weighty expounding.

· 1 ·

The Law of the Father

In the myth proposed by Freud in *Totem and Taboo* the all-powerful father of the primal horde domineered over his sons and enjoyed an exclusive sexual monopoly on their mother and sisters. Eventually, however, the sons discovered the solution to this problem, which was of course to kill the tyrant and eat him (Freud 1950: 141–2). Even so, the father refused entirely to die; he lived on in his sons' guilty consciences. Indeed, as Freud says,

> the dead father became stronger than the living one had been [because] what had up to then been prevented by his actual existence was thenceforward prohibited by the sons themselves, in accordance with the psychological procedure so familiar to us in psycho-analysis under the name of 'deferred obedience'. They revoked their deed by forbidding the killing of the totem [animal], the substitute for their father; and they renounced its fruits by resigning their claim to the women who had now been set free. They thus created out of their filial sense of guilt the two fundamental taboos of totemism, which for that very reason inevitably corresponded to the two repressed wishes of the Oedipus complex. (Freud 1950: 143)

So the taboos that resolve the oedipal dilemma issue from the dead father and become the origin of totemic culture.[1]

For Jacques Lacan the oedipal crisis is also the matrix of culture, but, as

1

'matrix' would imply, it is less an absent father than an absent mother who precipitates sons (and daughters) into civilised life. For the child's oedipal rite of passage from the 'imaginary' to the 'symbolic', though occasioned by the paternal No, is paid for by the 'disappearance' of the mother (the loss of a seemingly exclusive merger with her).[2] Deprived of the immediate gratifications supplied by the mother, the need for which is repressed and driven into the unconscious to form the basis of desire,[3] the child acknowledges the symbolic: language, discourse, the law of the father, a mode of representation and meaning characterised by substitutions, displacements and deferrals of desire. Thus desire itself as well as the symbolic order is founded on a fundamental lack brought about by the loss of a world of immediate experience but more specifically by the loss of the mother around whom that world was organised. The lost presence of the mother will be endlessly sought but never recovered, except by such symbolic means as the famous *fort/da* game played by Freud's grandson – in which the child learned to symbolise absence (that of his mother when she left the room, Freud argued) by casting away and retrieving a wooden reel while saying '*fort*' and '*da*' ('(gone) away' and '(back) here' (Freud 1961: 8–11)).[4]

Freud's grandson and Lacan's cryptic theories seem of little relevance to *A Midsummer Night's Dream*, and yet they can play something of a reel-like role in our attempts to retrieve some lost or at least dispersed meanings in the play.[5] A psychoanalytic vocabulary, annotated with an eye to Elizabethan customs and institutions, can help to point out features of the play that had in Shakespeare's time a local habitation but no name.[6] The very structure of the play, for instance, can be likened to the *fort/da* experience, with the lovers 'gone away' from Athens and from themselves in the nightmare wood, then reeled back into the symbolic of marriage by a more flexible patriarchy. Or, as part of this loss-and-retrieval pattern, take what might be called the mystery of the missing mothers.

MISSING MOTHERS AND STINGY STEPDAMES

What is mysterious about mothers in *A Midsummer Night's Dream* is that all of them are either dead (the mother of Titania's Indian boy) or puzzlingly absent (especially the mothers of Lysander and Hermia, not to mention the mother of the heroine in *Pyramus and Thisbe*, a role given to Robin Starveling but never played). At first glance there is not much mystery in this. After all, Shakespeare is under no obligation to clutter the stage with his characters' mothers – or with their grandmothers, grandfathers, uncles, aunts or cousins – and certainly in his other comedies he is no more forthcoming with mothers than he is here. Why, then, is it so particular in *A Midsummer Night's Dream?* Because in it such a ferocious stress falls on fathers and on patriarchal authority, and such curious mention is made of stepmothers, that the absence of proper mothers looms larger than in other plays, inviting further consideration.

On the psychoanalytic view, a dearth of mothers should yield an abundance of desire. And so it does; the play opens with Theseus keening over the fact that the consummation of his marital desires is suspended like the new moon just four frustrating days beyond his reach:

> Now, fair Hippolyta, our nuptial hour
> Draws on apace. Four happy days bring in
> Another moon; but, O, methinks, how slow
> This old moon wanes! She lingers my desires
> Like to a step-dame, or a dowager,
> Long withering out a young man's revenue.

Theseus' impatience should come as no great surprise, since he has never suffered lingering desire very gladly. With Perigenia, Aegles, Ariadne and Antiopa, as Oberon reminds us a bit further on (ii.i.78–80), the amorous hero spared no time posting marriage banns and waiting out lunar changes; he just took his ravishing pleasures and went his way. And surely now, having as he says 'wooed thee with my sword' and 'won thy love doing thee injuries' (i.i.16–17), he might well have done the same with Hippolyta. Why, then, does he marry her? Primarily, of course, because Plutarch says he did; the marriage comes with the myth, motives do not. Perhaps marriage itself under these circumstances is a form of ravishment – a notion I will consider further on. For the moment let us attend to Theseus' rhetoric, particularly to the conspicuously far-fetched simile in which he likens the waning of the old moon to a stepdame or a dowager lingering out a young man's revenue.

This stingy dowager figure becomes more meaningful later in the scene when an unfigurative dowager, Lysander's aunt, comes to our attention. At this point, having been denied Hermia, Lysander is even more frustrated than Theseus. Thus he proposes an escape from father-dominated Athens into the wood where, he says,

> I have a widow aunt, a dowager
> Of great revenue, and she hath no child.
> From Athens is her house remote seven leagues;
> And she respects me as her only son.
> There, gentle Hermia, may I marry thee.

(i.i.156–60)

Lysander's dowager aunt is just the reverse of Theseus' tormenting stepdames and dowagers; she will hasten a young man's desire, not hinder it. In fact, in Lysander's fairy-tale here, love will find its marital consummation under the auspices of a substitute mother whose 'great revenue' suggests a kind of wish-fulfilment treasure at the end of desire's rainbow. Unfortunately for the lovers, however, this flight from the repressive father back towards the lost mother takes its route through the sylvan imaginary, a territory of narcissistic and aggressive desire where Demetrius speaks for all in saying, 'And here I am, and wode [mad] within this wood' (ii.i.192).

Lysander's real mother is palpably missing, possibly dead; certainly, as one who is never seen, heard or mentioned, she is theatrically dead. But dead mothers, or repressed ones, remain elusively alive in the imaginary, where they appear as a series of substitutive (m)others issuing promises of fulfilment which they can only partially and passingly keep. In Theseus' case their names are Perigenia, Aegles, Ariadne, Antiopa, Hippolyta, Phaedra and (Plutarch adds but Shakespeare tactfully omits) Anaxo, Peribea, Pherebaea, Joppa and Helen. In Lysander's case the absent mother reappears in more maternal and chimerical form as a widow aunt, a benign fairy-tale stepmother in a welcoming home deep in the wood.[7] Unfortunately, even in this surrogate form, the mother remains irretrievably *fort*, not *da*. Lysander no sooner appears in the wood than he informs Hermia that 'to speak the troth, I have forgot our way' (ii.ii.36) – appropriately enough inasmuch as his aunt is herself but a roundabout 'way' to the real mother. Thus they never find the aunt's house, and by the time they emerge from the wood she has become so irrelevant that her inconsiderate nephew neglects even to send her a wedding invitation. What satisfaction the lovers can obtain must be achieved, it seems, in the daylight world of Athens, not in the moonshiny wood or over the rainbow.

Even so, Lysander's aunt helps explain the far-fetchedness of Theseus' simile about stingy stepdames and dowagers and the lingering out of desire, a simile that turns out to be not so far-fetched after all. For the proverbial stinginess of stepdames comes from their being mothers in name only. Testifying to the irrecoverable loss of the biological mother,[8] they stand for the indirect substitutive mediations of the symbolic, which do indeed defer the desires of young men and women (and of old men and old women and everyone in between). However, the mention of two kinds of stepdames in the play calls attention to the ambiguity of the symbolic. For on the one hand, as in Theseus' simile, the symbolic impedes desire by interposing cultural institutions like marriage between the individual and the absent mother, but on the other hand, as Lysander's kindly dowager attests, it perpetuates the mother in sublimated fashion and mediates desire in a new mode.[9] In short, culture restrains and displaces the crude thrust of imaginary impulse by making it observe the symbolic grammar of social co-operation.

Two other stepdames merit consideration. One is Titania, who has substituted herself for the Indian queen (I take it) as 'mother' of the changeling child demanded by Oberon. I'll return to Titania more appropriately in a later chapter. Meanwhile there is another stepdame who has some bearing on the play without being in it. I mean Phaedra, who is of course Theseus' next wife. It is she who, in ancient myth and drama, falls in love with her stepson Hippolytus while Theseus is off journeying and who when scorned by Hippolytus commits suicide but leaves a note accusing the son to his father, thereby ensuring his death. But these tragic affairs are all in the future, beyond the scope of the comedy, and the audience would have been quite oblivious of them if Shakespeare had merely chosen to call Theseus' bride Antiopa instead of Hippolyta. That he could very easily have done so is pointed out by D'Orsay W. Pearson, who observes that in the sources available to Shakespeare the wife of Theseus and mother of Hippolytus was most frequently called Antiopa, not Hippolyta (1974: 296-7). By choosing the latter name, the feminine form of Hippolytus, Shakespeare inevitably recalls the story of Theseus' son and his tragic death.

Why call attention to this story? Clearly (to anyone properly obsessed with stepdames) because Shakespeare wanted to emphasise the grisly future consequences of a missing Amazonian mother and a passionate Cretan stepdame.[10] In keeping with this, Hippolyta's first speech, in which she likens the coming new moon 'to a silver bow / New-bent in heaven' (9–10), also presages the unhappy future. Her simile evokes the bow-carrying huntress Diana in her lunar role as Phoebe–Cynthia–Luna and reminds us that Hippolyta's son came to grief in part because of his worship of the chaste goddess of the hunt who, at Ephesus, as Shakespeare knew, served as matron deity of the Amazons.[11] Thus for the hapless Hippolytus the replacement of the mother by not one but two stepdames involves him in a symbolic register of dangerous complexity. If the symbolic defers desire, so does the chaste goddess whom Hippolytus follows; and if it also mediates desire, so would the passionate Phaedra whom he disdains. With Hippolyta, Diana and Phaedra all competing for the role of mother, Hippolytus' sense of self must surely be fairly well shredded long before his body is torn apart on the seashore.

UBIQUITOUS OEDIPUS

The dearth of mothers in *A Midsummer Night's Dream* is brought to our attention by a plethora of stepdames and dowager aunts, and also of course by the forbidding presence of fathers. This is entirely fitting inasmuch as Shakespeare appears to be dramatising the cultural double-bind that attends the oedipal crisis – a deferred crisis in this case, the customary mother–father–infant configuration transformed into one featuring father–daughter–lover. On the one hand, if Hermia wishes to undergo the rite of passage from the imaginary to the symbolic, she must yield up her desires to patriarchal management. On the other hand, if she repudiates the symbolic, the cost is either death itself or the death of desire in a nunnery.

For both Freud and Lacan, the oedipal crisis is properly resolved when the child acknowledges the phallic fatherly No, represses its longing for the mother, abandons the pleasure principle and resigns itself to the deferral of desire. But for Lacan this No is a more broadly cultural matter than it is for Freud. It is spoken not necessarily by the father as a person decreeing family rules but by a 'father function', hence potentially anyone, an older brother or sister, even the mother (e.g. the Elizabethan mother banishing the wet-nurse); and the voice that utters the No speaks ultimately in the name of society itself issuing its perennial demand for repression, sublimation and order.

By way of broad historical illustration, for instance, consider the oedipal crisis facing England as a result of the Reformation. When during the reign of Henry VIII the reformers discredited both Mother Church and the Catholic cult of Mary, they obliged their followers to repress the Mother as intercessor and negotiate directly with God the Father and, more immediately, with Henry, spiritual father of England (Ong 1967: 188–202; Barber 1980: 196). The loss of the divine Mary might have been mitigated by her reappearance under the rule and in the name of Queen Mary, but of course Bloody Mary made a poor substitute for the Mary of the *Pietà*. Thus in a kind of *fort/da* game played in the religio-political unconscious, the lost Virgin Mother was finally reeled back in again by means of a highly symbolic new cult, that of the Virgin Queen Elizabeth, a cult which, as Louis Montrose observes, may have provided Elizabethans 'with a resource for dealing with the internal residues of their relationships to the primary maternal figures of infancy' (Montrose 1983: 33). Insofar as Elizabeth reaffirmed Henry's paternal No to Mariolatry, she assumed the function of the father while deftly substituting herself, a virginal step-mother of sorts, for the repressed Mother of God.

In *A Midsummer Night's Dream* the paternal No takes a similarly broad social and political aspect inasmuch as it is voiced not by Egeus alone but by Theseus and Athenian law as well. 'For you, fair Hermia', says Theseus,

> look you arm yourself
> To fit your fancies to your father's will;

Or else the law of Athens yields you up –
Which by no means we may extenuate –
To death, or to a vow of single life.

(i.i.118–22)

Hermia's desire is not just her business or her family's business but state business as well. In fact, since the only apparent business of the state in this play is to govern desire, Shakespeare's Athens seems to operate in accordance with Lévi-Strauss' dictum in *The Elementary Structures of Kinship*: 'The rules of kinship and marriage are not made necessary by the social state. They are the social state' (Lévi-Strauss 1969: 490). That being so, daughterly desire must be routed through the will of the father to make the marriages that make the state.

Why do Athenian fathers merit such sacred authority over their daughters? Because they are authors by act of nature. Theseus explains this a bit further on when he tells Hermia how she was 'composed':

be advised, fair maid.
To you your father should be as a god –
One that composed your beauties, yea, and one
To whom you are but as a form in wax
By him imprinted and within his power
To leave the figure or disfigure it.

(i.i.46–51)

As Barbara Freedman shrewdly observes (1991: 169–70), Theseus' simile refers to the heavily waxed (for better erasure) pages of Renaissance tablets ('My tables – meet it is I set it down', Hamlet says of the Ghost's command (i.v.108)). Thus as 'a form in wax', Hermia is a sign imprinted by her godlike father in the passively receptive material of her mother, the symbolic action of sealing obscuring the sexual action of the penis printing its form on the waxy womb (Thompson and Thompson 1987: 188). Like all children in such a society, Hermia is both biologically and symbolically created by the father.[12]

Theseus' version of Hermia's conception apparently comes, if like a crab it can go temporally forwards, from the patristic view that man is to woman as spirit is to matter. Following Aristotle, Aquinas held the woman's role in reproduction to be entirely passive. A kind of material cause, she supplies the stuff of life to which the father, the formal cause, gives shape.[13] This notion of biological conception became a model for verbal conception. Writing or speaking, that is, was regarded as a stamping of pure (masculine) concepts into the impure (feminine) matter of words, a view deriving

ultimately from the notion sacralised in *Genesis* that women and words are
belated supplements to men and ideas (Bloch 1989: 9–15).

In Theseus' account of it, however, no mother was present at Hermia's
conception. Egeus was there 'as a god', but the woman's part disappears, or
at best it appears in the metaphor of wax. Somewhat confusedly, Hermia
herself has now become the wax on which the paternal seal was imprinted,
and it is she who is now being asked to assume the feminine passivity
associated with her conception by allowing herself to be imprinted again
with what Lacan calls *le nom du père*, a phrase which in English loses the pun
on *nom* (name/No): 'It is in the *name of the father* that we must recognise the
support of the symbolic function which, from the dawn of history, has
identified his person with the figure of the law' (Lacan 1977: 67). In this
context Lacan's description of the ambient symbolic provides (with a
change of pronouns) an appropriate annotation of Theseus' account of
Hermia's plight:

> Symbols in fact envelop the life of [woman] in a network so total that
> they join together, before [she] comes into the world, those who are
> going to engender [her] 'by flesh and blood'; so total that they bring to
> [her] birth, along with the gifts of the stars, if not with the gifts of the
> fairies [!], the shape of [her] destiny; so total that they give the words that
> will make [her] faithful or renegade, the law of the acts that will follow
> [her] right to the very place where [she] *is* not yet and even beyond [her]
> death. (Lacan 1977: 68)[14]

At this point in Hermia's experience, the name-of-the-father embraces the
family father (Egeus), the state father (Theseus) and, in its most awesome
form, the patriarchal law of Athens. The symbolic has petrified into a
dictatorship of the signifier, endowed with the power to give life and
therefore of course to impose death.[15]

Even so, death seems an excessive penalty for daughterly disobedience.
Why introduce so lethal an option here? Well, for one thing, from an
Elizabethan reformer's perspective, death is not at all excessive. 'The
ancient privilege of Athens', that is, was also the contemporary privilege of
Geneva, death being precisely the punishment Calvin decreed for children
who disobeyed their parents.[16] However, the death-decreeing law here
issues less from Elizabethan society than from comedic tradition. Death is
generically suitable, inasmuch as comedies like to summon up ominous
characters and situations that will throw a fright into the action but that can
be made to vanish with the sunrise and a sense of relief. Moreover, the
threat of death nicely fills the need of the plot for something extreme to
motivate the lovers' flight from Athens. Finally, however, such a threat

makes the confrontation of Egeus and Hermia a life-or-death analogue to the encounter between Theseus and Hippolyta during the recent war. For as Theseus' 'I wooed thee with my sword' suggests, during the battle there must have been a climactic moment when the Greek hero, sword upraised, cried to the Amazonian queen 'Yield or die!' Yield, that is, to my masculine power, to the phallic sword that proclaims an Athenian No to deviant Amazonian society.

But of course Theseus and Hippolyta would not be back in Athens preparing for marriage if the duke's 'Yield or die!' had not also meant 'Yield *and* die – on our wedding night!'

As this suggests, Oedipus is not courting Hermia alone; the oedipal crisis assumes a cultural dimension that extends well beyond the nuclear family. In order to govern desire, all cultures sort people into genders and take care to police the borders between them, which are both horizontal (men | women) and vertical ($\frac{men}{women}$).[17] Given such divisions, the Amazons presented a special problem to the cultural constabulary of ancient Greece. In the first place, they mocked the principle of male dominance by establishing an independent society that excluded and denigrated men. Then, too, they violated the distinction between men and women by arrogating to themselves the masculine art of warfare, by excising their breasts (*Amazon* = 'breastless') or at least one of them (in the interests of less painful archery), and most of all by disdaining marriage. Of course for purely reproductive purposes they were obliged to rely on men, recruiting sexual partners from neighbouring tribes; but all male children born of these transient unions were either killed, mutilated or returned to the tribe of their fathers.

Hence Amazons constituted an indefinable gender, neither male nor female but something in between (duBois 1982: 34–42), and therefore a source of wonder and fear. Like satyrs, centaurs, cyclopes, manticores, harpies and hosts of other monsters, their existence was a threat to the identity of Greek society even as it defined that identity by contrast.[18] This threat became (mythically) very real indeed when in an attempt to recover Hippolyta, as Plutarch tells it, the Amazons invaded Athens, camped within the city, and advanced as far as the temple of the Muses before being repelled.[19]

Clearly Hermia is no Amazon, and yet in this context her perverse love for Lysander, as Egeus views it, and her bold resistance to patriarchal authority compose a faint reflection of Hippolyta's past. For both of them the institution of marriage is called on to regularise wayward desire. This is in keeping with the claim by Lévi-Strauss that human societies are formed in part by a kind of communicative circulation of women in which daughters, sisters, wives and mothers function as symbolic objects of exchange analogous to words passed around in dialogue (Lévi-Strauss 1969)[20] – and we have just seen that Theseus' concept of paternity marks daughters as signs of their fathers. The principal agency of this cultural dialogue is marriage, and marriage rules, like gender distinctions, serve as boundary markers distinguishing 'us' from 'them'. Those whom we refuse to marry, we also refuse to think of as fully human. Mere animals, monsters or barbarians, they are gross libidinal creatures lacking the restraints of culture. 'The primordial law', says Lacan, echoing Lévi-Strauss, 'is therefore that which in regulating marriage ties superimposes the kingdom of culture on that of a nature abandoned to the law of mating' (1977: 66). Hence by rejecting marriage, the Amazons automatically place themselves beyond the cultural pale, and from this standpoint Theseus' marriage to Hippolyta represents an imposition of the law of culture on unruly nature.

In psychoanalytic terms Hippolyta suffers castration in having to renounce her desire for the masculine phallus and resign herself to her 'proper' gender. From an Athenian perspective, marriage will rescue her from an anomalous Amazonian status of not-man, not-woman and define her as a 'real' woman, thereby reaffirming male superiority and the authenticity of Athenian society. Like Hermia receiving the imprint of her father's divine form, Hippolyta need only wait until her 'sealing-day', as Theseus calls it (I.i.54), to receive the stamp of culture. In this light, the wedding, though it seems loving enough on one level, is also, on another, an act of rapacious civilising in which the unisexual and antimarital Hippolyta is deflowered. In the process she suffers a kind of death by sublimation, insofar as the wedding that celebrates her new status as Theseus' wife is also the funeral that registers the demise of her Amazonian self.

TRIANGULAR DESIRE

If even an Amazonian queen cannot escape the institution of marriage, then the symbolic appears to be ubiquitous in Athens and desire takes a triangular form. Of course the oedipal is always triangular, but in the absence of mothers here the triangle is formed by the father's intervening not between child and mother but between daughter and lover. This is illustrated on stage when Egeus enters with Hermia, Lysander and Demetrius to register his paternal complaint. 'Stand forth, Demetrius', he directs, and 'Stand forth, Lysander'. When he adds, perhaps with an embracing gesture towards Demetrius, 'My noble lord, / This man hath my consent to marry her', he and Demetrius merge as one figure opposing, possibly even standing obstructively in between, Hermia and Lysander.

The triadic disposition of bodies on stage visually allegorises the displacement of the imaginary's dyadic reflections by the symbolic.

The lack of any difference between Lysander and Demetrius –

> I am, my lord, as well derived as he,
> As well possessed; my love is more than his;
> My fortunes every way as fairly ranked,
> If not with vantage, as Demetrius'
> (I.i.99–102)

– emphasises the arbitrariness of Hermia's choice of Lysander and of
Egeus' choice of Demetrius. The question is not whether Lysander or
Demetrius is the better man, or whether Hermia or Egeus is the wiser
chooser, but who has the authority to control desire. And the answer is, the
law, which is little more than the father writ large; law and the state insist
that desire be routed through the father. Thus Hermia is being asked to
marry not only Demetrius but also Oedipus – to submit, that is, to the
Athenian phallocracy. When Theseus renders judgment in the case, he
raises the phallic law over Hermia's head much as he did his phallic sword
over Hippolyta's in battle, demanding 'Yield or die!'

However, this demand, like that of Theseus to Hippolyta, tempers its
menace with an element of the seductive. Theseus, Egeus, Demetrius and
the law unite in a kind of cultural wooing of Hermia. The state threatens
death, to be sure, but it also promises life, approval, status, a place – all the
love-tokens of belonging which society offers its members in exchange for
repressing desire and behaving sensibly. Unfortunately, all societies are to
some extent liars, especially in their courtship of women. They are like
Demetrius, that 'spotted and inconstant man' who made promises to
Helena but then broke them, reports of which Theseus admits to having
heard but forgotten (I.i.111–14), and, having now heard again, seems to
forget again, perhaps because they remind him of his own spotted and
inconstant past. As a result Athenian society seems dangerously close to
courting Hermia the way Demetrius courted Helena and Theseus courted
Perigenia, Aegles, Ariadne and Antiopa. No wonder she accepts Lysander's offer to flee to the matriarchal wood. Not that she can truly recover
the paradisal pre-oedipal world of the mother but that a marriage under the
auspices of an unknown but presumably welcoming 'stepmother' holds
more promise at this point than one compelled by the desire of the father
codified into state law.

Thus when Hermia rejects Demetrius again, she rejects Egeus, Theseus
and the oedipal state as well. Such an act strikes ultimately at the triangulation of desire and constitutes an inside threat to Athenian culture

correlative to Hippolyta's outside threat. Repudiating the law of the symbolic and the tyranny of the signifier, she will embrace the dyadic imaginary and let her desire be guided by her own eyes. The route she might have followed is described when Theseus, having issued his ultimatum, calls Egeus and Demetrius to join him, and receives Egeus' obedient reply – 'With duty and desire we follow you' (i.i.127).

However, because triangulation is inescapable in Athens, even Theseus must walk the hypotenuse. In this respect Egeus' words 'With duty and desire we follow you' are somewhat curious. In the first place, they are highly ironic in being addressed to Theseus at all, because Theseus, though cast as avatar of order and law here, has been in the past, as we have seen, a prime example of the subversiveness of desire. The concatenation of his sexual episodes illustrates the nomadic nature of desire, which in its search for the oasis of ultimate content is analogous to signification in its pursuit of a transcendental signified. And as the business of logocentrism is to bring meaning to an illusory halt at words like 'truth' and 'fact', so the business of society is to make desire do more than merely pause at what it thinks it wants. The master metaphor for this effort of society to arrest desire is marriage. Unless its members marry not only one another but also a language, a sense of self, professions, cities, homes, social groups, political parties, ideologies, behavioural codes and so forth, there will be no society at all, only a medley of philandering impulses.

From this standpoint Theseus is submitting his wayward desire to the forms of culture by marrying Hippolyta nearly as much as she is by marrying him. He too is obliged to defer to Oedipus and the law, to the 'name-of-the-father'. This Lacanian term is surprisingly relevant in this context because it draws our attention to another mystery in *A Midsummer Night's Dream*, the mystery of Theseus' missing father. However, that is a mystery that must be explored more carefully in Chapter 3. For the moment, we need to look at another curious example of triangular desire – Egeus. For, after all, Egeus is experiencing a crisis of sorts himself, as would have been the case even in the best of circumstances, even if Hermia had been obedient to his wishes, because then he would have been giving his daughter away, something Shakespearian fathers do not do gladly. In fact, most of these fathers act as if any daughter of theirs who wants to marry is an adulteress.

Egeus' predicament is particularly interesting. If he is trying to force Hermia to undergo symbolic castration, demanding that she forsake phallic power, he is also undergoing it himself as well. Normally castration occurs in childhood and represents an interdiction of incest by the symbolic father who incorporates the law (Wilden 1968: 188). In Shakespeare the incest most often in need of interdiction has to do not with mothers and sons, despite *Hamlet*, but with fathers and daughters, and the crisis occurs not in childhood but at the point of marriage. In his portrayal of the fathers of Juliet, Hermia, Portia, Ophelia, Desdemona, Cordelia and Miranda, suggestions of incest are decently repressed. But in *Pericles* the repressed returns in the form of King Antiochus, who enjoys a manifestly incestuous relationship with his daughter – manifest to the audience but not to his daughter's suitors. Antiochus manages to keep both his daughter and his secret by presenting to each of her suitors a riddle: if the suitor solves it, he wins her hand; if he does not, he loses his head, which is then mounted on the palace wall alongside those of earlier and equally unsuccessful rivals. By the time Pericles comes on the scene, the wall of the palace is as studded with heads as the face of the royal taxidermist is creased with smiles.

King Antiochus is the explicit exception that proves the force of the interdictive rule, since all other Shakespearian fathers honour it, including Egeus. Not that Egeus would not like to have Lysander's head on his wall too. For although he calls for the death of Hermia in Act 1, the death he really covets is made clear at the end of Act 4. When the sleeping couples are discovered and attempt to explain, Egeus blurts out hysterically 'Enough, enough, my lord; you have enough. / I beg the law, the law, upon his head' (iv.i.153–4). *His* head now, not hers. Nevertheless, like Shakespeare's other fathers, Egeus sublimates whatever incestuous desires he may have by laundering lust at the font of capitalism. This strategy enables fathers to possess their daughters – not carnally like Antiochus but economically like Shylock ('my ducats, and my daughter!'). Unlike Shylock, however, who loses ducats and daughter at once, Shakespeare's more prudent fathers keep close watch on their virginal private property, feeding them and housing and clothing them, and graciously accepting their gratitude, all until that unavoidable Saturday when they must go to market: 'As she is mine', Egeus cries, 'I may dispose of her', and 'she is mine, and all my right of her / I do estate unto Demetrius' (i.i.42, 97–8).

Giving away a daughter in marriage, then, can be a kind of belated castration for a father. With this gift he again endorses the incest taboo, this time irrevocably, acquiescing to the demands of the law that he himself represents by placing his daughter for ever beyond his reach. Whatever it may be for daughters, for fathers marriage is a painful parting, only slightly anaesthetised by the pleasurable opportunity to engage in one final piece of tyranny, choosing the right husband himself.[21] Actually, like so many of Shakespeare's heavy fathers, Egeus attempts to choose not so much a husband for his daughter as a son-in-*law* for himself – the conventional term taking on special significance in this context. Since these sons-in-law are so uniformly distasteful to the daughters, we might suspect that they are chosen at least partly as a vindictive consolation for the father's own loss ('If

I can't keep her, let her suffer through life with this young lout'). But Egeus also chooses Demetrius because he, unlike Lysander, has conceded to the triangularity of desire – so willingly, it seems, that he has courted the father even before the daughter, a tactic that produces Lysander's impertinent 'You have her father's love, Demetrius; / Let me have Hermia's. Do you marry him'. Lysander has no doubt been reading Lévi-Strauss, for if the anthropologist is right – about women and especially daughters being units of social exchange that mediate between males – then the proposed marriage of Demetrius and Hermia is in some degree instrumental to the real 'marriage' of Demetrius to Egeus. Hermia is simply the ring Egeus places on Demetrius' finger, bawdy meaning and all.

'And why not?' the disgruntled Egeus might ask. After all, Hermia is merely a daughter. It is not as though Egeus were arranging the marriage of a son who could ensure his immortality by perpetuating his family name. Instead, like all daughters, like all illegitimate sons for that matter, Hermia offers Egeus nothing in compensation for his death. The laws of incest prevent him from reproducing himself through her, and the laws of patriarchy decree that the children she does produce will bear another grandfather's name. Unless Egeus has sons and they acquire wives, Hermia's marriage is his funeral. His only consolation is that 'As she is mine, I may dispose of her'. And so he would if he could, reducing her to a piece of sexual property to be conferred on whomever he chooses.

But as Jessica, Juliet and Hermia rebelliously demonstrate, Shakespeare's daughters do not always welcome the opportunity to become units of cultural exchange between fathers and their sons-in-law or indeed between anyone except themselves and the lovers of their own choosing. They find the immediate reciprocations of the imaginary more attractive than the triangulations of the symbolic, the courtship of Lorenzo, Romeo or Lysander more appealing than that of Oedipus.

PARADISE LOST, OR *FORT/DA*

With the exit of Theseus and company, Hermia and Lysander are left on stage to contemplate their plight and perhaps, the audience may hope, to explain how things have come to such a sorry pass. But Shakespeare is not much in the giving mood as regards exposition. What preceded the oedipal crisis of the opening is left largely to our conjecture. Nevertheless, we do get a few clues to what has happened, and what they add up to is a tale of paradise lost and only partially regained. The first evidence of this is when Hermia tells Helena that

Before the time I did Lysander see,
Seemed Athens as a paradise to me.
O, then, what graces in my love do dwell,
That he hath turned a heaven into a hell!
(ı.i.203–7)

This would not be surprising news if it came during the hellish nights in the wood, but the unfortunate fall Hermia speaks of has already taken place in Athens. At first we might think that by 'hell' she means the unhappy experience she has just been put through by Egeus. But in that case she ought to have said 'Before the time *my father* did Lysander see'. As it is, not the exposure and parental rejection of her love but that love itself – the seeing and hence loving of Lysander – has precipitated the loss of an Athenian paradise for Hermia.

Why Athens was once so paradisal is suggested a bit further on when Hermia tells Helena that she and Lysander intend to meet

. . . in the wood, where often you and I
Upon faint primrose beds were wont to lie,
Emptying our bosoms of their counsel sweet.
(214–16)

And this in turn looks forward to its elaboration by Helena in Act 3, when she thinks Hermia has joined with the men to humiliate her:

O, and is all forgot?
All school-days' friendship, childhood innocence?
We, Hermia, like two artificial gods,
Have with our needles created both one flower,
Both on one sampler, sitting on one cushion,
Both warbling of one song, both in one key,
As if our hands, our sides, voices, and minds,
Had been incorporate. So we grew together,
Like to a double cherry, seeming parted,
But yet an union in partition;
Two lovely berries moulded on one stem;
So, with two seeming bodies, but one heart;
Two of the first, like coats in heraldry,
Due but to one, and crowned with one crest.
And will you rent our ancient love asunder,
To join with men in scorning your poor friend?
It is not friendly, 'tis not maidenly:

Our sex, as well as I, may chide you for it,
Though I alone do feel the injury.
                    (III.ii.201–19)

What to make of this description of a maidenly paradise that seems to idealise well beyond recognition any mere 'school-days' friendship'? Let me suggest a couple of ways of looking at it.

First, we are surely meant to hear in Helena's complaint at least a muted echo of Hippolyta's situation, inasmuch as she too has lost the feminine friendships of her Amazonian past. Similarly, Titania has lost her former votary, the mother of the changeling child she refuses to give to Oberon: 'Full often hath she gossiped by my side, / And sat with me on Neptune's yellow sands', etc. (II.i.125 ff.). In some degree, what has happened to Hippolyta and to Titania is now happening to Hermia and Helena; feminine community is suppressed by masculine conquest under the cultural auspices of love and marriage. Theseus wins Hippolyta's love doing her injuries, Oberon compels Titania's obedience through humiliation, and in Helena's imagination Lysander and Demetrius, in collaboration with Hermia, are similarly humiliating her.

However, what Helena remembers seems more intimate than female fellowship. She describes a fusion so Siamese-twinlike as virtually to defy division, a 'union in partition' formed by a kind of monozygotic and polymorphic melding of hands, sides, singing voices, minds and hearts. What has been lost seems as much biological as it is social – 'two seeming bodies, but one heart' – almost as though some memory of the original union of infant and mother were invading Helena's story of childhood friendship. Of course an 'emptying [of] bosoms', as Hermia calls it, requires words, but hers and Helena's merger of secret selves and bodies seems to have been so perfect and natural that words took on corporeal form and met like clasped palms or mirrored gazes. Helena's sense of loss is familiar enough. As Mark C. Taylor says, Hegel 'postulates a state antecedent to consciousness in which self and other (subject and object) remain undifferentiated. This condition, however, is strictly unconscious (*bewusstlos*). For conscious beings, such a state (represented as a paradisiacal or infantile innocence) is always present as lost and can never be regained' (Taylor 1980: 187). Less theoretically, according to psychoanalysts like Grunberger and Kohut, 'we idealize ourselves and others in an attempt, never to be achieved, to recapture an Edenic world that we either vaguely remember from our youth or have a strong sense of experiencing during infancy and childhood' (Westlund 1967: 86).[22] *Edenic* is appropriate: Helena's lament records a fall from paradisal innocence and is imbued with a yearning for a lost plenitude.

If twentieth-century patients share Helena's sense of loss and longing, so evidently did Athenians of the fourth century BC. At any rate, so says Aristophanes when his turn comes to speak about love in Plato's *Symposium* (189c–193e, Plato 1961: 542–6). The power of love, he says, is no longer understood, because we humans are sorrily diminished since the ancient days when our race consisted of three genders – male, female and hermaphrodite. Males descended from the sun, females from the earth and hermaphrodites from the moon, 'which partakes of either sex' (190b). The hermaphrodites were strange globular male–female creatures with two faces and twice the normal number of hands and feet and other bodily members. Powerful and energetic, 'such [was] their arrogance that they actually tried . . . to scale the heights of heaven and set upon the gods' (190c). However, this unwise scheme came to the attention of Zeus, who with the help of Apollo first split the hermaphroditic bodies in two and then mercifully patched up their wounds, leaving the navel as a reminder of their folly. As a result each separate half passionately longed to reunite with its complement and, unable to do so, was in danger of extinction. In compensation Zeus rearranged the hermaphrodites' genitals so that they could engage in sex and reproduce. At this point in the myth, Aristophanes apparently forgets about the original male and female genders and regards the newly heterosexual hermaphrodites as the source of all humans. Thus it came about, he explains, that

> we are all like pieces of the coins that children break in half for keepsakes – making two out of one, like the flatfish – and each of us is forever seeking the half that will tally with himself. (191e)

> And so all this to-do [among the sexes] is a relic of that original state of ours, when we were whole, and now, when we are longing for and following after that primeval wholeness, we say we are in love. (193a)

So it seems to have been with Helena and Hermia, who in their 'ancient love' formed two halves of a single self that was subsequently divided, not by Zeus but by the distracting appearance of Lysander and Demetrius, to whom they transferred their love, as if seeking in displaced form the lost half that would make them complete again.[23] Now, in the derision of the wood, the vestige of that Siamese love is again 'rent' by a conspiracy inspired by men.

Aristophanes' myth explains an even older myth, not about the hermaphrodites but about Hermaphroditus. This is the story of how Hermaphroditus acquired his androgynous shape, a story recorded by Ovid and translated by Golding. According to Ovid, the 15-year-old

Hermaphroditus, who 'wist not what love was' (Rouse, 1966, IV: 403), was
pursued and eventually caught by the lascivious water-nymph Salmacis,
who so wore herself out wrestling with the reluctant virgin that she prayed
'Ye Goddes of Heaven agree / That this same wilfull boy and I may never
parted bee', and, as Golding's immortal cadences record (IV: 460–70):

> The Gods were pliant to hir boone. The bodies of them twaine
> Were mixt and joyned both in one. To both them did remaine
> One countenance. Like as if a man should in one barke beholde
> Two twigges both growing into one and still togither holde:
> Even so when through hir hugging and hir grasping of the tother
> The members of them mingled were and fastned both togither,
> They were not any lenger two: but (as it were) a toy
> Of double shape: Ye could not say it was a perfect boy,
> Nor perfect wench: it seemed both and none of both to beene.

Since this amorous transformation appears in Book IV of the *Metamorphoses*,
which also contains the tale of Pyramus and Thisbe, Shakespeare could
hardly fail to run across it. If so, he would have noted that the hero's name
is a fusion of those of his parents, Hermes and Aphrodite. Hermaphroditus himself makes a point of it, albeit in Latin terms: 'O noble father
Mercurie, and *Venus* mother deere, / This one petition graunt your
son which both your names doth beare' (475–6). Thus Hermaphroditus'
narcissism is reflected in his self-loving name, as if he were self-sufficiently
both male and female even before the nymph's prayer is answered and he
becomes still more lovingly self-entwined. All of this seems relevant to
A Midsummer Night's Dream because Hermia's name is of course the
feminine form of *Hermes* and because Helena's name associates her,
if not directly with Aphrodite, at least with the mythic Helen whom
Aphrodite promised Paris in return for his awarding her the golden apple
for beauty.[24] Thus Ovid's minglings of two in one – Hermes and
Aphrodite, Hermaphroditus and Salmacis – may have helped inspire
Helena's idyllic account of hers and Hermia's symbiotic 'ancient love', now
so unhappily sundered. In sense, at any rate, there is not much to choose
between 'Two twigges both growing into one and still togither holde' and
Helena's 'double cherry, seeming parted' and 'Two lovely berries moulded
on one stem'.

During the time Helena and Hermia enjoyed their Siamese union in
partition, they can scarcely be said to have possessed individual identities.
Like the sense of plenitude in the sexually undifferentiated foetus in the
womb, their love was virtually the self-love of a single hermaphroditic
creature not yet sexually distinguished.[25] Once the 'double cherry' is

parted, however, they pass from a love based on sameness to one based more problematically on difference. Since difference differentiates, the girls' love for the young men brings into being new and distinct identities: females instead of androgynes, women instead of girls, Hermia–Lysander and Helena–Demetrius instead of Hermia–Helena – new and distinct but also changeable. For although love's mutual flame has been reputed to unite heterosexually separate selves – 'Two distincts, division none: / Number there in love was slain' – that flame, as 'The Phoenix and the Turtle' records, guttered out long ago. What remains is, at the worst, the kinds of ill-grafted and mismatched love that Lysander and Hermia deplore or, at the best, the kind that war, death and sickness lay siege to, or that Athenian law wedges apart.

LOVE: SYMBOLIC AND IMAGINARY

The arrival of the young men seems to signal the girls' graduation from a kind of symbiotic and static imaginary into a differentiating and mutable symbolic. Not that the two registers are ever so discrete. Consider for instance their merger in Egeus' description of Lysander's surreptitious courtship of Hermia:

> This man hath bewitched the bosom of my child.
> Thou, thou, Lysander, thou hast given her rimes
> And interchanged love-tokens with my child.
> Thou hast by moonlight at her window sung
> With feigning voice verses of feigning love,
> And stolen the impression of her fantasy
> With bracelets of thy hair, rings, gauds, conceits,
> Knacks, trifles, nosegays, sweetmeats – messengers
> Of strong prevailment in unhardened youth.
> With cunning hast thou filched my daughter's heart,
> Turned her obedience, which is due to me,
> To stubborn harshness.
>
> (i.i.27–38)

From the troubled father's point of view, this crafty courtship has taken place entirely within the territory of the imaginary, where false feigning passes for true faining and where Hermia's 'fantasy' receives a delusive 'impression' of Lysander. But the enchantments of the imaginary are clearly coupled with the seductions of the symbolic. Unable to present himself in person to Hermia's admiring gaze, Lysander represents himself in a metonymic series of love-tokens, rhymes, songs and conceits. When the name-of-the-father blocks the yearning gaze, love must be smuggled to and fro inside signifiers as transient and slippery as desire itself – 'rings, gauds, conceits, / Knacks, trifles, nosegays, sweetmeats'. Such a shifty series of tokens and proxies lends Lysander's courtship a veneer of superficiality and hints faintly at Demetrius' falseness with Helena – enough at any rate to inspire Hermia's later remark, mostly jesting but perhaps also slightly anxious, about 'all the vows that ever men have broke, / In number more than ever women spoke' (i.i.175–6).[26]

Thus Hermia's and Helena's childhood innocence was innocent most of all, it seems, of the disjunctions of the symbolic. The young women fell from a paradisal past in which words and looks were true reflectors of feelings, fusing two into one, to a present in which they have become the source of division: Demetrius' false vows to Helena have left her bereft of him and envious of Hermia, and Lysander's token-laden courtship – combined of course with Athenian law – has brought Hermia to either the brink of death or the threshhold of a nunnery.

A similar mixture of imaginary and symbolic appears when the lovers are left alone to speak antiphonally of love's vicissitudes. Lysander begins:

> Ay me! For aught that I could ever read,
> Could ever hear by tale or history,
> The course of true love never did run smooth;
> But either it was different in blood –
>
> *Hermia*   O cross, too high to be enthralled to low!
> *Lysander* Or else misgraffed in respect of years –
> *Hermia*   O spite, too old to be engaged to young!
> *Lysander* Or else it stood upon the choice of friends –
> *Hermia*   O hell, to choose love by another's eyes!

Hermia too has been studying tales and histories, especially those of Ovid and Virgil:

> My good Lysander!
> I swear to thee, by Cupid's strongest bow,
> By his best arrow with the golden head,
> By the simplicity of Venus' doves,
> By that which knitteth souls and prospers loves,
> And by that fire which burned the Carthage queen,
> When the false Troyan under sail was seen;
> By all the vows that ever men have broke,
> In number more than ever women spoke;

In that same place thou hast appointed me,
Tomorrow truly will I meet with thee.
(i.i.168–78)

Lacan's notion of the unconscious is relevant here. For him the unconscious is not Freud's deep seething cauldron of impulses but a network of relations that connects us to other people and to outside ideologies, institutions and practices. His famous claim that 'the unconscious of the subject is the discourse of the other' (1977: 55) is evidenced here by the fact that Lysander's and Hermia's doleful sense of what love is derives not from introspection but from (anachronistically) reading tales, histories, Ovidian mythology, Virgilian epics and no doubt a good many Petrarchan sonnets too. Thus their antiphonal style echoes the dualistic back-and-forthness of (imaginary) love, but is complicated by the (symbolic) triangularity introduced by the references to literature as an outside model. As though the 'mirror state' were moved from the imaginary into the symbolic, the stories of troubled love serve as a verbal glass in which the lovers' identity is reflected and created. Unfortunately, these lovers seem to have peered into the most dismal of textual mirrors, where even bright love is fated to be devoured by the jaws of darkness. So even as they defy (or at least defer) the definitions Athenian law and patriarchy would impose on them, Hermia and Lysander acquiesce quite readily to the fateful roles prescribed by literary 'law'. The audience, wearying of all this secondhandedness, might be prompted like Sidney's muse to murmur 'Fool, look in thy heart and love'. But, alas, there is no natural untutored heart to look in; culture, quicker than the fool's glance, always writes its messages on the heart first. Nevertheless, for the lovers this literary process seems so natural that Hermia pronounces unhappy love 'an edict in destiny' (i.i.151), as though love's crosses were written indelibly in the stars and not in books.

To be sure, books can be as fettering as fate, especially if we include scripts. For insofar as the love of Hermia and Lysander is tied to the plot of Shakespeare's play, and their speech to his script, unhappiness is simply their lot. It comes with the territory, and the territory is generic: the script that governs the characters is itself governed by New Comedy, as the learned members of the audience would suspect when Egeus as *senex iratus* hauls his daughter on stage and demands that true love be frustrated. In calling for Athenian law, that is, Egeus calls also for the generic law of New Comedy, which calls in turn for lovers to endure a period of alienation and frustration before being incorporated into society by way of marriage. And of course the instrument of rescue, and sometimes of confusion, in the plays of Plautus and Terence is the 'tricky slave', a role for which Puck seems well qualified; and the fortunate *metabasis* is often brought about by an implausible action, like Theseus' sudden change of mind about the law at the end of Act 4.

So the troubles of Hermia and Lysander *do* stand as an edict in destiny, 'sentenced' as they are by (and in) the texts Lysander has read, and by and in the enveloping texts of Shakespeare's play and its generic forerunners. This metadramatic dimension of the lovers' experience thus reinforces the realistic stress in the opening scene on how the pre-scripts and pre-texts of culture govern the play of youth. Insofar as we humans enter the symbolic by acquiescing to and identifying with *le nom du père*, all the tribulations of the opening scene issue from patriarchy and patrinomy. Theseus sums it up in short when he tells Hermia that Egeus' godlike authority over her derives from the fact that he is her begetter. Typically, an authority grounds authority on the 'natural'; yet in Theseus' phrasing the natural is quickly translated into the cultural: the act of conception involves Egeus, a genetic printing machine, sealing his fatherly copyright in Hermia's daughterly wax (I.i.47–51). Thus metaphorised, the act of conception underwrites the patriarchal law itself, which, like the graphic torture machine in Kafka's penal colony, stamps its imprint on everyone. Even the script of the play, setting down the law for and demanding obedience of its actors and characters, is patriarchal.

And from all of these paternal prescripts the lovers propose to escape by fleeing through the wood into the embrace of the mother. But, alas, she is not the real mother but an aunt, a mother substitute. If that gives our hopes for the lovers' freedom a slight pause, still the widow aunt's house lies beyond the wood, and surely the wood offers itself as a natural sanctuary from an overly symbolic Athens. So it would seem anyhow.

· 2 ·

Desire, the Eye and the Gaze

In the opening scene of *A Midsummer Night's Dream* the heavy hand of the symbolic lies across the action and characters. The love of Hermia and Lysander ought to be a direct unmediated affair of two melding hearts but is governed instead by triangularity and deferral. Even those who rule are ruled: the sudden desires of the duke himself, short as any dream in the past, are now lingered out in the interests of his and Hippolyta's solemnities. Deferral lies not in nature but in second nature, in the symbolic; Theseus' desire waxes, he laments, as the old moon wanes, but the moon itself is quickly eclipsed in his speech by stepdamish metaphors. Given his own obligatory postponements, it is appropriate that Theseus should rule against an immediate decision on Hermia's part:

> Take time to pause; and, by the next new moon –
> The sealing-day betwixt my love and me,
> For everlasting bond of fellowship –
> Upon that day either prepare to die
> For disobedience to your father's will,
> Or else to wed Demetrius, as he would,
> Or on Diana's altar to protest
> For aye austerity and single life.
>
> (i.i.83–90)

Hermia and Lysander do take time to pause, not out of deference to law and cultural mediation but in favour of escaping into the wood where love comes by nature, pauselessly. At least that is how love comes in soft pastorals written with an eye to poetic conventions by bookish young men living in cities. And, as we have seen, that is how the love of Hermia and Lysander has come too, less like the blowing rose than like a poem modelled on other poems – Virgil, Ovid, Petrarch. There is no return from the symbolic to a lost idyllic nature, only to imaginary sylvan paradises where the leaves in the trees derive from those in books, and, as Orlando later demonstrates, vice versa: 'O Rosalind! these trees shall be my books' (*As You Like It*, III.ii.5). But that remains to be seen. Meanwhile, in Athens, the paternal No, the law, Demetrius' vows, Lysander's tales and histories, all seem mobilised in a grand cultural conspiracy against the originality of true love.[1]

BLIND CUPID

With the arrival of Helena, however, a shift occurs. The previous stress on language in its formal and institutional modes gives way to the voice and especially to the eye as more natural media:

> Call you me fair? That fair again unsay.
> Demetrius loves your fair. O happy fair!
> Your eyes are lodestars, and your tongue's sweet air
> More tuneable than lark to shepherd's ear
> When wheat is green, when hawthorn buds appear.
> Sickness is catching. O, were favor so,
> Yours would I catch, fair Hermia, ere I go;
> My hair should catch your hair, my eye your eye,
> My tongue should catch your tongue's sweet melody.
> Were the world mine, Demetrius being bated,
> The rest I'd give to be to you translated.
> O, teach me how you look, and with what art
> You sway the motion of Demetrius' heart.
> (I.i.181–93)

The fact that Helena has just entered and knows nothing of Hermia's trials lends a certain irony to her envious remarks. 'To be to you translated' is one thing if Hermia is the happy focus of male desire, but quite another if for that very reason the Damoclean sword of Athenian law impends over her.[2] Thus Helena's pastoral depiction of a starry-eyed lark-voiced Hermia appears to anticipate the lovers' flight to the sylvan sanctuary of nature rather than to reflect the distraught maid of Athens. Yet her final couplet may give us pause. Does the appeal of Hermia's eyes lie in nature or in art?

We may pause again a bit further on, not over eyes but over a lack of eyes, when Helena concludes the opening scene with a monologue summing things up and casting blind Cupid in the role of villain:

> How happy some o'er other some can be!
> Through Athens I am thought as fair as she.
> But what of that? Demetrius thinks not so;
> He will not know what all but he do know.
> And as he errs, doting on Hermia's eyes,
> So I, admiring of his qualities.
> Things base and vile, holding no quantity,
> Love can transpose to form and dignity.
> Love looks not with the eyes, but with the mind,
> And therefore is winged Cupid painted blind.
> Nor hath love's mind of any judgement taste;
> Wings, and no eyes, figure unheedy haste.
> And therefore is Love said to be a child,
> Because in choice he is so oft beguiled.
> As waggish boys in game themselves forswear,
> So the boy Love is perjured every where.
> For ere Demetrius looked on Hermia's eyne,
> He hailed down oaths that he was only mine;
> And when this hail some heat from Hermia felt,
> So he dissolved, and showers of oaths did melt.
> (i.i.226–45)

The winged Cupid who is painted blind here is a bit confusing. According to Erwin Panofsky, Helena is casting back to a medieval tradition in which Cupid was painted with a bandage over his eyes to represent the blindness of vulgar sensuality – the dread *amor carnalis*, *mundanus* or *profano* from which any decent Christian lover should take flight – instead of his being painted clear-sighted to represent the lucidities of divine love, *amor sacro* (Panofsky 1962: 122–3). If this is so, then Helena is apparently also mocking the mystic vision of Renaissance neoplatonists like Ficino, Pico and especially Bruno, who, far from associating blind Cupid with lust, took Plato's lead and regarded him as emblematic of the fact that the most spiritual forms of love transcend sight, and even for that matter intellect (Wind 1968: 58; Kristeller 1943: 256–8).

It is not clear what tradition of iconography Helena is honouring or deriding. What is clear is that she is not championing the mind over the eye, because the one is as bad as the other: 'Nor hath love's mind of any judgement taste'. Witness, she might have added, my own mind, so lacking in judgement that it keeps me enthralled to the perjured and indifferent Demetrius. Like most fond lovers, Helena's theory is better than her practice. Her plight is like that of Shakespeare's bemused lover in the late sonnets, who laments his unreliable eyes or his errant judgement or both:

> O me, what eyes hath love put in my head,
> Which have no correspondence with true sight!
> Or if they have, where is my judgement fled,
> That censures falsely what they see aright?
> > (Sonnet 148)

Is there a solution to this recurrent dilemma? Helena's complaint suggests that if lovers were equally blind to both Cupids, if they simply saw with what the sonnet calls 'true sight' and not with their ill-judging minds, all would be well.[3] Seeing with the eyes alone sounds ideally objective, and yet in its erasure of the mind or unconscious it becomes a visual analogue to Macbeth's murderous resolution that in the future 'the very firstlings of my heart shall be / The firstlings of my hand' (iv.i.147–8). Macbeth longs for an unmediated bodily action whereby the heart's bloody impulses will spurt into the world unimpeded by the pauser, reason; and Helena longs for a kind of natural seeing undistorted by the too easily infatuated imagination. But their mutual hope to collapse triangularity into a single straight line of desire is an unlikely one. When Hermia wishes her father could see Lysander with her eyes, Theseus corrects her, 'Rather your eyes must with his judgement look' (i.i.56–7). This is a repellent notion – 'O hell', she declares later, 'to choose love by another's eyes' (140) – yet it seems unavoidable: rejecting the guidance of her father's eyes, she nonetheless submits to the sorrowful 'view' of love presented in the tales and histories read by Lysander.[4]

Thus the need for a purer mode of seeing looms large, and when Helena says Hermia's eyes are 'lodestars' we seem to have found it. For this starry image appears to elevate love to an ethereal altitude where it becomes, as Shakespeare idealises it in Sonnet 116,

> 　　　　　　　　　an ever-fixed mark
> That looks on tempests and is never shaken;
> It is the star to every wandering bark,
> Whose worth's unknown, although his height be taken.

Burning serenely at this great height, love is at the furthest remove from the substitutive shifts and changes of sublunary affairs, in which quick bright things come to confusion. Moreover, associating true love with the luminously visible seems a way to avoid the annoying deferrals of the symbolic, because seeing requires no pausing, just an opening of one's eyes. That is exactly what Lysander, Demetrius and Titania do in the forest. They open their eyes and are smitten on the instant with love for the wrong ladies and a far wronger jackass: not much of a recommendation for the innocent eye. On the other hand, these lovers' eyes are by no means innocent if we take into account Puck's flowery glamorisings.

Helena's speeches on the role of eyes and looks in love glance forward to the eye-engendered infatuations of the forest and invite a comparison with the workings of the symbolic in Athens. So, to complement the emphasis I've been placing on the symbolic register, let me focus on the imaginary and rephrase the plight of the loved and unloved in terms of some modern and ancient theories about seeing and desiring.

SIGHTING, SITING, FASCINATION AND THE VEIL

Helena's likening of Hermia's eyes to lodestars calls on a familiar enough metaphor in the rhetoric of love, in whose pages starry-eyed lovers are as populous as the Milky Way. Lodestars, however, are not ordinary stars – in fact are not even stars at all, since there is only one of them, albeit with several names: Polaris, the North Star, the polestar, the lodestar, Star of the Sea. Its names might be various but the star itself is not, and because of this it served since at least the ninth century as a guide for travellers and especially for navigating sailors. In Shakespeare's day it guided them, they hoped, along a latitude. To get across the Atlantic, for instance, mariners sighted on the polestar with astrolabe, quadrant or cross-staff, determined its height above the horizon, and then, checking periodically, traced a latitude to their destination.[5] This procedure seems to have been familiar to Shakespeare when he wrote about love being 'the star to every wandering bark, / Whose worth's unknown, although his height be taken'.

Many a navigator would have agreed cursingly that Polaris' 'worth's unknown', because for a long while its navigational worth depended on the assumption that its heavenly lodging was directly over the geographic pole. Even after that notion was jettisoned, its distance from the pole was officially but erroneously listed in the sixteenth century as $3\frac{1}{2}°$. (In fact it was slightly less than $3°$. In Homer's time it was $12°$ and of negligible use for navigation; today it is a more helpful $1°$ (Taylor 1971: 12, 206, 210)). Moreover, though it appears stationary to the casual observer, the star actually circles the pole. Hence wandering barks wandered a great deal more when the sky was overcast and a compass was required to locate north – because what the compass pointed to, it was assumed, was the 'lodestar'. That is, until 1600 when William Gilbert proved otherwise in his *De Magnete*, Polaris was traditionally thought to be an ethereal lodestone that drew or 'led' magnetised needles towards it. This idea was useful for sonneteers like Samuel Daniel:

> Drawn with the attractive virtue of her eyes,
> My touched heart turns it to that happy coast,
> My joyful north, where all my fortune lies
> *(Delia*, 48)

– and it was seemingly useful for mariners also, since, theoretically, longitude could be calculated as a deviation of the compass needle from true north. Unfortunately, however, as a ship proceeded along a given latitude the compass variation did not remain constant. As a result, until the invention of the marine chronometer in the eighteenth century, it was safer to rely on latitude alone – to sail to a point directly east or west of your destination and 'run the line' – than to go at an angle and rely on the capricious attractiveness of the lodestar (Landes 1983: 107–8).

Sighting on Shakespeare's lodestar image can help us chart a somewhat wandering way among the imagery of eyes and eyesight in *A Midsummer Night's Dream*. For instance, determining one's site by sighting is a use of seeing that confirms its traditional association with truth. It goes without saying that at least since Plato, western philosophy has tended to assume that knowing is assimilable to sight. Seeing is believing, *I see* means 'I know', not to know is 'to be in the dark', we focus on issues or shut our eyes to the truth, and so forth.[6] In Shakespeare's time navigation was a very practical affair of the eyes, a matter of plain sighting. But of course sight depends on light, and just the right amount of it. Too little light keeps us in the dark – 'I'll believe in black holes', the astronomer Philip Morrison prudently declared, 'when I see one' – and too much light dazzles rather than illuminates, as Plato's ascending cave-dwellers discovered, or for that matter as Elizabeth's wandering mariners found out much later. Pilots sighting on the sun with a cross-staff had to shield their eyes with coloured glass; but the glass created so much distortion that they were then obliged to invent the back-staff, which enabled them to turn away from the sun and sight on its shadow instead.

Seeing is at its best when diffused light is reflected from a surface; and yet surfaces render sight suspect, because they presuppose an invisible far side, under side, or inside where appalling things may lurk, like Hamlet's imposthume 'That inward breaks, and shows no cause without / Why the man dies' (*Hamlet* IV.iv.27–9). To learn the inward truth about the human body 'imposthumously', Hamlet goes to school in the graveyard and studies skulls, corpses and such sore decayers of your whoreson dead body as water and worms. The great make-up artist who masks these unappealing truths, he discovers, is really life itself, but he perversely associates it with woman – 'Now get you to my lady's chamber and tell her, let her paint an inch thick, to this favor she must come' (*Hamlet* v.i.192–4). Needless to say, when truth's favour is skull-white, cosmetic painting will always be in vogue.

Whether the hidden truth is appalling or appealing, the metaphors it attracts characteristically derive from woman. Truth is then figured as coyly unforthcoming, veiled, seductive, vainly clothed, inviting, hard to achieve, a cornucopia always strip-teasingly beyond, beneath, below or within (Doane 1989: 119–25).[7] In the Renaissance, nature was herself a fallen woman, a latterday Eve bearing the brands of her former sins but also traces of her original loveliness. Those traces hinted of divinely invisible things, of truths never fully manifest. To enjoy the lady's favours meant to pass beyond the domain of the eye, even for Baconians, who took the testimony of the eye with a grain of judgement. So vulgar love passed from the seen to the unseen, to an orgasmic experience in which a woman was 'known' in non-visual ways; and so neoplatonic lovers, travelling in the other direction, graduated from the visible beauty of the courtly lady to an ecstatic experience of a beauty that transcended vision and led ultimately, they hoped, to an apprehension of God. Not, however, to God as a divine spectacle. As Shakespeare's reading of classical authors would have made plain, divinities have always been shy about making a spectacle of themselves, especially to mortal eyes. Apuleius records how the night-guest Eros simply vanished when the foolish Psyche, though warned not to, *did* try to look on him; and Ovid, in addition to numerous stories of gods concealing their divinity in animal disguises, tells of more harrowing experiences: Pentheus torn apart for spying on the rites of Bacchus, Semele going up in flames after witnessing Zeus unveiled, and Actaeon, glimpsing the equally unveiled Artemis, transformed into venison for his own hounds (after which, however, he could look on Artemis all he liked through the eyes of animals, according to Bruno).[8]

Even for less ambitious pursuers of knowledge than these, the equation of seeing and knowing generates a goal as seductive but also as elusive as satiety or a terminal signified. This is because knowing is invaded by desire, and truth by allure. The feminine allure of Hermia's eyes, for instance, is like the lodestar's magnetism, a power that could only be explained in Shakespeare's day as a form of mystical sympathy like that of the soul – yet surpassing the soul, Gilbert claimed, because it is not 'bound to a human body' (*De Magnete* V: 12; Zilsel 1941: 4). Like a stellified goddess, Hermia draws the gaze of Demetrius' eyes and, as Helena ruefully notes, 'sway[s] the motion of [his] heart'.

The motion of Demetrius' heart is not alone in being swayed by Hermia's eyes; all eyes are magnetised by hers. Lysander and Demetrius would possess her as love object, Egeus as daughterly property, and the state as legal subject. And Helena would possess her even more exclusively, desiring 'to be to [her] translated'. Clearly Hermia commands a more than natural magnetism, perhaps even a dangerous capacity to beguile gazes – in which case her artful looks reflect in benign form what in witches was called 'fascination'. Cornelius Agrippa supplies a vivid description:

> Fascination is a binding, which comes from the spirit of the witch, through the eyes of him that is so bewitched, and entering to his heart. . . . Know, then, that men are most bewitched when, with often beholding, they direct the edge of their sight to the edge of the sight of those that bewitch them; and when their eyes are reciprocally intent one upon the other, and when rays are joined to rays and lights to lights, the spirit of the one is joined to the spirit of the other and fixeth its sparks. So are strong ligations made, and so most vehement loves are inflamed with only the rays of the eyes; even with a certain sudden looking on, as if it were a dart or stroke, penetrating the whole body. (Agrippa 1974: 154–5)

Little wonder that judges of the Inquisition obliged a witch under indictment to enter the courtroom backwards so they could see her before she could see them (Kramer and Sprenger 1970: 228). However, what Agrippa describes here is not just a 'looking on' but a taking possession of, even an act of visual congress featuring 'strong ligations', spirits joining, loves inflamed and a 'penetrating of the whole body'. Seeing becomes a form of touching, as that word was understood in Elizabethan parlance.[9]

If visual fascination could verge on sexual possession, then it behoved society, especially masculine society, to exercise careful control over women's eyes. The ideal of purity in such matters would be the Virgin Mary, and in this connection the lodestar is again interestingly relevant, for it 'was not only precious because it was the sailor's star, the Stella Maris or Star of the Sea, that never moved; it was also by tradition the Star of Mary' (Taylor 1971: 100). This association evidently arose from a fancied etymological connection between the *mare* of Stella Maris and *Mary* (a mistake like that made in translating Ovid's *ros maris*, 'sea spray', into English 'rosemary'). As part of the confusion, the mariner's compass rose, which was shaped like a star to emblematise Polaris, got its name because the rose was Mary's flower. In several ways, then, the lodestar became Marianised, taking on the brightness, distance, purity and truth of the Virgin Mother. Or, for that matter, of the Virgin Queen, as Fulke Greville claims in one of his sonnets (No. 82):

> Under a throne I saw a virgin sit,
> The red and white rose quartered in her face;
> Star of the north! and for true guards to it,
> Princes, churches, states, all pointing to her grace.

These virginal virtues would accrue to Hermia also, Theseus says, were she to enter a nunnery in obedience to the law. And yet the duke has reservations:

> For aye to be in shady cloister mewed,
> To live a barren sister all your life,
> Chanting faint hymns to the cold fruitless moon.
> Thrice blessed they that master so their blood
> To undergo such maiden pilgrimage;
> But earthlier happy is the rose distilled,
> Than that which withering on the virgin thorn
> Grows, lives, and dies in single blessedness.
> (I.i.70–8)

There is more of Protestant England in Theseus' speech than pagan Greece. Although virginity was a compelling religious ideal in medieval England, with the Virgin Mary serving as the ultimate model for nuns, after the Reformation the stress on companionate marriage made 'the assumption that a woman would marry . . . so universal that it was seldom explicitly articulated' (Henderson and McManus 1985: 72). Both historically and in Theseus' anachronistic speech, the rose protected by the 'virgin thorn' yields to the rose whose bud is maritally plucked and distilled into fragrant offspring who will perpetuate beauty.

Sequestration in a nunnery is an appropriate punishment for someone with eyes as alluring, or for that matter with a face as alluring, as Hermia's. For in Helena's 'O, teach me how you look', the word 'look' chiasmically implies in Hermia both a looking and a being looked at and hence breaks down the distinction between the two. Because how they look is a major part of how she looks, Hermia's eyes not merely look but attract looks. Of course her appearance includes more than her eyes, but it is focused there and in her face, in keeping with the idealising tendency of some Renaissance literature to disregard such mundane features of the body as legs, hips, stomachs and often even breasts. The effect of this focus on the feminine face is somewhat to diminish female autonomy. For though there be some who are 'the lords and owners of their faces' (Sonnet 94), a woman's face belongs, as Susan Stewart says, 'to the other; it is unavailable to the woman herself' (1984: 125). To be sure, all faces are 'for the other' insofar as they are invisible to their possessors and are the most 'readable' feature of the body. Bottom, whose ass's head in the woods and whose asininity in Athens are visible to everyone but himself, testifies to that. But in western culture a woman's face is especially alienated, caught and defined by the male gaze it has itself caught and defined. Since alluring feminine faces create male desire, and vice versa, the Christian monastic reaction is to sacralise the removal of the feminine face from the sexual marketplace. Hidden in a nunnery, the face that 'takes the veil' conceals how, in both senses, the woman 'looks' and so preserves mystery and virtue at once.

In recommending the earthlier happiness of marriage over the cold comforts of sequestered virtue, Theseus gives the female gaze freedom to range, as long as it restricts itself to a husband's face. The difference between a nunnery and a marriage, however, is not quite the night and day one he makes it seem, and the point is subtly made through the imagery of hawking that Shakespeare habitually employs of women suspected of sexual flightiness.[10] Because taking the veil is an institutional equivalent of a demure lowering of the eyelids, it is interesting that Theseus associates it with mewing – 'For aye to be in shady cloister mewed' – since mewing is a major phase in the process whereby falcons are taught to 'master . . . their blood'. Even more directly analogous to lowering the eyelids or taking the veil is 'seeling', the drawing of a thread through a bird's eyelids so its eyes can be partially closed against the excitements of light. This association would emerge more obviously in the theatre where the 'aye' in Theseus' 'For aye to be in shady cloister mewed' could not be distinguished from 'eye'.

Beneath the rhetoric about the blessedness of virginity lies the practical need to keep the alluring feminine eye properly downcast and the feminine face modestly veiled. But marriage also seels the eyes of a woman. Only a few lines later Theseus speaks of the 'sealing-day betwixt my love and me', which refers of course to the sealing of marital vows but also may suggest seeling as the first step in the taming of a wild Amazonian creature. Since Theseus' past has not been a model of sexual tameness, either, it is mildly amusing that he should speak so eloquently on behalf of a marital mastering of blood. But given the sexual double standard, his own eyelids are safe; the married male eye was not noticeably downcast either in ancient Greece or Elizabethan England. On the other hand, when the marriage-bound Hermia leaves for the wood with Lysander, she does in effect take the veil with respect to Demetrius. 'Take comfort', she reassures Helena, 'He no more shall see my face' (i.i.102).

THE LOOK AND THE GAZE

The notion that there is a kind of natural unmediated seeing available to lovers, or anyone else, has been discredited by students of sight like Maurice Merleau-Ponty, Ernst Gombrich and Rudolph Arnheim. Purifying vision by separating the eye from the interfering mind, as Helena would like to do, cannot be managed, because, as Merleau-Ponty argued:

> Vision is not the metamorphosis of things themselves into the sight of them; it is not a matter of things belonging simultaneously to the huge, real world and the small, private world. It is a thinking that deciphers strictly the signs given within the body. Resemblance is the result of perception, not its mainspring. (1964: 171)

That is to say, perception is governed by the same processes that govern thought; or, as Arnheim puts it, 'visual perception is visual thinking' (1969: 14). There may be a kind of passive visual receptivity that occurs when you simply open your eyes and register a world of undifferentiated images in a glare of light, but since it is hard not to look at something, real perception takes place with the intended act, ranging from the merely casual glance to the deliberate instrumental sightings of mariners. Focusings of this sort highlight – or, depending on our metaphors, aggressively confront, excise, capture and steal, or more gently greet, open towards, caress and fall in love with – a portion of the visible.

But stripped of metaphor, these are purely optical operations, whereas theorists like Sartre and Lacan are concerned with the extent to which visual experience involves more than (or not even) the eye. They are concerned rather with '*le regard*', which for convenience of distinction we can refer to in Sartre as the 'look' and in Lacan as the 'gaze' (Sartre 1956: 340–400; Lacan 1978: 67–104). Not of course that the concept was unknown prior to Sartre and Lacan. After all, a witch's powers of 'fascination' had nothing to do with visual acuity; meeting her glance meant opening the bedroom window of one's soul to her succubine powers. And the perennial beguilements of woman have always been marked by an appeal to something beyond sight, something in which seeing is infused with desire and hence with a longing to see more than meets the eye.

In *Being and Nothingness* Sartre conceives of the look as a weapon in a contest with the other for identity, status and the world. When I am alone and looking about myself, everything orients itself to me; I take visual possession of the world. But as the judges of the Inquisition were nervously aware, I cannot see without being visible, and therefore vulnerable. The moment I am seen by someone else, a mutual transformation occurs. This person, who had been no more than an object in my field of vision, an *it*, now pre-empts my role as 'seer' and assumes the status of a subject, a *he* or *she*. His or her look not only asserts ownership over what had been *my* world but also, by including me as part of that world, annihilates me as a subject. Now it is I who am reduced to the status of an object, an *it* (Sartre 1956: 340–5).

Given this conception of our visual dealings with one another, it is not surprising that in *No Exit* Sartre says 'Hell is other people'. If so, then looks are the devil's pitchforks. For example, Sartre imagines a mildly infernal situation in which he is peeking through a keyhole, in visual command of the scene within and wholly absorbed in what he sees, when suddenly he hears a footstep behind him. Without turning around, he is transformed from an unselfconscious observer into a shame-ridden voyeur (1956: 347–9). Even the footstep is unnecessary. Once the look has taken its toll on our imagination, an open door or window, a siren, the fall of a shadow, the ticking of a clock, one's name in a newspaper – almost anything can evoke it.[11] We can never look at others without realising that we too can be looked at. Our vulnerability is attested to by the fact that in our infancy we were seen long before we could see.

And that is only the beginning, since the world is very anxious to keep us in view. In the Renaissance the all-viewer was of course the Christian deity, of whom Nicholas of Cusa said, 'I exist in that measure in which Thou art with me, and, since Thy look is thy being, I am because Thou dost look at me, and if Thou didst turn Thy glance from me I should cease to be' (Cusa 1960: 16), an *esse est percepi* that Bishop Berkeley later expanded to include everything under the eye of divinity.[12] Less auspicious are the supervisors scrutinising the prisoners in Jeremy Bentham's *Penitentiary Panopticon*, the portrait of General Gabler glaring down at Hedda and Lövberg, or Big Brother's TV sets peering at the citizens in Orwell's *Nineteen Eighty-Four*. For most creatures, being visible is a curse – the field mouse nibbles at the hawk's shadow – but for humans visibility is a cage whose centre is everywhere, whose circumference is nowhere. In extreme cases, as in madness, the 'look' may become engulfing and terroristic. A manic-depressive patient describes his impressions as follows:

> my behavior was watched and discussed by the staff; nursing reports, patients' journals, were filled with hundreds of pages describing my appearance and movements; spies were sent into the Hall exclusively to

keep track of me, and to report any suspicious behavior to the hospital administration; therapists ignored their own patients and spent hours in endless discussion, looking at the ramifications of my case; TV cameras, hooked into the walls, taped my facial expressions; every morning, around 3 A.M., three thousand spotlights aimed directly into my eyes; staff prepared elaborate strategies to humiliate me, to expose me and leave me naked in front of the Hall; killers hid behind closed doors and waited until night to sneak into my room. (Glass 1989: 38)

In brief, 'The eyes of Texas are upon you', as the song warns, 'You cannot get away.'[13]

For Hermia, Athens is merely a suburb of Texas, as most Texans would blandly agree. She whose eyes have shined alluringly on Lysander is suddenly caught in the harsh gaze of the law, which threatens either to force her into Demetrius' bed, to mew her in a shady cloister, or to annihilate her altogether. In the last chapter I likened the Athenian law, the quintessentially symbolic, to Kafka's graphic torture machine. In the present context the law partakes of the imaginary and is analogous to General Gabler's portrait and the Sartrian look. Both convert the other into an object, a possession, in Hermia's case a possession of the state, which means that she must put on patriarchal spectacles and see as the law requires. 'I would my father looked but with my eyes', she complains, but Theseus replies, 'Rather your eyes must with his judgment look'. To control seeing in this way is to control identity. If Hermia can be made to see Lysander as her father does, as the state and the law do, she will have become a different person. But the sheer fact of being seen is also defining. Just as the sound of the footstep transformed the un-selfconscious 'Sartre' into a shame-ridden voyeur, so the law's judgemental gaze would transform the innocently self-centred Hermia and Lysander into guilty transgressors.

For Sartre the look seems almost always predatory, hostile and humiliating.[14] Like Hegel's 'master' with his slave, or like Athenian law with Hermia, it subjugates the subject as it defines her. Helena especially undergoes a series of definitions and increasingly degrading redefinitions brought about by the vagaries of the masculine gaze. In Athens, as Demetrius' love-looks shift from her to Hermia, her status declines; but in the wood his hostile looks so degrade her that it would be, she says, 'a place of high respect with me / . . . to be used as you use your dog' (ii.i.209–10). Well before Puck's flowering of eyes, both young women experience the defining power of the male gaze.

For Lacan, on the other hand, the gaze defines more variously, not necessarily in a spirit of competition and hostility. If the world keeps us in view, it is not always because we are a threat but sometimes because we are interesting or attractive, in which case the gaze is to be sought, not avoided. From it, we learn who we are, not in the Cartesian manner by gazing introspectively upon our self, but through phenomenological reflection, by encountering otherness in its various forms, beginning with the (m)other. Seeking to be the *désir de la mère* – a phrase meaning both 'desire for the mother' and the desire to be 'the mother's desire' – the infant who is all eyes, looking, staring, visually exploring, not only gazes but finds itself maternally gazed upon. Along with other part-objects like the voice and the breast the maternal gaze is introjected by the infant as a mental representation to form the somewhat fragmented basis of a lifelong desire to be looked both at and after. Thus the gaze does not merely humiliate or reify in the Sartrian manner, it also solicits the gaze of the other, which then becomes at least partly constitutive of one's subjectivity. Even the narcissistic gaze is constitutive, as when the infant sees its image in the mirror and grasps the inchoate coherence of its body, not precisely 'out-there', since the mirror image is not its real body, but in a midway zone between out-there and in-here, in the split between objectivity and subjectivity.

The mirror experience is perhaps better called a state than a stage, since we never outgrow the need to discover who we are by reflection, painful as those reflections can become: mirrors are not popular for long in burn wards or old folks' homes. No mirrors appear in the Greece of *A Midsummer Night's Dream* either, but substitutes abound in the glassy eyes of others. Rejected by Demetrius, Helena asks disconsolately, 'What wicked and dissembling glass of mine / Made me compare with Hermia's sphery eyne?' (ii.ii.98–9). The dissembling mirror that made her think herself as attractive as Hermia was really the opinion of others – 'Through Athens I am thought as fair as she' (i.i.227) – but whatever it was, a closer look at Hermia's eyes makes of them another equally dissembling mirror in which Helena now sees herself and concludes, 'I am as ugly as a bear' (ii.ii.94).

More traditionally the self-revealing glass is found in the eyes of the beloved, which is where Plato situated it in the *Phaedrus* (255d) when he said that the baffled lover 'cannot account for [his affliction], not realizing that his love is as it were a mirror in which he beholds himself' (Plato 1961: 501). This essentially narcissistic view of love is reflected later in Ficino's claim that lovers do not simply fall in love with someone else but become enamoured of the beloved's image in themselves: 'The lover carves into his soul the model of the beloved. In that way, the soul of the lover becomes the mirror in which the image of the loved one is reflected' (Couliano 1987: 31). Both the beloved, gazing on her exalted image reflected back to her,

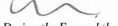

and the lover, gazing inwardly on this same image but seeing also his own soul, fall in love with themselves. How appropriate then that Shakespeare's lovers agree to meet 'Tomorrow night, when Phoebe doth behold / Her silver visage in the wat'ry glass' (I.i.209–10). Here is a wood in which even the moon does not simply cast forth light but gazes self-lovingly upon her own enchanting visage.

The Renaissance theory of love, with its symmetrical identifications between lover and beloved, anticipates Lacan's notion of the imaginary as a visual enclosure from which we could never escape without the mediation of a third term – the unconscious, the symbolic, the social world beyond. Thus we find Shakespeare sometimes canting these mirror metaphors away from the narcissistic in order to reflect public demands. Cassius, seeking to rouse Brutus to greatness, first gets him to acknowledge that 'the eye sees not itself / But by reflection, by some other things', and then laments that Brutus has 'no such mirrors as will turn / Your hidden worthiness into your eye, / That you might see your shadow' (*Julius Caesar*, I.ii.55–7). In Cassius' calculus, for Brutus *not* to look into the mirrors set up by his revolutionary friends is a kind of narcissistic blindness. This same strategy is employed more extensively by Ulysses to open Achilles' eyes to his own hidden virtues. Like Cassius, he obliges Achilles to admit that

> The beauty that is borne here in the face
> The bearer knows not, but commends itself
> To others' eyes; nor doth the eye itself,
> That most pure spirit of sense, behold itself,
> Not going from itself; but eye to eye opposed
> Salutes each other with each other's form.
> (*Troilus and Cressida*, III.iii.103–8)

In Achilles' case this is accomplished (or Ulysses would like to have it accomplished) by his gazing into the cultural mirror of opinion, good report, honour, fame. Then if he issues forth into battle, the heroic 'I' he fashions will survive time's assaults long after his own eye is dust, attaining immortality in stories and plays of the sort Shakespeare's audience is at this moment watching (although Achilles might prefer to remain un-remembered than to be preserved as ingloriously as he is in the ambergris of *Troilus and Cressida*). Ulysses explains this by reference to his mysterious proto-psychoanalytic author, who expressly proves

> That no man is the lord of anything
> Though in and of him there be much consisting,
> Till he communicate his parts to others;

Nor doth he of himself know them for aught
Till he behold them formed in the applause
Where they are extended
          (*Troilus and Cressida*, iii.iii. 115–20)

This is to say with Lacan that the subject is an entity that can conceive of itself only when it is mirrored back to itself from the standpoint of the other's desire. Discovering who I am by seeing myself from the outside, as a me, prepares the way for my understanding of myself as part of a community of others. The I is thus a locus of socialisation, and identity is akin to the Saussurian sign, deriving its value and meaning less from itself than from its location within a differential system.[15]

Situating the self in this way may not be easy. Lysander is no less well bred and good-looking than Demetrius, but mirrored by Egeus' eyes he becomes a presumptuous thieving interloper, by Demetrius' eyes a despised rival, and by Hermia's eyes an infinitely charming wooer. And in the mirror of the lugubrious stories he has read, he becomes a foredoomed lover against whom the tragic plots of true love and the forces of the universe are arrayed. Who, then, is he 'really'? Or who is Helena, for whom the opinion that she is as fair as Hermia in the eyes of all Athens means nothing as long as Demetrius 'thinks not so'? Gazing into Hermia's mirroring eyes, Helena sees both what she is not and what she would like to be. Her identity shifts from gaze to gaze but also as the same gaze changes: Demetrius loved her once, hates her now, and will love her again. Any identity these characters attempt to form on these shifting sands will be something of a mirage.

STYLES OF SEEING

When your I resides in another's eye, an eye through which you see yourself as well, then you are partly split and alienated from yourself and hence in some jeopardy, as indeed we all are even in our first gestures towards forming a sense of self, in the 'mirror state'. That is, the infantile gaze that discovers its bodily wholeness in the mirror image has affinities to Sartre's look, inasmuch as seeing itself from the outside, from the position of a mirroring other, it reduces itself to an object. The extreme version of this is exemplified by Helena, who uses Hermia as a mirror in whose mirrored perfections she becomes by contrast a degraded object. Helena's masochism in the wood is implicit in the self-punishing comparisons and felt lack that motivate her Athenian desire to take Hermia's place, to 'look' like her.

Looks are dangerous. By comparison to the ear, for instance, the eye is a fickle lodging-place for one's value, and to rely on it is to invite betrayal. For whereas the ear is always open to sounds, so that even if you reject what I say you must first listen to my voice and tacitly acknowledge my presence, the eye is a lidded and notorious rover. To say 'As long as you hear me, I am' seems a reasonably safe venture if I can manage to stay within earshot. But to say 'As long as you see me, I am' is to risk annihilation from a single blink or a distracted glance. Demetrius degrades Helena with Sartrian looks – 'For I am sick', he says, 'when I do look on thee' (ii.i.212) – which is bad enough; but he annihilates her when in response to her claim that she is perfectly safe in the wood 'When all the world [i.e. Demetrius] is here to look on me' he refuses to look on her at all – 'I'll run from thee and hide me in the brakes, / And leave thee to the mercy of wild beasts' (ii.i.226–8). By hiding, he not only annihilates her but also, by escaping her doting gaze, annihilates the repellent identity she has imposed on him.

What happens to Helena here happens to everyone else at some point. Demetrius himself runs afoul of Hermia's hateful gaze when she suspects him of killing Lysander: 'So should a murderer look', she says, 'so dead, so grim' (iii.ii.57). His 'look' – both his manner of looking and his appearance – makes him a murderer in her eyes, but her look of loathing annihilates him: 'So should the murdered look', he corrects her, 'and so should I, / Pierced through the heart with your stern cruelty'. And all the while her fair looks belie her fierce look: 'Yet you, the murderer, look as bright, as clear, / As yonder Venus in her glimmering sphere'. After reducing Demetrius to Helena's canine status with cries of 'Out, dog! Out, cur!' (65), Hermia ends the exchange by inflicting on him the punishment he inflicted on Helena: the only favour he will get from her, she says, is 'The privilege never to see me more' (iii.ii.79). And off she goes, leaving him, if not to die, at least to sleep – death's counterfeit.

These annihilating looks and the general antagonisms of the wood may remind us that falling in love is hard to distinguish from falling in hate. Coleridge noted that 'Sympathy constitutes friendship, but in love there is a sort of antipathy or opposing passion. Each strives to be the other' (*Table Talk*, cited by Reik 1957: 57). Similarly, Lacan claims that lovers caught up in the imaginary find themselves flailing back and forth between love and hate, master and slave, victim and victimiser; and Theodor Reik says love is a reaction-formation to feelings of envy, possessiveness and hostility: '"I love you" does not mean "I do not hate you" but "I have reversed all my hostile emotions and domineering feelings and have turned them into tenderness for you"' (1957: 66–7). All of these views seem perfectly illustrated by the lovers in the wood.

Even the much-beloved Hermia is not exempt from the antipathies of

love. By fleeing to the forest she may have escaped the basilisk stare of
Athenian law, but she encounters something equally frightening when she
and Lysander are asleep and she dreams of the male gaze at its most
vicious. She awakes crying:

> Help me, Lysander, help me! Do thy best
> To pluck this crawling serpent from my breast!
> Ay me, for pity! What a dream was here!
> Lysander, look how I do quake with fear.
> Methought a serpent eat my heart away,
> And you sat smiling at his cruel prey.
>
> (II.ii.145–50)

Considered from an outside perspective, Hermia's dream confirms what
Sartre and Lacan maintain, that the potency of the gaze has nothing to do
with eyes: the watching, smiling Lysander exists only in her fearful
imagination. Within the dream, however, the male gaze has a gruesome
bodily presence. Considered from this standpoint, the eating serpent is a
physical extension of the smiling Lysander's sadistic line of sight.[16] Its head
penetrates her heart, but its tail emerges from his eye – a grotesque way of
literalising the familiar metaphor of seeing as a kind of touching (as in 'to
lay one's eyes on' or, more to the present point, 'to feast one's eyes on'). To
be seen in this way is to be violated, as Athena and Diana felt when while
bathing they found themselves observed by Tiresias and Actaeon, or as
René Magritte demonstrated in his startling picture 'The Rape'[17] Hence
the snake takes on a phallic identity as it corporealises the metaphor of
visual violation.

The metaphor of seeing as touching, even as sexual touching (as here or
in the case of witches), would seem less metaphorical if you believed, with
a host of authorities including the Pythagoreans, Plato, Euclid, Galen,
Leonardo, Ficino, Agrippa, Bruno, Donne and Shakespeare, in the
extromission theory of vision, according to which the eye sends forth its
own rays in the act of perception (Edgerton 1975: 67 ff.; Hanson 1961:
180). These rays, composed of vapours distilled from the thinnest blood in
the heart, are discharged through the eyes as if through the muzzle of a gun
– or, more appropriately in this context, are fired from the eyes as though
the corneas were bent bows shooting forth love's arrows. To fashion
'Cupid's arrows' out of darting erotic glances was not, for Ficino, wholly
mythological; he thought the rays fired forth by the eyes to be 'equipped
with invisible pneumatic tips able to inflict severe damage on the person
shot' (Couliano 1987: 30).[18]

Titania could attest to the severity of the damage, provided the sequence

erotic glance → Cupid's arrow is carried several steps further in keeping
with Oberon's long speech about the origins of errant desire (ii.i.148–72).
In that speech he explains to Puck how Cupid's arrow, aimed at a 'fair vestal
throned by the west', missed its target when it was 'quenched in the chaste
beams of the wat'ry moon' and fell to earth, wounding the innocent 'milk-
white' western flower that afterwards, having become potently purple with
eros, became known as 'love-in-idleness' and now serves Oberon as an
aphrodisiac for Titania. Thus the sequence becomes love's glances →
Cupid's arrow → love-in-idleness → Titania's eyes → braying Bottom.
This sequence applies also to the flower-smitten Lysander and Demetrius,
and in each instance it comes to a halt when it reverts to its metaphoric
origin in 'erotic glance'. Comes to a halt, that is, because the arrows shot
with such passion from the afflicted eyes of Lysander and Demetrius and
especially of Titania thud harmlessly against the armour of Helena's
scepticism and Bottom's obliviousness.

Consider Titania's case. Before her eyes are charmed, the fairy queen is
far less subject to the defining male gaze than Hermia and Helena. After
all, to get a squire, Oberon has already brought to bear on his stubborn
queen both the male gaze and the regal look, whose awesomely combined
powers have turned the seasons upside down, drowned the countryside in
rainwater, and left the king precisely as devoid of a squire as he was before.
Undeterred, he tries again; if Titania will not lower her eyes before his
gaze, he will open them to strange sights:

> What thou see'st when thou dost wake,
> Do it for thy true-love take;
> Love and languish for his sake.
> Be it ounce, or cat, or bear,
> Pard, or boar with bristled hair,
> In thy eye that shall appear
> When thou wakest, it is thy dear.
> Wake when some vile thing is near.
> (ii.ii.27–34)

As I said earlier, the imaginary constitutes a closed dualistic system unless
there is recourse to the mediation of a third term – the symbolic, the
unconscious. Thus Oberon seeks to shatter Titania's exclusive identification with the Indian boy by introjecting his tyrannical charm as the
mediating third term. In this he imitates affairs in Athens, inasmuch as his
magic is the sylvan equivalent of the patriarchal law that governs desire in
Athens. Actually, his magic is more powerful than Athenian law. Hermia
must marry the man her father chooses, but the law can not compel her to

love him, whereas Oberon's charms are irresistible – they trip Cupid's bowstring and send love forth in volleys. The fact that they do not decree whom the arrows will strike suggests that desire is so fundamentally errant that merely to release it is a guarantee of grief; it will invariably strike someone incapable of loving in return.

In Titania's case it strikes Bottom, a somewhat more likely lover than a boar with bristled hair, but still sufficiently demeaning for Oberon's purposes. Once Titania has been properly humbled, Oberon reveals his strategy with a couple of puns:

> I'll to my queen and beg her Indian boy;
> And then I will her charmed *eye* release
> From monster's *view*.
>
> (III.ii.375–7)

His pun on I/eye effectively underscores the role of the 'charmed eye' in creating a 'charmed I'. Her eye charmed, Titania's I is redefined. The marvellous powers of the pansy, coupled with Oberon's verbal charm, have afflicted her with love's trick of seeing not with the eyes, as Helena said, but with a mind bereft of judgement. The gaze she is captured by is her own, as she said on first view of Bottom:

> So is mine *eye* enthralled to thy shape;
> And thy fair virtue's force perforce doth move me
> On the first *view* to say, to swear, I love thee.
>
> (III.i.134–6, my italics)

Bottom needs no lodestone eyes to attract Titania's loving looks; her eye is enthralled to a shape that her I, a more inward viewing device, has somehow endowed with beauty. Yet when Oberon says he will release Titania's 'charmed eye . . . From monster's view', there is a point to the ambiguity of 'monster's view'; for Titania is caught both in her charmed view of the assish monster and in his uncharmed view of her. What is embarrassing about her experience is not only what she acknowledges afterwards, that she has loved this repellent creature – 'O, how mine eyes do loathe his visage now!' (IV.i.79) – but also what she does not acknowledge, that he has not loved her. 'On the first view' of Bottom, Titania declares her love and marvels at his wisdom and beauty. But the 'monster's view' of her is so languid that it scarcely spans the distance between them. As befits a man-beast, Bottom dotes on nothing but his own needs – to get out of the forest mainly (III.i.143), and in lieu of that to get his head scratched, his stomach filled and his 'exposition of sleep' satisfied

(IV.I.23–38). That means he spends more time looking at helpful elves like Cobweb and Mustardseed than gazing into the eyes of a fairy queen. In fact, largely oblivious of the charms of fairyland, he soon closes his eyes to everything, though he is agreeably indifferent to playing the elm round which Titania sensuously winds her ivy arms as he drowses (IV.i.43–4). That is a good place to leave them for a while.

LOOKING AWAY

In the forest the merry-go-round of unattainable desire in Athens continues as a kind of dance within a fairy circle. If in Athens Helena loved Demetrius who loved Hermia who loved Lysander who loved but could not have Hermia, now in the forest this chase of love continues, once Lysander is anointed, with the last-named Hermia in pursuit of Lysander who pursues Helena who pursues Demetrius who pursues Hermia. As Enid Welsford saw it,

> The lovers quarrel in a dance pattern: first, there are two men to one woman and the other woman alone, then for a brief space a circular movement, each one pursuing and pursued, then a return to the first figure with the position of the women reversed, then a cross-movement, man quarreling with man and woman with woman, and then, as a finale, a general setting to partners, including not only lovers but fairies and royal personages as well. (1962: 348)[19]

'Our sense of the lovers' permutations', says David P. Young, 'is distinctly spatial; almost any discussion of them is apt to resort to diagrammatic figures' (1966: 94). Thus if the complexities of desire in the Athenian symbolic are triangular, in the wood they are circular – and appropriately so, since a grassy clearing in the wood is a likely site for 'fairy rings', those circles of grass made more brightly green, it was thought, by the dancing of fairy feet within them (but actually caused more mundanely by the outward propagation of a mushroom). Since setting foot within a fairy ring was hazardous – it could bring you under the power of the fairies – perhaps it is within such a ring that the unwitting Hermia and Lysander fall asleep, inviting Puck's application of love-in-idleness.

In any case we have a sequence of diagrams, beginning in pleasanter times with the straight-line reciprocations of gaze-like love, first between the budding schoolgirls, then, with the arrival of the young men, when the two couples face off to form a kind of square made of an exchange of looks and vows. However, when Demetrius breaks his vows, this mirroring love gives way to triangular complications. And now in the wood, as Demetrius and Lysander switch affections, we have triangles yielding to a circle of unrequited desire:

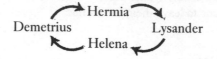

Then this clockwise motion of desire metamorphoses into a new triangle when Puck applies the antidote to Demetrius so that he and Lysander both love the astonished Helena: 'O spite! O hell! I see you all are bent / To set against me for your merriment' (III.ii.145–6). And finally, when the antidote is applied to Lysander, this triangle yields to reciprocation of love and friendship in all directions:

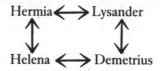

All of these figures and designs suggest that Shakespeare is less interested in characterisation in this play, at least with respect to the lovers, than with positioning. We find no malapropistic Mrs Quicklys here, no explosively bombastic Pistols or whelk-nosed Bardolphs, no arresting personalities like Hotspur or Falstaff, but rather two pairs of fairly identical twins who are best distinguished by their locations within a network of desire. Thus a self is a complex reticulation of desires, some going forth, some coming in. To keep to the terminology, desires are azimuths that enable us to locate identities by triangulation. If you draw azimuths of desire out from Lysander, Demetrius, Egeus and Helena, they will meet at Hermia. So with the others. As regards family and fortune, and probably appearance, Demetrius and Lysander are indistinguishable. Even their own desire does not distinguish them, because they both desire Hermia; hence we locate them by drawing back-azimuths from Hermia and Egeus. The one desires Lysander, and the other desires Demetrius, and therein lies a world of difference. By the same token, 'Throughout Athens [Helena is] thought as fair as [Hermia]', but Demetrius loves Hermia, not Helena – another world of difference.

Most of the circular back-and-forthing is defined by who looks at whom and in what way. That can get very complicated if you try to chart everyone's glances. In general, however, the women's gazes remain fixed on the proper beloved, and the spinning heads are on male shoulders, with Lysander glancing from Hermia to Helena and back again, and Demetrius from Helena to Hermia (in Athens) and now back again.[20] This male whiplash effect illustrates the fickle and foolish version of desire that Shakespeare usually calls doting, a state of stunned adoration brought on by that electrifying first glimpse of the other as vision. Lysander, for instance, has never really looked at Helena before. When he does, he is astonished at what he sees: 'Transparent Helena! Nature shows art / That through thy bosom makes me see thy heart' (II.ii.104–5). Here at last is seeing as nature and right reason meant it to be:

> Reason becomes the marshall to my will
> And leads me to [Helena's] eyes, where I o'erlook
> Love's stories written in love's richest book.
>   (II.ii. 120–2)

'Reason' marshals Lysander the way he was already going, down the byways of book-inspired illusion. The 'transparent Helena' he now spies through the pure lens of nature is merely the latest edition of the lady of love he extracted once before from 'tale and history' and called by the name of Hermia (I.i.132–3). In the present case, however, Helena is not just modelled on 'stories written in love's richest book'; she is the book itself. In a Petrarchan age – but only more obviously than in other ages – love goddesses are bound in calf, and their lovers, like the pedants in *Love's Labour's Lost*, must dine on paper and drink ink.

Shakespeare never tires of dispelling the illusion of an unmediated nature while seeming to invoke it. A fresh and lovely Helena appears to Lysander because he now sees with an eye made one with nature by Puck's application of the flower juice. Yet Puck's action equally emphasises, at a purely bodily level, the distorting role of mediation, even when the medium is nature itself. Lysander's eyes enable vision and warp it at the same time, as any lens does, thus making him a visual predecessor of Heisenberg's 'uncertainty principle'. This go-between get-between aspect of sensory mediation is repeated at the level of culture. Loving, seemingly the most spontaneous and natural of activities, always ends up repeating, with an air of discovery, someone else's clichés – 'O Helen, goddess, nymph, perfect, divine!' Demetrius babbles on, seeing Helena as if for the first time (III.ii.137) – even as Shakespeare is at this moment repeating Petrarch's, albeit in a demystifying cause. As for Lysander, love's stories worked their transformative magic on his reading eyes less conspicuously perhaps in Athens but no less compellingly than Puck's flowers do in the forest.

The compelling aspect of desire overrides the individuality of choice. It is not Lysander who chooses but desire, working unconsciously, using Lysander as its agent in finding an object for its attentions. Thus Lysander has no idea what he is seeing. Helena is a kind of blur into which he quite literally reads his own interpretations. This suggests that sometimes the best way to see someone is by not looking at them. If Lysander has never really looked *at* Helena before, neither has he ever really looked away from Hermia until now. When he does, he is astonished at what he sees:

> Hang off, thou cat, thou burr! Vile thing, let loose,
> Or I will shake thee from me like a serpent!
> *Hermia.*   Why are you grown so rude? What change is this,
> Sweet love?
> *Lysander.*   Thy love? Out, tawny Tartar, out!
> Out, loathed medicine! O hated potion, hence!
>
> (iii.ii.260–5)

Here is a version of a Hermia who was perhaps always there but whom Lysander could not see as long as he was glamorised by her looks and his looking. Looking away from her enables him to register those disconcerting features of the beloved to which love must be blind in order to be so rapturously loving. 'Yes, now that I actually look at Helena I see that Hermia *is* rather, well, short – not to mention keen and shrewish too when she is angry!'

What Lysander discovers is what all lovers discover sooner or later, that the beloved he or she is, not necessarily a tawny Tartar, but decidedly imperfect.[21] All this the world well knows, of course, but to the young every cliché is first a revelation, perhaps especially so in Hermia's case. For despite her tribulations with the state in the opening scene, she is the cynosure of desire. Everybody is looking at her – Lysander, Demetrius, Egeus, Helena, Theseus, the law – and wanting her to fulfil some desire in them. As a result she seems plenitude itself, capable of satisfying the 'want' in others, especially in Lysander, Demetrius and Helena. After all, *eros* means 'lack, want and hence desire': the illusion that everything I find absent in myself is abundantly present in this wonderful creature. Of course, precisely because of that, one part of me envies and dislikes her. She is like that 'fair vestal throned by the west' of whom Oberon speaks: so insufferably complete, serene and 'fancy-free' that my own shortcomings and insecurities surface the more painfully by contrast (ii.i.157, 164).

But love quickly represses envy and resentment and converts desire into deification, as Demetrius does Helena in the line quoted earlier. Surely it is no accident that the Demetrius who awakes to catalogue Helena's divine perfections has just been scornfully rejected and degraded by Hermia. Nor any accident that Helena herself trotted all the more worshipfully after him when he rejected and degraded her earlier. The more unworthy I am, the more need I have for love, especially from a divinity. Who is worthy of the Helena Demetrius now describes? Not him or me, perhaps only an Apollo. Hence if I could somehow suspend the laws of nature and obtain her love it would transfigure my faults and redeem all my losses, raise Atlantis and . . .

Must give us pause. Say I *do* obtain her love. What then? Why, then she too is smitten by arrowing Eros. In my enchantment I had forgotten that *eros* works both ways so that if she wants me she must herself be wanting. That is an unfortunate discovery if I had hoped to perfect myself through her, as Alcibiades hoped to do through Socrates (*Symposium* 218d); yet it is fortunate too, because it means she is capable of love, as Socrates seemed not to be (219c). Thus the much-desired and seemingly replete Hermia is sufficiently incomplete to want the Lysander who wants her. More than that: when she tells Helena where she and Lysander intend to meet after fleeing Athens –

. . . in the wood, where often you and I
Upon faint primrose beds were wont to lie,
Emptying our bosoms of their counsel sweet.
(i.i.214–16)

– her choice of a location suggests that, like Helena later, she too longs to return to the scene of childhood bliss and wholeness. Indeed, by comparison to the envious Helena, Hermia actually 'wants' a very great deal, having lost not only childhood but also paternal love, state approval, social identity and possibly her freedom or even her life as well. But it is primarily in the forest, where she is entirely dependent on Lysander, that Hermia's aura of plenitude and wholeness evaporates. Thus her nightmare occurs precisely while Lysander is glancing away from her and gazing happily into the heart of 'transparent Helena' (ii.iii.103 ff.). This looking away from her is represented in her dream as a looking at her with a new sadistically judgemental gaze: Lysander's blind Cupid removes his blind-fold and reveals the lidless killing stare of the serpent.

A sight not to be suffered gladly. Let us clap a blindfold over Cupid's eyes again by shifting to a larger issue raised by this notion of discovering something by looking away from it. For this kind of looking implies the anamorphic gaze.

· 3 ·

The Anamorphic Gaze and Theseus' Dream

At the end of the last chapter I suggested that looking away is also a kind of looking back, as though the Lysander who stares dopily at Helena is also looking at Hermia, seeing her the way mariners sighted on the sun by studying its shadow with a back-staff or the way Hamlet sees Ophelia, 'with his head over his shoulder turned' (*Hamlet*, II.i.94), as he departs for good, or maybe the way Socrates looked at everything, according to Aristophanes (Plato, *Symposium* 221b), with a 'sidelong glance' that presumably discerned what could not be seen from straight on. If so, the need for such a look in assessing Hermia and Helena would seem even more acute because of the paradisal union the girls once enjoyed. If each is the lost half of the other, then to look at Helena is to see what has been lacking in Hermia since the two were sundered.

From the women's point of being viewed, the situation is inverted. 'Point of being viewed' because since Hermia and Helena escape Puck's anointings it is not so much how they see as how they are seen that gets emphasised. For them the ordeal in the forest consists in changing places: Helena learns how it feels to be the cynosure of the male gaze, and Hermia how it feels to be doubly disregarded. Each is reduced to crying in effect 'Why are you looking at me that way, I'm not her!' even as each is being obliged to see the world from the other's perspective and herself from the world's perspective. Indeed all the lovers seem to be holding a mirror before them; look at Lysander and you see Demetrius, at Hermia and you see Helena, and so on. This mirror viewing reflects something more general in *A Midsummer Night's Dream*, something that calls on both characters and audience to practise a kind of Socratic sidelong glance that might be called the anamorphic gaze.

ANAMORPHIC DOUBLING

Anamorphism, a visual device well known and much used by Renaissance painters, is a perspectival technique designed to present one image if viewed from directly in front of the painting and another if viewed from an angle. The most famous instance is Holbein's 'The Ambassadors'. Looked at straight on, the painting displays the familiar figures of the two Frenchmen and, in the foreground between them, an indistinguishable image, a kind of elongated pale blur that might be a flying saucer with holes in it but that, if the puzzled viewer moves to the right and glances back and down, turns out to be a skull lying at the ambassadors' feet.[1] The eye sockets of the skull are large and distended, and their vacant gaze seems to focus nowhere and everywhere, taking in the ambassadors but also the side-angled viewer of the painting and, beyond, all who think they see without being seen. The uncanniness of the painting comes not just from the unexpected appearance of death in it – *Et in Arcadia ego* – but from the association of death with being-seen-seeing. In the very moment of power, as the viewer is taking possession of the painting visually, she is nullified, much as Sartre was shamed by the sound of the footstep behind him as he peered through the keyhole. The effect is like that sought by the director Carl Dreyer for his film *Vampyr*:

> Imagine that we are sitting in an ordinary room. Suddenly we are told that there is a corpse behind the door. In an instant the room we are sitting in is completely altered: everything in it has taken on another look; the light, the atmosphere have changed, though they are physically the same. (Arnheim 1969: 89)

As with the painting, the room takes on 'another look', acquiring a gaze as well as a different appearance, both of which are in excess of the sheer physical facts, which remain precisely as they were. Nothing changes, and everything changes.

In *A Midsummer Night's Dream* Shakespeare does something similar to Holbein by creating a linear version of anamorphosis, converting the painting into a play which the audience sees from three different perspectives.[2]

We do not have to change seats during a performance to find the proper anamorphic angle; Shakespeare does our moving for us by making the 'seen' – that is, the scene – change, in effect presenting us with a painting in three panels. First he gives us a straight-on look at Athens, then shifts our perspective by obliging us to consider the night in the forest, then brings Athens back in the third panel and says, 'Look again'. The anamorphic effect arises from the fact that fairyland, though not exactly a blurry skull at the base of Theseus' palace, is a kind of crazed mirror of the Athenian world.

Because Shakespeare is adapting a graphic technique to a linear form, the anamorphic acquires a parenthetical quality. Since the affairs in Athens cannot be entirely resolved until the day of the wedding, what happens in the forest is a kind of embedding or, more precisely, a recursive function. The play puts Athens on 'hold' while a more urgent 'call' is taken concerning marital insurrections in fairyland and dislocations in nature. The two calls are more than merely modally related. If the Athenian problem cannot be addressed until the fairyland problem is solved, it is not just because the latter is more urgent but because the two are causally connected; fairyland is a phase in the Athenian plot.

What, then, does fairyland cause in Athens? Most obviously, it brings about the corrective realignments among the lovers that prepare for the multiple marriage finale. However, Puck's and Oberon's machinations only make the lovers at the end of Act 4 *willing* to marry. That they *can* marry is a result of Theseus' surprising dismissal of the law. 'Surprising' because in Act 1 the law was said, by Theseus himself, to be irrevocable. 'Fit your fancies to your father's will', he told Hermia, 'Or else the law of Athens yields you up – / Which by no means we may extenuate' (I.i.116–20). But at the end of Act 4, when Egeus invokes that same law, Theseus doffs it aside with a cryptic 'Egeus, I will overbear your will' (IV.i.178). Why so great a change? Who knows? – we have neither seen nor heard of Theseus since his exit in the opening scene.

Or have we?

Perhaps we have, but from an anamorphic angle.

That is, one way to explain Theseus' cavalier dismissal of the law is by registering the full effect of Shakespeare's device of doubling the roles of Theseus and Hippolyta with those of Oberon and Titania. I say 'Shakespeare's' because this practice, which has become almost automatic in the late twentieth century, issues from the playwright as much as it does from inventive directors like Peter Brook or Robin Phillips.[3] The effect of this doubling is that the actors who play the paired parts become visual puns. Listen to Oberon and Titania upbraiding one another about their love for Hippolyta and Theseus in Act 2 Scene 1, then cock your head to one side and, despite differences in costume, you see the bodily presence of Theseus and Hippolyta themselves. Or, rather, of the actors who play them. But since we have already assigned the names Theseus and Hippolyta to these actorly bodies, when they appear as Oberon and Titania they cannot help evoking ghostly images of their Athenian counterparts. All the more so because just when we are asking ourselves 'Isn't that Theseus, and isn't that Hippolyta?' we are also asking ourselves 'Isn't this the same subversion of hierarchical and patriarchal order that we just saw so ruthlessly dealt with in Athens?' For in Athens we heard that Theseus has won Hippolyta's love 'doing [her] injuries', and we saw Egeus, Demetrius and the law combine in an effort to win Hermia's love doing *her* injuries, and now we see Oberon trying to win Titania's love doing *her* injuries. It is all Athens in another key or mode.

To make the parallel with anamorphism more exact, let me take another angled glance at the opening scene and observe that Oberon and Titania are invisibly present there in the persons of Theseus and Hippolyta. Not that Theseus and Hippolyta are blurred the way Holbein's skull is in 'The Ambassadors'; we see the duke and his betrothed as clearly as we do the French ambassadors. Yet something is there that we cannot see or fully make sense of – Oberon and Titania.

Naturally, this seems a perverse claim: how can we expect to see Oberon and Titania when they have yet to make an entrance as characters? Ah, but the anamorphic is perverse by nature – that is to say by artifice: how can we expect to see Holbein's skull when we have yet to move to a position from which it is visible? Nevertheless, when we first encounter 'The Ambassadors' straight on, the skull is there, in the white paint that came from Holbein's brush; and while we watch the opening scene of *A Midsummer Night's Dream* the fairy king and queen are there too, In the stuff Shakespeare painted his plays with, the bodies of actors.

DREAM VISIONS IN FAIRYLAND

Let me trace out the anamorphic effect of this curious doubling, with the aim of seeing how it affects Theseus' dismissal of the law in Act 4. Most immediately, if Oberon and Titania are present in the opening scene in shadowy shape, that is in actorly shape – 'The best in this kind are but shadows' (v.i.210) – then we get a glimpse of a different, more troubled other side to the seemingly cheerful obverse shown us by Theseus and Hippolyta in this scene. But nothing can be discerned until we have a change of scenes and costumes, and an exchange that invites us to recognise the doubling that has taken place:

Oberon   Tarry, rash wanton: am not I thy lord?
Titania   Then I must be thy lady; but I know
            When thou hast stolen away from fairy-land,
            And in the shape of Corin sat all day,
            Playing on pipes of corn and versing love
            To amorous Phyllida. Why art thou here,
            Come from the farthest steep of India,
            But that, forsooth, the bouncing Amazon,
            Your buskined mistress and your warrior love,
            To Theseus must be wedded? and you come
            To give their bed joy and prosperity.
Oberon   How canst thou thus, for shame, Titania,
            Glance at my credit with Hippolyta,
            Knowing I know thy love to Theseus?
            Didst thou not lead him through the glimmering night
            From Perigenia, whom he ravished?
            And make him with fair Aegle break his faith,
            With Ariadne and Antiopa?

                                        (ii.i.63–80)

Elliot Krieger supplies a perceptive gloss on this:

> The suggestion of an erotic connection between the rulers of the
> fairy world and the rulers of Athens transforms the fairies into spiritual
> manifestations of the sexual drives of Theseus and Hippolyta: Titania
> represents in the realm of spirit Theseus's physical desire, held in abey-
> ance during the four-day interval before the wedding, for Hippolyta;
> Oberon represents Hippolyta's desire for Theseus. The destructive
> jealousy with which Oberon and Titania confront each other replaces,
> then, the injury, the actual martial opposition between their two races,
> with which Theseus 'wooed' Hippolyta. (Krieger 1979: 56)[4]

If we factor in the implications of theatrical doubling, these erotic connections between fairyland and Athens suggest a rather sharp discord within the
pre-marital harmonies of Theseus and Hippolyta in Act 1. If Oberon's
difficulties reflect Theseus' state of mind, then the somewhat Chaucerian
Theseus of the opening scene, duke of bright corners and exemplar of order
and government, he whose rough courtship has brought the Amazonian
queen so properly to heel that he can refer to it with urbane self-assurance –

Hippolyta, I wooed thee with my sword,
And won thy love doing thee injuries;

But I will wed thee in another key,
With pomp, with triumph, and with revelling
(1.i.16–19)

– this same duke may nevertheless be hearing in some corner of his mind unnerving forehints of Horace Walpole's remark about comedies ending in marriage because after that the tragedy begins.[5] After all, winning love by doing injuries is not the most auspicious form of courtship in the best of cases, and it would seem particularly questionable when one's beloved is an Amazon. Consider, for example, some Amazonian precedents.

As mentioned earlier, Plutarch says that at one point in the continued conflict between the Greeks and the Amazons the latter invaded Athens and very nearly conquered it (Bullough 1957: 386–7). Had this invasion succeeded, dreadful consequences would surely have ensued. If not killed outright, the Athenian stalwarts might well have suffered the fate of the men captured by Spenser's Radigund, the evil Amazon who obliged her male captives to wear feminine attire and spend their days at women's work (*Faerie Queene*, v.iv.21 ff.). Perhaps Theseus would have been reduced to spinning flax and tow like the wretched Artegall, until some sojourning female warrior like Britomart freed him and set the earth back on its axis again.

Fortunately, Theseus was spared such humiliations. Still, he may have other anxieties about his duchess-to-be. After all, the Elizabethan view of Amazons was somewhat anamorphic. From one perspective, as devotees of their goddess Diana, they appeared as noble, valiant, beautiful and chaste (Shepherd 1981: 13–14). From another they were cunning, cruel and tyrannous – and possessed, Spenser wrote, of a 'wandering fancie [that] after lust dir raunge' (v.v.26). Thus Artegall says he fights Radigund because of 'the faith that I / To Maydenhead and noble knighthood owe' (v.iv.34), and when Britomart kills Radigund, chastity and marriage triumph over lust and 'licentious libertie' (v.v.25). Given the unnatural disobedience and sensuality to which some of these Amazons were prone, Theseus can hardly rest easy despite having conquered Hippolyta and persuaded her to marriage. Who knows whether she will replace his crown with a set of horns, or his throne and sceptre with a joint-stool and distaff?

Not that Hippolyta says anything to suggest as much. Her first speech seems perfectly acceptant of the coming 'solemnities'. But it is hard to know how she responds to the unpleasantness with Hermia. As a woman, especially an Amazonian woman, she can hardly regard with indifference this show of masculine force. As a bride-to-be for whom marriage is the gate to Athenian citizenship, can she simply hold Theseus' arm and smile as he decrees death or virginity for women who reserve some right of choice in marital matters? Does she see in Hermia's resistance a rebuke to her own submissiveness? Or *is* she submissive? Is Theseus' 'Come, my Hippolyta. What cheer, my love?' (I.i.122) merely routine solicitude, or has he sensed something amiss with Hippolyta, and if so, what – outrage, dismay, fear, shame? But Hippolyta keeps her counsel, and so remains an enigma to us as well as to Theseus.[6]

What cheer, then, for the anxious duke? What cheer especially four nights later when he is scheduled for another engagement with this man–woman whose sexual desire is a mystery? Who knows the extent of her requirements? Perhaps she will demand more than he has to give – or, worse, as a devotee of Diana disdain all he has to offer – or, worse yet, insist on assuming an 'Amazon-on-top' position! What does a warrior monarch do in such a case besides casting uneasy glances at his betrothed and murmuring, 'What cheer, my love?'

Well, as W. Thomas MacCary suggests (1985: 146–9), perhaps he dreams about his plight, or rather has a nightmare about it. In his nightmare he finds himself transformed into a fairy king married to a fairy queen even more uncontrollable than he fears his Amazonian queen may turn out to be. This stubborn imperious creature, refusing to honour either his masculinity or his royalty by yielding a changeling boy, instead makes '[the child] all her joy', forswears his own bed and company, and spends her time dancing in the wood with her elves. Not much cheer here for Oberon. Nor for Theseus, whose ducal body fits within the fairy king's robes far too snugly for comfort – especially when Hippolyta's body is so visible in Titania's.[7]

In fact, since Hippolyta's body *is* every bit as visible in Titania's as Theseus' is in Oberon's, is she not dreaming too? After all, it is she of whom Theseus asks, 'What cheer, my love?' And certainly she has as much reason as he to be troubled about their forthcoming marriage, especially after observing how things are done in Athens. Hence what happens to Titania is as much Hippolyta's nightmare–dream as it is Theseus'; and as a result, affairs in fairyland must be interpreted from two perspectives. Let me try to simplify this by dividing the experience of Hippolyta–Titania into two phases, before and after she is charmed by Oberon. The first phase focuses on the dispute over the changeling child.

I DO BUT BEG A LITTLE CHANGELING BOY

Why does Oberon beg a little changeling boy? To serve, he says, as his squire. But Oberon needs a squire the way Portia needs a ring when she demands hers back from Bassanio at the end of *The Merchant of Venice*. That is, Oberon's desire for the boy is an example of what Lacan calls 'demand': 'Demand in itself bears on something other than the satisfactions it calls for. . . . [It] annuls [*aufhebt*] the particularity of everything that can be granted by transmuting it into a proof of love' (1977: 286). Oberon's demand 'annuls the particularity' of the boy by transforming him into a symbol of what Oberon really desires, the gift of Titania's love and obedience. From an Hegelian–Sartrian point of view, it appears that the boy is a subject reduced to an object (a slave) in a contest for marital dominance – even, some have argued, a sexual object, not for Titania but for Oberon (Kott 1964; Cutts 1968; MacCary 1985). However, if Shakespeare intended the boy as a Ganymede figure for a pederastic Oberon, or meant him to have any importance in his own person, surely he would have put him onstage.[8] By not doing so, he does to him theatrically what Oberon and Titania do to him rhetorically – transform him into a signifier in a system of communication.[9] For Titania also wants him less for himself than as a token of love. She tells Oberon exactly why she will not surrender the boy:

> Set your heart at rest.
> The fairy land buys not the child of me.
> His mother was a vot'ress of my order,
> And, in the spiced Indian air, by night,
> Full often hath she gossiped by my side
> And sat with me on Neptune's yellow sands,
> Marking the embarked traders on the flood,
> When we have laughed to see the sails conceive
> And grow big-bellied with the wanton wind;
> Which she, with pretty and with swimming gait,
> Following – her womb then rich with my young squire
> Would imitate, and sail upon the land
> To fetch me trifles, and return again,
> As from a voyage, rich with merchandise.
> But she, being mortal, of that boy did die;
> And for her sake do I rear up the boy,
> And for her sake I will not part with him.
>
> (ii.i.121–37)

Titania describes a fellowship with her votaress Indian queen as idyllic as that enjoyed by Hermia and Helena or, more to the Theseus-as-Oberon point, by Hippolyta in her Amazonian past – a feminine world rich with all the mysteries of fertility, conception, pregnancy and birth that women can treat with easy familiarity but that can be conveyed to Oberon only through imperfect analogies to masculine trade and money-making. The analogies work both ways: the sails of the merchantmen imitate pregnancy by conceiving and growing big-bellied with the wanton wind, and the pregnant votaress, seeing this, imitates the ships by sailing upon the land 'as from a voyage, rich with merchandise'. But although a profitable rhetorical trade is conducted here between women's and men's 'business', there is no question which has priority in terms of nature and grace. Pregnancy is primary and ideal; it can only be imitated by merchantmen, who are then imitated in turn, with light mockery, by the Indian queen.

This is a picture that Oberon, who sees no sign of himself or even of the Indian king in it, can hardly be expected to admire.[10] His response is curt: 'How long within this wood intend you stay?' For her part, Titania takes obvious but melancholy pleasure in the recollection. For the skull in the corner is the child in the womb. Male of course, it kills the mother and brings an end to Titania's idyll, just as the arrival of men has curtailed the idylls of the other women in the play.[11] And now, for Titania, here is another man, a fairy-man, demanding of her as stepmother another kind of birth and death, that she yield up the boy and let the past die.

Thus the fairyland dispute, like that in Athens in the opening scene, is a displaced version of the oedipal crisis. The Athenian version of the crisis took a father–lover–daughter configuration, with Egeus' paternal No delivered to Hermia with respect to marriage. In fairyland we have the classic father–mother–child triangle, except that the child is a changeling and the parents are step-parents. Because the child is absent from the scene here, the theatrical focus falls on the 'mother's' reaction to the paternal No that would separate the child from her. Titania, not the child, suffers symbolic castration: she has to surrender a desire for the phallus of masculine privilege but also her symbolic association with her beloved votaress. Like Hermia and Helena, she longs for a paradisal feminine past prior to or outside of marriage; and so her desire, like theirs, is founded on loss, made even more irremediable in her case by death. To part with the changeling is to acknowledge this loss and the futility of trying to perpetuate an imagined completeness associated with pregnancy by playing stepmother to the boy. Life with Oberon will not compensate Titania for the loss of these illusions; but on the assumption that fairyland has turned Protestant during the Reformation, she will find her likeliest compromise in companionate marital love.[12]

From Oberon's standpoint, acquiring the changeling child erases the point of contentious difference between him and Titania by dissolving her ties to an idealised female past. Similarly, Hippolyta's marriage to Theseus will represent a castration of her Amazonian attempt to possess the phallus.

Ceasing to live a life of masculine privilege, she will submit to her role as Athenian wife (though just how submissive she will be is the point at issue). Thus Titania's giving up a male child seems the dream equivalent to Hippolyta's giving up a masculine life.

But this is to stress merely one aspect of Theseus' anxieties about his Amazonian bride. Such sacrifices guarantee the duke an obedient wife, under which heading chastity presumably falls too. But if we key on Titania's speech about the pregnant votaress, the stress falls not just on obedience but also on motherhood. Amazons, after all, were hardly model mothers. According to Elizabethan authorities,

> Not only did the Amazons refuse to suckle their sons but – according to their enemies – they often slew them at birth. At best they banished them to the fathers for rearing. Or – a third account, preferred by violent antifeminists – these outrageous mothers dislocated the boys' joints and then enslaved the cripples at spinning. (C. T. Wright 1940: 453)

This is a far cry from the attitude expressed by Titania in recounting the scene on the beach. Immortal herself (accented by her line 'But she, being mortal, of that boy did die'), she does what immortals inexplicably do from time to time, envy humans. It comes as something of a surprise that Titania, the beautiful queen of fairyland, can want for anything; but of course immortals have always found themselves wanting – why else would Apollo chase Daphne so, or Aphrodite dote on Endymion, or Zeus descend swan-like upon Leda? What Titania lacks and yearns for here is not sex but pregnancy. She gazes on the Indian queen as Helena gazes on Hermia in the opening scene, desiring 'to be to [her] translated' (i.i.191). Indeed, she depicts her votaress in full sail with such imaginative sympathy that she seems to make it her own – and surely she (and by means of her, Hippolyta) must imitate this voyaging onstage as she tells of it, herself the votaress and Oberon perforce the fairy queen to whom the trifles are given – but not the boy.

Thus Hippolyta-as-Titania experiences a moment when the phallus is not male but female.[13] Her story about her votaress proceeds as if she had been present during the opening scene and heard Theseus' patriarchal account of conception (i.i.47–51) – as of course in the form of Hippolyta she had. As though in retaliation, her story is as devoid of husbands as his was of wives, though hers gives at least a rhetorical nod in the direction of men. Delightful as all this is, it has a certain pathos too, inasmuch as Titania's desire focuses on that specific feature of humans that marks their greatest lack. Creatures that give birth must die, as the fate of the Indian queen makes clear. With her death, the phallus of femininity is lost to

Titania, replaced by the boy whom she can only 'step-mother'. Real motherhood is barred to her by death – the death of the Indian queen but also, more fundamentally, the death an immortal would have to become subject to, and by definition cannot, to enter a world in which children are created, not stolen.

Thus in her role as Titania, Hippolyta experiences a past quite different from her own, one in which she longs for and imitates not male behaviour but femininity and motherhood. For Titania, motherhood was never possible, and even her imaginative association with it through the Indian queen is lost; how irretrievably is evidenced by her inability to express it except in the rhetoric of masculine trade. When she begins her speech by saying 'The fairy land buys not the child of me', she has already conceded the game by thinking of the boy not as a heartfelt be-all and end-all but as a commodity to be bartered for.[14] After all, as Puck said, 'She never had so sweet a changeling' (ii.i.23), which implies that the Indian boy is merely another item in a series and risks raising questions like 'How many changelings had Queen Titania?' Whatever the answer, stepmotherhood is apparently as close as fairy queens can get to biological motherhood.

Not so, however, for Amazonian queens like Hippolyta, once the moon has beheld the night of her and Theseus' solemnities. But will an Amazonian queen even want to be a mother? Presumably she will, once she has passed through the dream of fairyland in the shape of Titania. For on this view Titania's loss and the desire it occasions represent the unconscious loss and desire of the Amazonian queen as well. They represent, that is, precisely what Hippolyta has had to repress in order to *be* an Amazon and what must be readmitted to consciousness, therefore, if she is to become, as she *is* soon to become, not merely the wife of Theseus but also the mother of Hippolytus.

MY MISTRESS WITH A MONSTER IS IN LOVE

The second phase of Hippolyta's nightlife role as Titania is stage-managed by Theseus–Oberon, who gets his will by magical means. If his own imperial gaze has proved ineffectual, he will capture Titania's gaze and refocus it with an aimlessness that would have gratified Cupid:

> The next thing then she waking looks upon,
> Be it lion, bear, or wolf, or bull,
> Or meddling monkey, or on busy ape,
> She shall pursue it with the soul of love.
>   (ii.i.179–82)

According to Jan Kott, this prepares the way not merely for an arousal of 'animal love' in Titania but for its consummation in her bower (Kott 1964: 220–1).[15] In this vein David Ormerod (1978) reminds us that Pasiphaë was just such a lascivious matron and suggests that the encounter of Titania and the onocentaurian Bottom in a labyrinthine wood carries overtones of monstrous doings beneath the palace at Knossos (but see Lamb 1979: 478–82); and Homer Swander attributes to Titania a 'savage, knowingly destructive lust' that is consummated with Bottom in an offstage fairyland bower beyond the woods (Swander 1990: 102).

Swander's argument situates the supposed ravishment of Bottom decorously offstage, primarily because that is the only place it could occur. His argument makes much of the fact that Titania's bower is not the same as the flower-canopied bank 'where the wild thyme blows' and where, according to Oberon, 'sleeps Titania sometime of the night' (ii.i.249, 253). If it *were* the same, Swander says, then 'it is especially easy and attractive to believe that no sexual act occurs between the Queen and the Ass' (1990: 92). Since he believes such an act should occur, he argues that her bower is really in fairyland, which is distant from the wood, and that it is there where Bottom is taken and there where he is ravished.[16]

Peter Brook was not so delicate in his famous production of 1970. Roger Warren describes his staging of the pre-ravishment phase:

> As [Titania] fell in love with Bottom, she lay on her back and curled her legs around his, clawing at his thighs, gasping and gabbling in sexual frenzy as she said:
> And I do love thee. Therefore go with me.
> I'll give thee fairies to attend on thee,
> And they shall fetch thee jewels from the deep,
> And sing while thou on pressed flowers dost sleep
> (iii.i.147–50)
> – whereupon Bottom jumped on top of her.
> (Warren 1983: 57–8)

Whereupon many critics jumped on top of Peter Brook, crying that the real victims of rape here are Shakespeare's text and theatre. As for the theatre, a Titania-jumping Bottom, or a Bottom-jumping Titania, is hardly what Shakespeare could have had in mind for his manor-house production, certainly not what the Office of the Revels would countenance for court performances, and not even what the Shoreditch Theatre in the licentious liberty of Holywell could display. All of Shakespeare's (and any other Elizabethan playwright's) bed-tricks occurred invisibly offstage.

And as for the text, any bedding of Bottom would have to be hidden not only from Elizabethan audiences but from Oberon as well. That the fairy king, twice said to be 'jealous' of Titania (ii.i.24, 81), should be willing to gain a squire at the expense of acquiring horns, especially when his rival is an ass, strains credulity. Of course the conjuring Oberon could not have known Titania would dote on an ass; what he had in mind was 'ounce, or cat, or bear, / Pard, or boar with bristled hair' (ii.ii.30–1). The creatures he cites are all noted for their ferocity and hence would be the most likely to repel, not invite, sexual overtures. Hence his charm calls for Titania not to enjoy her new-found love, whatever he or it may be, but to 'love and *languish* for his sake' (29) or, as he said earlier, to '*pursue* it with the soul of love' (ii.i.182). On learning that Titania 'waked and straightway loved an ass', Oberon says 'This falls out better than I could devise' (iii.ii.34–5), thereby revealing, Brook says, the 'hidden play': 'It's the idea, which has been so easily passed over for centuries, of a man taking the wife whom he loves totally and having her fucked by the crudest sex machine he can find' (Ansorge 1970: 18). That such an idea was passed over for centuries comes as no great surprise, since Oberon, not a man but a fairy king, does not choose a 'sex machine' or anything else (J. R. Brown 1971: 133). What is surprising is that Oberon would opt to be present at the time – as the stage direction at the opening of Act 4 Scene 1 implies: 'Enter Queen of Fairies, and Clown, and Fairies; and the King, behind them'[17] – and that afterwards, looking upon the now-sleeping couple, he could merely observe wryly to Puck, 'Seest thou this sweet sight?' (45). Either we critics and directors mistaketh quite, or fairy kings regard such matters very differently from other Shakespearian husbands, most of whom express some anxiety about their wives' fidelity and none of whom assumes that the best way to teach a wife obedience is to encourage her to make a cuckold of you.

A third deterrent to this ravishing interpretation is Bottom himself, to whom I will return momentarily. Let me note first that part of the difficulty lies in Shakespeare's having composed something of an anamorphic picture of Titania's bower. Take, for instance, Titania's words as she gathers Bottom and herself for . . . for whatever she is gathering them for:

> Come wait upon him; lead him to my bower.
> The moon methinks looks with a watery eye;
> And when she weeps, weeps every little flower,
> Lamenting some enforced chastity.
> Tie up my lover's tongue, bring him silently.
>
> (iii.i.192–6)

A straight-on look at the phrase 'enforced chastity' yields an image of chastity forced or violated, in which case the watery-eyed moon must be Diana, goddess of virginity, who quite properly weeps on such unhappy occasions. Indeed her watery eye, reflected in the eyes of every little flower, disperses a panoptic sex-censuring gaze throughout nature – hardly the kind of gaze or the kind of goddess Titania would want to invoke if she had carnal designs on Bottom. Nor can one imagine a lunar Diana and a myriad flowerets dripping with grief at the thought of Bottom yielding up whatever chastity he has to yield up; the speech would make better sense if a salacious Bottom were hauling Titania off to his hay-stall, not she leading him dumbly to her bower. Still, if we opt for a Titania so bent on ravishing Bottom that she can dismiss the moon's weepy protests, then her 'Tie up my lover's tongue, bring him silently' would apparently be the equivalent to 'Enough said, let's get down to business.'

So the straight-on meaning of 'enforced chastity' is 'chastity forced'. Looked at askance, however, it means just the opposite, 'chastity compelled', the kind Hermia would exemplify if she were to get herself to a nunnery, perhaps the kind she does briefly exemplify when out of deference to 'human modesty' she obliges Lysander to sleep apart from her. This reading would invoke a different kind of moon altogether, one who grows teary-eyed when chastity is preserved: certainly not the prudish Diana, but rather the more amorous Luna or Selene, who fell in love with Endymion long ago and who still inspires the lunacy of country lads and lasses in woodland bowers on the eve of May and at Midsummer Night. By this token the weepy flowerets are not 'Dian's buds' but 'Cupid's flowers' (iv.i.72), who should have little cause to weep if a deflowering is forthcoming. Later on, when Oberon exhibits the sleeping Titania and Bottom to Puck, these flowers, now 'flouriets', are weeping anew. For as Oberon reports,

> that same dew, which sometime on the buds
> Was wont to swell like round and orient pearls,
> Stood now within the pretty flouriets' eyes
> Like tears that did their own disgrace bewail.
>   (v.i.52–5)

What flouriets are these, and what is their disgrace? Surely they must be Dian's buds bewailing the disgrace of having been transformed into Cupid's flowers during the bower episode – bewailing, that is, the humiliation of Titania, brought about not by the demise of her married chastity but simply by her degrading but unconsummated desire for Bottom.

Most arguments for a sexual consummation rely less on the text than on

mythic or fictional parallels (Pasiphaë and the bull, the sexual escapades of
Apuleius) or simply on the director's capacity to divine a subtext. Yet there
are a couple of instances in which Titania appears to speak of country
matters. The first is in Act 3 Scene 1 when she tells her fairies to
light tapers for Bottom 'To have my love to bed and to arise' (166).
Anamorphically hidden within a simple statement about his getting up after
sleeping is a phallic arousal on Bottom's part, indeed *of* Bottom's part. In
the Brook production the line was chanted by the fairies as they led Bottom
offstage, one of them thrusting an ithyphallic arm up between his legs.

The next instance occurs after their reappearance in Act 4 Scene 1,
when Titania enfolds the drowsy Bottom in her arms and murmurs,

> So doth the woodbine the sweet honeysuckle
> Gently entwist; the female ivy so
> Enrings the barky fingers of the elm.
> Oh, how I love thee! How I dote on thee!
>
> (41–4)

Woodbine and honeysuckle are innocent enough, but the enringed finger
is a familiar Shakespearian metaphor for coition (Carroll 1985: 152–5),
most explicitly in *All's Well* when Bertram sets the conditions for Helena's
becoming truly his wife (III.ii.57–60), and the ivy enringing the elm is a
variation on a vine-and-elm topos that Peter Demetz has charted from the
first century BC to modern times (though, surprisingly, without mentioning
A Midsummer Night's Dream). Beginning with Catullus (*Carmen* LXII), the
marriage of feminine grapevine and masculine elm signifies the fruitful
union of husband and wife (Demetz 1958: 521). By the Renaissance the
topos had become widespread, only now it was 'combined and contrasted
with the motif of the ivy, clinging to its tree in an amorous embrace of
intense sexual connotations' (526). Shakespeare employs both topos and
countertopos in *A Comedy of Errors* when the faithful Adriana encounters a
man who looks exactly like her husband and, embracing him, says 'Thou
art an elm, my husband, I a vine', adding that 'If aught possess thee from
me, it is dross, / Usurping ivy, brier, or idle moss' (II.ii.173, 176–7).
Adriana is unaware that in fastening on a man who is not her husband she
is herself the 'usurping ivy'. Similarly, as Titania clings to Bottom, her lines
identify her as the invasive ivy entwining an elm that is not her husband. Of
course if Adriana can play the usurping ivy role in broad daylight on the
streets of Ephesus without betraying her married chastity, so can Titania in
her bower.

This is not to deny that Titania is sensually taken with Bottom; she is.
But the question is how far her sensuality goes, and indeed how far it can

go. Surely a good part of Oberon's punishment of Titania centres in the physical and metaphysical impossibility of a fairy queen to couple with an ass. Add to this the impossibility of exhibiting such a coupling in Shakespeare's theatre and, if we still opt for a sexual act, then it must be accomplished verbally, not actionally, in which case Titania's onstage metaphors here serve as verbal substitutes for the unstageable. It seems to me that Titania's sexually ambitious metaphors are evidence not of what she and Bottom did or are doing but of what at worst she thinks she would like them to be doing. Such metaphors, like those of treasure-laden merchant ships earlier, are the only way to express the mystery of desire as it goes about its strange business in the psyche of a fairy queen.

To expand on this a bit: insofar as desire presupposes lack, we must imagine that Bottom has something that Titania lacks. One glance at Bottom makes this seem absurd; and yet as we saw earlier, Titania's admiring portrayal of the Indian queen implies a desire on her part to be an Indian queen, big with an Indian prince. But what has Bottom got that Titania could possibly desire? Perhaps the most obvious thing a fairy queen lacks and Bottom abundantly possesses is his 'mortal grossness'. That is how she phrases it when she tells Bottom that she will 'purge [his] mortal grossness so / That [he] shalt like an airy spirit go' (III.i.154–5). Unfortunately for her, the last way in the world Bottom could 'go' is like an airy spirit; not even Titania has such transformative powers. And yet she cherishes him most passionately, not in any airy form but in his utmost physicality. This follows logically enough from her speech to Oberon expressing her admiration for 'lower' things – a woman, a human, pregnancy, mortality – even as she neglected her allegiance to 'higher' things – a 'man', a royal husband, wifely obedience, immortality. It follows also from Oberon's accusing her of loving the mortal Theseus. Thus Oberon engineers a punishment that caricatures her desire: she is obliged to descend to the level of brute matter, to the very Bottom itself, and be enthralled by it. When she dotes on Bottom's 'shape' (III.i.134), his 'amiable cheeks' and 'fair large ears' (IV.i.2–4), when she obliges her elves to cater to each of his corporeal needs, and finally when she winds his drowsy bestial body in her arms, what else is she doing but desiring his mortal grossness?

And not simply his 'grossness' but his 'mortal grossness', a significant addition. In a play in which death is often invoked but always shied away from or apparently transcended (except in *Pyramus and Thisbe* (Lyons 1971; Farrell 1989)), Titania comes at it from the other side. Her 'tragedy' is not like that of mortal lovers, whose grand but fatal passion is 'short as any dream' because the jaws of devouring time do their business quickly (I.i.144). Unlike humans Titania is not in flight from time and its henchman mortality; she flutters at their window like a moth at a lantern, trying to find her way into a world of sexuality, pregnancy, birth and (the price of all the others) death, and being frustrated by her immortal ungrossness. Her love for Theseus, her wish to be the pregnant Indian queen, her stepmothering of the queen's child, and now her passion for Bottom: all reflect a desire for mortality. In this light her surrender of the changeling child marks her reconciliation not merely to Oberon and patriarchy but also to her immutable destiny as an immortal. Titania's 'tragedy' is that she is ineligible for the role of tragic heroine; fairy queens cannot fall – not at least into time and death.

Yet in a sense she does fall, not into time or death and not even into bed with Bottom, whose more than mortal grossness is its own impediment to any sexual derring-do in Titania's bower. As Edward Berry observes, 'Of all the many incongruities in this episode, the subtlest, least expected, and most characteristically Shakespearian, is the bestial lover's lack of interest in sex' (1984: 122). Even Kott says, 'Bottom appreciates being treated as a very important person, but is more interested in the frugal pleasure of eating than in the bodily charms of Titania' (1987: 52). Thus despite a major campaign in which she sends armies of elves to hop in his walks, gambol in his eyes, and fetch and feed and scratch as well, she can no more capture his loving glance than Oberon can hers. From the standpoint of Theseus' therapeutic 'dream', this suggests that it is not Hippolyta–Titania's sexual desire alone that is being purged but the unseemly aggressiveness and desire to dominate men that, in his anxious imagination, might well attend it. Thus the presumptuously masculine Amazon becomes the presumptuous Queen Titania, who then becomes the aggressive lover of Bottom, so domineering as to disabuse us of the notion that tyranny is an exclusively masculine pursuit.[18] If Oberon has imposed his will on her with flowers and charms, she imposes hers on Bottom no less irresistibly, first tethering his body – 'Out of this wood do not desire to go. / Thou shalt remain here, whether thou wilt or no' (III.i.146–7) – and later his unmelodious braying – 'Tie up my lover's tongue, bring him silently' (196). In between, the love she displays is imbued with regal narcissism:

> I am a spirit of no common rate.
> The summer still doth tend upon my state;
> And I do love thee. Therefore, go with me.
> (148–50)

This 'I-therefore-you' style of love seems almost as self-centred and inconsiderate in its imperiousness as Bottom is in his bestial oblivion. But Bottom's oblivion outfaces Titania's; when her loving 'therefore' takes aim at him, it turns into a *non sequitur* of heroic proportions. Thus in the bluntest way Titania is lessoned about the limits of queenly command, and Amazonian queens are asked to take note.

In fairyland kings demand, command, punish and finally forgive. When Oberon displays for Puck the sleeping queen and her entwined beloved, Oberon says, 'Seest thou this sweet sight?':

> Her dotage now I do begin to pity.
> For, meeting her of late behind the wood,
> Seeking sweet favours for this hateful fool,
> I did upbraid her and fall out with her.
> For she his hairy temples then had rounded
> With coronet of fresh and fragrant flowers;
> And that same dew, which sometime on the buds
> Was wont to swell like round and orient pearls,
> Stood now within the pretty flouriets' eyes
> Like tears that did their own disgrace bewail.
> When I had at my pleasure taunted her,
> And she in mild terms begged my patience,
> I then did ask of her her changeling child;
> Which straight she gave me, and her fairy sent
> To bear him to my bower in fairy land.
> And, now I have the boy, I will undo
> This hateful imperfection of her eyes.
>
> (IV.i.45–62)

The quality of mercy is not entirely constrained in Oberon, but it is by no means free and generous either, coming as it does only after he has got his humiliating way. Still, Titania's disgrace, reflected in the flouriets' weeping eyes, moves him to pity; and if pity depends on taking the perspective of others, of feeling what wretches feel, then Oberon's own vision has been modified for the better. His sarcastic 'Seest thou this sweet sight?' summarises his entire project to restore marital order by doctoring Titania's eyes and standing coldly by to observe her humiliation. This is his version of the smiling sadism Hermia's dream attributes to Lysander; and insofar as this is also Hippolyta's 'dream', it represents *her* anxieties about a Theseus who won her love doing her injuries. But then, in a forecast of Prospero's 'The rarer action is / In virtue than in vengeance' (*The Tempest* v.i.27–8), Oberon not merely sees Titania's disgrace but feels it, and so breaks his charm.

Unpleasant as Oberon's methods are, we can only judge them by Titania's response; and from the moment of her awakening she is not only unembittered but quick both to love – 'My Oberon!' (IV.i.75) – and also to obey: when he asks for music she immediately cries, 'Music, ho! Music, such as charmeth sleep!' (82). Moreover, when the fairies reappear at the end of the play to bless the marriages, the king and queen are in such perfect accord that her troupe of elves merges with his train as harmoniously as the song she instructs them to sing:

> First, rehearse your song by rote,
> To each word a warbling note.
> Hand in hand, with fairy grace,
> Will we sing, and bless this place.
> [*Song and dance*]

Surely songs and dances of this sort will not only ward off moles, hare-lips, scars and other 'blots of Nature's hand', as Oberon assures us, but also persuade the angry moon to dry up contagious fogs, quiet the rambunctious winds, set the seasons in order and restore fertility to beast and human. However, before such glorious restorations can be made, Theseus must dismiss the law – and to see clearly and obliquely why he does this we have to return to the opening scene and another instance of anamorphism.

ANAMORPHISM, REALISM AND THE LAW

One thing the blatant trickery of the anamorphic teaches us is the more subtle trickery of the 'natural'. For the realism produced by linear perspective in our first straight-on view of Holbein's French ambassadors is just as much the product of craft and art and the geometry of pictorial representation, including the precise placement of the viewer, as the anamorphic unrealism of the skull is. What is palpably apparent in, say, surrealism or cubism is kept hidden in realism: the skull of artifice, whose hollow-eyed glance says to the viewer what the skull says in Holbein's painting – 'Caught you!' What has been caught and exposed is not our blithe sense of immortality but rather our blithe acceptance of the reality of what we thought we saw to begin with: all of the clearly recognisable objects in 'The Ambassadors' apart from the anamorphic skull.

Because the skull is not merely blurred but invisible in dedicated realistic works, we think we are not being watched. But there is the cunning of it. Knowing we will come this way, realism sets a trap for our gaze as craftily as anamorphism does. Seeing us before we even arrive on the scene, it takes our measure, cataloguing the regularity of our habits, what we want and expect to see – our tiresome predilection for recognisable hands and faces and bowls of fruit and French ambassadors – and, noting all of this, it lines us up just so, as if we were sitting for the painting instead of viewing it. There we stand, wide-eyed as a spotlighted deer. We never know what hits us – until anamorphism or some other perversely artificial device gives away the game.[19]

In the opening scene of *A Midsummer Night's Dream* something is hidden also, and hidden in full view, just as the artifice of perspectival realism is. I do not mean the shadows of Oberon and Titania cast by the bodies of Theseus and Hippolyta, but rather the invisibly visible artifice of patriarchy embodied in the law, in the name-of-the-father. For the one thing everyone in this scene accepts, even Hermia and Lysander, is the authority of the law, which no one except Egeus seems to like but which everyone acknowledges as given and unalterable. This is what Pascal calls the 'mystic basis of authority', the fact that authority is often honoured simply because it exists, and continues to exist simply because it is honoured. 'Laws', he observes, 'are obeyed not because they are just but because they are thought just: it is necessary that [justice] be regarded as authentic, eternal, and its beginnings hidden, unless we desire its imminent collapse' (Pascal 1962: 140–1). Yet although it is wise to keep 'beginnings hidden', it is also tempting to seek legitimacy in origins, especially natural ones, as Theseus does when he chides Hermia for not honouring her quasi-divine genetic source:

> To you your father should be as a god –
> One that composed your beauties, yea, and one
> To whom you are but as a form in wax
> By him imprinted and within his power
> To leave the figure or disfigure it.
>
> (I.i.47–51)

But this appeal only confirms Pascal's wisdom about keeping beginnings hidden; for it does not take much of a sidelong glance to see who is missing from this act of genetic composition. If patriarchal authority rests on the act of conception, then mothers have as natural a right to be considered 'gods' as fathers.[20] What is glaringly absent from Theseus' justification of patriarchy calls our attention to what is glaringly absent from the scene itself – mothers. Glaringly absent, that is, now that we notice. Before Theseus' speech we might have vaguely sensed that something was missing from this scene, but the theatrically given – simply who is present on stage – is a kind of law in itself, so naturally persuasive that it takes an anamorphic glance, prompted unwittingly by Theseus, to reveal what ought to be there but is not.

As this speech indicates, and as I mentioned at length in the opening chapter, Shakespeare supplies us with plenty of patriarchal fathers and a decided absence of mothers. That being the case, we ought to be taken aback somewhat to encounter also, or not to encounter, a missing father. Not, again, that every non-appearing father or mother or great-uncle should be reported as missing, since nothing is missing in a play unless its absence is somehow announced, the way the non-materialising battle of Gaultree Forest in *2 Henry IV* is, or as Hamlet's long-delayed revenge is. Here, the absence of Theseus' father becomes apparent in the opening scene, announced by the fact that his name is possessed by that acme of fatherhood, the man whose identity is totally absorbed by paternity, Egeus.

That is, any Elizabethan familiar with the Theseus of mythology would know that his father's name was Aegeus and could hardly help being momentarily puzzled when an older man appears on stage, cries, 'Happy be Theseus, our renowned Duke!' (i.i.20) and is called homophonically 'Aegeus/Egeus' by the duke. For a moment or two the very notion of paternity and patriarchy is as blurred as the skull in Holbein's painting. Has the royal father come before his son the duke to lodge a complaint? If so, then surely the specialty of rule hath been neglected, and degree, both familial and political, is given a fearful shake. An even fearfuller shake is given to our sense of time if we recall that Aegeus ought by all rights to be underground, or rather underwater, instead of in court. For the scholars in the audience would know that Theseus' marriage to Hippolyta took place well after he killed the Cretan minotaur and, returning with Ariadne, forgetfully flew the black sail that caused his despairing father to fling himself into what became the Aegean Sea.

Gradually, however, this blur takes recognisable shape. 'King Aegeus' evaporates, leaving the despotic father of Hermia. Nevertheless, the association between the two has been made, and is reinforced by the fact that in upholding the law Theseus bows to the will of a man who represents, quite literally, *le nom du père*. Perhaps there *is* a skull in this scene after all, casting a ghostly authoritarian gaze on Theseus. For the law Theseus cannot abrogate is 'the ancient privilege of Athens' (i.i.41), a law he inherits from his father's reign, as he inherited it from his, and so on. The monarch Theseus is as ruled by patriarchy as his subjects.

Up to a point, anyhow. At the end of Act 4, when Egeus invokes the law again, with even better justification than before, Theseus cavalierly dismisses both father figure and patriarchal law without a hint of explanation. If the play is a kind of *fort/da* game writ large, the *da* that would normally represent a recovery of the lost mother becomes here a *fort* that does away with the commanding father. I mean 'does away with' not entirely meta-phorically. For Egeus' death is implicit in Theseus' overruling his demand for Lysander's death. The situation is very like that in *Othello* when Brabantio hales his would-be son-in-law before the Senate, demands his death, and is himself officially overruled (Act 1 Scene 3). We learn the significance of this much later, when Gratiano addresses Desdemona's dead body: 'Poor Desdemon! I am glad thy father's dead. / Thy match was mortal to him' (v.ii.211–12). In *A Midsummer Night's Dream* Hermia's match is not mortal to Egeus but something evidently akin to it. When Theseus issues his judgement, Egeus turns abruptly silent, exits shortly thereafter and disappears from the play. At the performance of *Pyramus and Thisbe* he is, or should be, as conspicuously absent as Hermia's mother was from the opening scene of the play.[21]

In freeing Hermia and Lysander from *le nom du père*, Theseus also frees himself, especially if we hear an echo of 'Aegeus' in 'Egeus'. The name-of-the-father resides in the law itself, and to repudiate the law, if only in a particular instance, is to deny its total dominion and hence to expose the ghostly skull of its 'natural' authority for what it is, a self-serving construction of patriarchal culture. To see this, however, Theseus must position himself differently, taking a sidelong Socratic glance at the law. That is just what the play has done for him by casting him in the role of Oberon during the middle of the play and obliging him, in his private version of a midsummer night's dream, to come to terms with his marital anxieties. Not only his marital anxieties, it would seem, but also his tendencies towards phallocratic tyranny – the Theseus who won Hippolyta's love doing her injuries. For one solution to his anxieties about Hippolyta is precisely the solution Egeus resorts to when his authority is called in question: sheer force, death, sequestration. As Egeus, with the uneasy acquiescence of Theseus, seeks to humiliate Hermia by force of law, so Oberon humiliates Titania by force of love-in-idleness. When Titania capitulates, Oberon recants. If the parallels hold, perhaps we can assume that authoritarian excess has been purged not only from fairyland but also from Theseus and Athens.[22] At any rate, Theseus releases the awakened lovers from the power of the law in an act analogous to and consequent, I suppose, upon their earlier release from the power of Oberon's spells.[23]

Both acts of liberation depend on the earlier freeing of Titania from her entrancement with Bottom, which, along with the transfer of the changeling child, marks a restoration of hierarchy in royal marriages. Titania can now pass almost seamlessly into Theseus' world, translated into Hippolyta by means of her doubled role. Having resumed her proper status as obedient and loving wife, she is twice addressed by Oberon as 'my queen' (iv.i.84, 94), just before, after a quick change of costume, she reappears onstage as Hippolyta and is addressed by Theseus as 'fair queen' (108) –

which, given the duke's scepticism in such matters, is as close as his tongue
can get to 'fairy queen'.

This confirmation of the presence of Titania in the body of Hippolyta
affirms the rightness of Theseus' marriage. For if we go back to Oberon's
jealous accusations about Titania's love for Theseus –

> Didst not thou lead him through the glimmering night
> From Perigenia, whom he ravished?
> And make him with fair Aegles break his faith,
> With Ariadne and Antiopa?
>
> (ii.i.77–90)

– we can now see that Titania is cast in the role of desire itself, figured as a
kind of sensual glimmering in the night that promises Theseus the ultimate
in fulfilment just beyond Perigenia with Aegles, just beyond Aegles with
Ariadne, just beyond. . . . So it goes with desire. And there, just beyond all
of these transient desires, flits Titania herself, beckoning. Why? If my
argument about Titania's desire for mortality is plausible, then surely it is
because Oberon is justified in his jealousy. Titania does – or, by now, did –
love Theseus, yearning across the gap separating immortal from mortal. As
she wanted and imagined herself to be the pregnant Indian queen, so in
furthering Theseus' love affairs, she wanted and imagined herself to be
Perigenia and Aegles and Ariadne. But fairies being fairies, following
darkness like a dream, she could come no closer than imagining. Nor, it
seems, could Theseus himself. For this line of argument implies that the
amorous hero was not really pursuing the mortal women he briefly loved
and left but rather the enduring illusion of Titania that took up residence in
each of them before drifting out of reach like desire itself.

This would bespeak a tragic love if it were not for the fact that Titania
now stands beside Theseus in the shape of Hippolyta. Through the magic
of an actor's body Titania finally achieves the corporeality she sought, and
with it Theseus, even as he achieves the elusive Titania he sought, in the
body of his queen to be. Thus Theseus' marriage to Hippolyta receives
a kind of teleological certification, and his earlier infidelities a kind of
exoneration, because it was she all the time he longed for. And, thanks to
the tyrannies of Oberon, his anxieties about her Amazonian desires in bed,
in council chamber, and in the royal nursery have been put to rest. With
Oberon assuming the role of stepfather to the changeling child, patriarchal
authority is restored in fairyland and hence can be relaxed in Athens.

But of course Theseus knows nothing about all this. When he dismisses
the Athenian law he exhibits much the same kind of irrationality as the male
lovers in the wood. As a result, his famous speech extolling the virtues of

reason takes on the character of Lysander's flowery-eyed explanation of why he suddenly loves Helena: because 'The will of man is by his reason swayed' (II.ii.115). Theseus will have nothing to do with 'antic fables' or 'fairy toys' (v.i.3), although as a mythic character he is an antique fable himself and as a player he is an antic onstage (Edwards 1968: 51–6; Barkan 1986: 252), indeed an antic twice over, having played a fairy king as well as an Athenian monarch. In this light, Hippolyta's musing comment –

> But all the story of the night told over,
> And all their minds transfigured so together,
> More witnesseth than fancy's images
> And grows to something of great constancy;
> But, howsoever, strange and admirable.
>
> (v.i.23–7)

– grows more meaningful if she, like the awakened Hermia, is seeing things 'with parted eye / When every thing seems double' (IV.i.188–9) and is perhaps hearing echoes of her own double, the awakened Titania, murmuring 'My Oberon! What visions have I seen! Methought I was enamoured of . . .' (IV.i.75–6). Ah, but neither fairy queen nor Amazonian bride can tell what she thought she was enamoured of. What she *is* enamoured of is Duke Theseus, and all the rest is a dream. Perhaps they can get Peter Quince to write a ballad of this dream. It could be called 'Theseus' Dream'.

· 4 ·

Liminality: Puck's Door

RITES OF PASSAGE

Near the end of the play, as the nobles and workmen exit, Puck makes his entrance to deliver a song-like speech about time (v.i.366–86). Just now, he says, is the time when lions roar, ploughmen snore, graves gape and fairies frolic. That the fairies might frolic all the better, he says, 'I am sent with broom before, / To sweep the dust behind the door' (385–6). Just what this means is unclear. Are fairies especially averse to dust?[1] Is Theseus a lax palace-keeper? It is not even clear what the actor who plays Puck is supposed to do – sweep the dust in the room behind the door or sweep the dust behind the door somewhere else, presumably outside. The ambiguous meaning swings on the hinge of Puck's line rather like the door itself.

Puck's door, like his ambiguous line, is a liminal object. Quite literally part of the limen, or threshold, it stands between inside and outside, partakes of both, is neither wholly one nor the other – a man knows not where to have it. That's how it is with thresholds and boundary points. That's how it is, for instance, with Pyramus and Thisbe's wall. Meant by their fathers to divide the lovers, in its role as 'vile wall' it does just that, but in its role as 'O sweet, O lovely wall', a wall with a chink in it, it also joins them. For that matter it must join the two fathers as well. Since Shakespeare does not say who put up the wall, we are left to wonder which side belongs to whom. Worse yet, what about the hole in the wall? Does it belong to one father or the other; does legal possession include the air

72

within the hole; and where, then, does the hole begin and end? Such confusions suggest why a particularly elusive band of Old West desperadoes, who earned their outlaw status by plying their trade within the world of law before disappearing outside it, called themselves the Hole in the Wall Gang.

The fairies are themselves something of a hole in the wall gang inasmuch as their hideout is similarly difficult to locate. They have recently come from India (II.i.69, 124), but to regard even vast and exotic India as their home seems unduly confining for such evanescent spirits. In this play, at any rate, fairyland seems less a specific place than simply where the fairies are at any time. Where they often are, it seems, is in flight – girdling the globe at an indeterminate altitude, not so high as to be confused with angelic aerialists, nor so low and ominously as to be confused with ghosts and evil spirits, with whom they share the night, but not for the same reasons. Noting the approach of dawn, Puck urges Oberon to make haste (III.ii.378–87), but Oberon assures him that, unlike evil spirits who fear the exposures of the sun, the fairies are 'spirits of a different sort', he himself having frolicked many a time with Aurora at dawn and even in full daylight (III.ii.388–93). Still, darkness is their natural element, as Puck repeats near the end of the play when he says they

> do run
> By the triple Hecate's team
> From the presence of the sun,
> Following darkness like a dream
> (v.i.378–81)

Perhaps during the day the elves curl up under acorns and in hidden bowers, or maybe at the dawn their spirits move wraith-like on, leaving behind the cobwebs, peasblossoms and mustardseeds they have temporarily animated. At any rate, Puck's lines suggest that the fairies circle the earth each night, running before the sun in pursuit of darkness, and hence are always on the shadowy side of the planet. That means that they flourish wherever humans lie sleeping and, more important, dreaming. Thus they flood the stage at the end of the play just as everyone traipses off to bed – at the magic hour of midnight.

What Puck's door and Pyramus and Thisbe's wall do with space, midnight does with time. The 'iron tongue of midnight', Theseus says a few lines earlier, 'hath told twelve', adding no doubt with a teasing smile, 'Lovers, to bed; 'tis almost fairy time'. And indeed it is; the night turns on the iron hinge of twelve, allowing fairy visitors to enter and swinging the festive first of May towards the more prosaic second of May. More largely, the first of May and Midsummer Night are calendrical hinges, the former helping mark the seasonal rotation from spring to summer, the latter turning summer itself in the direction of autumn. Provided of course that Titania and Oberon are not brawling and making the seasons change their wonted liveries.

That is where country festivals come in, to ensure the happy wedding of spring and summer. Like weddings, they are a kind of *rite de passage*, the phrase used by Arthur Van Gennep, whose beliefs about society, as described by Mary Douglas, are right at home, or palace, in the present context:

> He saw society as a house with rooms and corridors in which passage from one to another is dangerous. Danger lies in transitional states, simply because transition is neither one state nor the next, it is undefinable. The person who must pass from one to another is himself in danger and emanates danger to others. The danger is controlled by ritual which precisely separates him from his old status, designates him for a time and then publicly declares his entry to his new status. Not only is transition itself dangerous, but also the rituals of segregation are the most dangerous phase of the rites. (Douglas 1966: 96)

Van Gennep's view of society and its rituals is especially hospitable to open doors:

> the door is the boundary between the foreign and domestic worlds in the case of an ordinary dwelling, between the profane and the sacred worlds in the case of a temple. Therefore to cross the threshold is to unite oneself with a new world. (Van Gennep 1960: 20)

Thus Puck, wielding his broom at the portal to Theseus' palace, properly combines both a domestic task with fairy foreignness; and the fairies in general unite the profane and the sacred, since they are here to bless the newly-weds, their offspring and the palace itself.

In the opening chapter I said the structure of *A Midsummer Night's Dream* is something of a *fort/da* experience writ large, the lovers being lost and then found again by Athenian society. Viewed in a festive light, this movement out and back reflects the 'Saturnalian pattern' that C. L. Barber sees in Elizabethan May-games and in Shakespearian 'festive comedy' generally (1959: 16–57). From an anthropological perspective, it mirrors, as many of the comedies do (Garber 1980; Berry 1984), the tripartite pattern of Van Gennep's transitional rites, in which rites of separation (instigated by the opening scene) lead to rites of liminality/marginality (in the wood) followed by rites of aggregation (as the new status of the lovers is acknowledged and they are admitted into Athenian society at the end of Act 4).[2]

Thus while they are detained by Puck and Oberon in the forest, the lovers take on the amorphous status of persons suspended *en route* from one to another social identity: unbaptised infants, unburied bodies, homeless ghosts, sequestered neophytes, untenured faculty and so on. This indefinable inbetweenness is what makes the liminal dangerous, a kind of hole in the skein of symbolic differences, a phase in which everything is 'ambiguity and paradox, a confusion of all the customary categories' (Turner 1967: 97). As Edward Berry says, 'In the course of a single night the lovers experience all of the confusions of the liminal phase: they wander, they dream, they act madly, they are bewitched, they are "translated"; their loss of self is its own disguise' (1984: 71).

To supplement the discussion of Holbein's 'Ambassadors' in the previous chapter, we could regard the anamorphic as a special visual instance of the liminal. The uncertain identity of Holbein's anamorphic skull lies in the divide between a straight-on and a side-angled Socratic view of it. His painting is like Pyramus and Thisbe's wall. Looked at straight on from either side, the wall is a blocking two-dimensional surface. But the hole is a blur of inbetweenness that redefines the wall by reorienting the viewer's gaze, transforming a two-dimensional into a three-dimensional structure, specifically one with a far or other side. Neither strictly 'Capulet' nor 'Montague' as it were, the wall unites in the act of separating. The hole itself is analogous to Holbein's anamorphic skull. Considered straight on, it looks like a tunnel of love uniting hero and heroine. Unfortunately, it does not quite unite them – 'I kiss the wall's hole, not your lips at all' – and so, considered from a retrospective angle, after their deaths, it symbolises the not-quiteness of desire and prefigures the mortal holes made in their bodies by the sword of Pyramus.

A good deal has been made, properly and profitably so, of the influence on Shakespeare's play of Ovidian metamorphosis (William C. Carroll 1985; Barkan 198). The liminal, however, is not quite metamorphosis itself but an arresting phase within it – a border checkpoint where travellers from one state to another must pause and have their credentials confirmed. Such confirmations do not come easy, because it is precisely at borders and boundary lines, with one realm ahead and another behind, that identities become indefinable. Consider, for instance, the cause of all the turmoil in nature and fairyland – the changeling child. In the lexicon of fairyland, the term 'changeling' did not mean a child the fairies stole from humans but the child they left behind in exchange, the one with hare-lip, scars, moles, marks prodigious, all the defects that made disappointed parents want to disown it (Briggs 1967: 115–22; Brooks 1979: 27). By incorrectly assigning the name 'changeling' to the boy in his play, then, Shakespeare calls special attention to his liminal status. Not only is he a foreigner in fairyland, but he is also arrested between youth and adulthood and between fairy queen and fairy king. Worse yet, he is caught theatrically in the middle, neither in the play nor out of it, or both in and out of it. We hear so much about him that we expect him to make an entrance at any moment, but he never does. He remains suspended on the theatrical threshold, waiting in the dressing room perhaps or sleeping on a bank where the wild thyme blows.[3]

Since *A Midsummer Night's Dream* seems especially intent on exploring liminal midpoints and margins, let us leave the changeling boy arrested on the verge, and Puck suspended broom in hand, while we consider the matter more extensively.

THE MOON, LIKE TO A SILVER BOW

Take the moon for instance. Whatever the hole in the wall may be metaphysically, in practical terms it is a kind of makeshift window; and that may remind us that one solution to the vexing problem of lighting the stage for the play of *Pyramus and Thisbe* is Bottom's idea of leaving a casement open for the moon to shine in. But since that depends on the moon shining that night, a great haste is made to discover whether or not it does: 'A calendar, a calendar!' Bottom cries, 'Look in the almanac. Find out moonshine, find out moonshine', and Quince, looking, announces, 'Yes, it doth shine that night' (iii.i.48–54).

But doth it? It certainly shines a great deal before that night. Theseus' desire is lingered by the old moon's waning light; Lysander 'hast by moonlight' sung love-songs below Hermia's window; Hermia will chant hymns to the 'cold fruitless moon' if she denies her father; Lysander and Hermia are to meet in the wood 'when Phoebe doth behold / Her silver visage in the watery glass'; Titania's fairy tells Puck she travels 'swifter than the moon's sphere'; Peter Quince makes arrangements for his company to meet according to the moon; the wood in *Pyramus and Thisbe* is lit by moonlight and the stage by 'Moonshine'; and at midnight, as everyone prepares to depart for bed, Puck says the 'wolf behowls the moon'. By this point we are inclined to agree with Hippolyta when she says, 'Well shone, Moon. Truly the moon shines with a good grace' (v.i.263).[4]

Perhaps the moon shines so well and so much because, like everything else in this play, it is double. For there are two moons, an old and a new, and Shakespeare is so precise about this and about the exactly four days separating the one from the other that surely we ought to follow Bottom's advice and find out moonshine ourselves. When we do, we discover how curious it is that Shakespeare should have chosen the exact lunar phase he did, because it promises very little in the way of moonshine. When the lingering old moon has fully waned, its image will disappear from the sky for at least one night – the night of the 'new moon', so called, though no moon is visible – before the new moon actually makes its silvery/slivery appearance. The night when the new moon does become visible as 'a silver bow' is the night the solemnities take place and *Pyramus and Thisbe* is performed. If that is the night of 1 May (iv.i.132), four days from the time of the opening scene, then the action begins on 27 April, and the lovers spend the next three nights in the wood, beginning, as Lysander twice says, 'tomorrow night' (i.i.164, 209) – therefore the nights of 28–29 and 29–30 April and 30 April/1 May (Paolucci 1977). During these three nights the moon ought to be virtually invisible, appearing first as a sliver of old moon for two nights, then in total darkness the night of 30 April/1 May, then as a sliver of new moon appearing briefly around sunset on the evening of 1 May (and perhaps not even then, since the new moon is often invisible for several days).

What, then, is the status of the moon during this period, especially on the crucial night of its disappearance? Is it still the old moon, has it become the new moon, or is it something anomalous in between – something like Puck's door, Pyramus and Thisbe's wall and the non-appearing changeling boy? Surely it has the same dual character they have. For the two crescents it forms, new and old, curve in opposite directions, the new moon 'wi' the auld moon in hir arm', as the 'Ballad of Sir Patrick Spens' puts it, and the auld wi' the new in its. Like facing parenthesis marks, the crescents visibly embrace the past and the future. Or, instead of being a parenthetical arm embracing its past, perhaps the new moon is an archer's bent bow flexed towards the future. That is how Hippolyta puts it – 'like to a silver bow / New-bent in heaven' – when she reassures the anxious Theseus that the night of their wedding will arrive in due and natural course.

Hippolyta's bent bow image is crescent with mythological implications, at least two of which deserve a glance. Applied to the frustrated Theseus, for instance, the bent bow suggests the centaur, a familiar figure for lust. Beryl Rowland notes that the centaur 'was an archer, and traditionally, as may be seen in the Pentateuch, the bow and arrow (*keschess*), was often used as the symbol for the normal male act of *ejaculatio seminis*' (1974: 53). The bent bow image would thus evoke Theseus' somewhat centaurian sexual past as he hunted about the Near East and brought down such game as Perigenia, Aegles, Ariadne and Antiopa. It would also emphasise the fact that the affairs of the wood all take place while the bow of his current sexual desire is strung and bent but, alas for him, as yet unreleased.

At the same time, the bent bow evokes Hippolyta's past by figuring as a symbol of Diana in her lunar aspect. This association often appears in paintings by Renaissance artists who were inspired by a Greek sculpture of the fourth century BC depicting Diana in knee-length tunic, shod in buskins, with bow in one hand while the other is drawing an arrow from her quiver (Hall 1974: 102). In such a posture she could aptly serve, as she did at Ephesus, as a patron deity of the Amazons, themselves fierce devotees of the bow, especially when men came within range. Diana, though tricked by Apollo into killing Orion, normally was less concerned to make men the target of her arrows than to make sure she did not become the target of theirs, not even the target of their gaze, as the over-bold Actaeon discovered.[5] In this light, then, the bent bow image frames Hippolyta in her dangerous aspect, suggesting an unsubdued strain of Amazonian queenliness within the Athenian bride-to-be.

So it seems that if the moon itself is liminal, tediously making its three-night way between its oldness and newness, so too is the bent bow image that describes it. Within that image reside two contesting interpretations, and the question is which is to dominate. Is it the defiant Amazon's bow or the lusty duke's? The question itself remains in suspension as the events of the wood move transitionally towards a defining answer.

Moreover, to complicate things, the Diana represented by the bent bow image is herself ambiguous, in part because there are two bent bows, one formed by the old moon, one by the new. The old moon, as Theseus declares at the start, lingers desire, and hence enforces chastity, as it properly should during these treacherous pre-marital days and nights. Here is Diana in her traditional role, keeping a sexually safe distance between lovers, the same Diana, 'cold fruitless moon', to whom Hermia will chant faint hymns should she enter a nunnery. But Elizabethans also knew of another Diana, one who served to unite rather than separate lovers, provided their love was chaste. She played a role in Lyly's *Sapho and Phao* and *Gallathea*, capturing the lascivious Cupid and assuming the part of a chaste Venus in promoting love affairs. Similarly in *Pericles* she sanctions both the reunion of her high priestess Thaisa with Pericles (v.ii.241–50) and the marriage of Marina and Lysimachus (Purdon 1974: 175–8); and, in modified form, she is the 'Diana' (maid, not goddess) in *All's Well* who helps Helena play the bed-trick on Bertram. In *A Midsummer Night's Dream* it is this Diana who lends her virtue and *virtu* to 'Dian's bud', enabling it to overcome 'Cupid's flower' (iv.i.70) not to promote virginity but to restore the love of Titania for Oberon and of Demetrius for Helena.

Thus the two bent bows of Diana, the old representing celibacy, the new chaste love, appropriately face away from one another while enclosing the moon itself, giving Diana a Janus-like indeterminacy as her appearance shifts from the one to the other as the four days elapse. And of course this indeterminacy is reflected in Theseus and Hippolyta, who during the four-day interim are no longer their old selves nor quite yet their new married selves. Theseus is poised between seducer and husband, and Hippolyta between man-hating Amazonian queen and loving Athenian duchess. Even within the ritual framework of marriage, as betrothed but yet unwed, the two are obliged to occupy a liminal state before their desire is solemnised and the bent bow, whoever it belongs to, is sprung.[6]

FORECLOSURE AND THE LIMINAL

In the opening scene Hermia and Lysander come to grief because their desire is being forced into the geometries of cultural triangulation, whereas if they had their choice they would, like Romeo and Juliet and all self-absorbed lovers, withdraw from society and do nothing but gaze narcissistically into one another's eyes. At any rate that is how they view their situation and why they flee from Athens into the wood. What happens in the wood seems to stand in diametric contrast with what happens in Athens, and a set of binary opposites offers itself to the teacher as readily as blackboard to chalk. Palace and wood usher in culture/nature, order/disorder, law/impulse and reason/imagination, to cite a few of the obvious contrasts.

Placing palace and wood in dialectical opposition like this is highly inviting and probably unavoidable even with the best of intentions, but also a bit too easy. Doing so ignores, for instance, the fact that what happens in the wood, though it partly contrasts with, also repeats and intensifies what happens in Athens.[7] Theseus' inability to impose the rule of patriarchy in the palace is mirrored by Oberon's frustrations with Titania and the changeling; and the male rivalry and odd-woman-out pattern of the lovers in Athens is merely aggravated and inverted in the wood. Shakespeare is not piping a pastoralist tune about shedding civilisation and the symbolic in order to return to a golden age of the imaginary. His lovers are as laden with the accoutrements of city life as weekend campers in Yosemite or the Yorkshire Dales. Although in their recollection Hermia and Helena fell from a natural 'union in partition' when the young men introduced them to the differentiations of the symbolic, even this lost paradise is characterised by an exchange of confidences ('counsel', i.i.216, iii.ii.198), which implies not so much a primordial oneness as differences shared. Similarly, the 'sister's vows' mentioned by Helena (iii.ii.199) presuppose a fear of alienation; and her eulogy of their cherry-like two-in-oneness builds to a strange heraldic shield metaphor – their bodies were 'like coats in heraldry, / Due but to one and crowned with one crest' (iii.ii.213–14) – as though the natural and bodily were already taking cover behind an aegis of signifiers in a world of warring differences. Despite Helena's paean to the past, it is clear that there was and is no uncorrupted state of nature to which the lovers can return.

To what then do they return? Taking a cue from Demetrius' line about being 'wode within this wood' (II.i.192), perhaps we could say they do not return at all but simply enter a mad maze-like scene, a forest of mirrors and mirror-states through which they pass like Alice through her looking-glass, into the schizophrenic wonderland so admired by Deleuze and Guattari in *Anti-Oedipus* (1983: 51–138), though rather less esteemed by schizophrenics themselves.[8] Certainly the lovers' experience in the wood amply satisfies Deleuze and Guattari's characterisation of schizophrenia as a condition in which social boundaries are transgressed, meanings proliferate wildly and unified selves disintegrate.

Although Lacan is oblivious of the charms of schizophrenia, he too associates it with the anti-oedipal. Schizophrenia is a consequence of what he calls forclusion or foreclosure:

> It is an accident in this register [i.e. the symbolic] and in what takes place in it, namely, the foreclosure of the Name-of-the-Father in the place of the Other, and in the failure of the paternal metaphor, that I designate the defect that gives psychosis its essential condition, and the structure that separates it from neurosis. (Lacan 1977: 215)

That is, foreclosure (repudiation or default) is a rejection not so much of an individual father as of the cultural signifier, 'the paternal metaphor'. In contrast to Freudian repression, which is a neurotic process taking place within the symbolic, foreclosure is a rejection of the symbolic itself, a refusal to submit to the act of repression and alienation by which one crosses the threshold from the imaginary to the symbolic, from the bodily immediacy of the mother to the verbal mediations of the father. Unfortunately, to refuse this invitation of Oedipus is not only to escape his tyranny but also to forfeit his hospitality and protection. Unwilling or unable to situate herself within the symbolic order, the schizophrenic must encounter her demons outside it, in the imaginary, rather like Hermia and Lysander when they repudiate the paternal metaphor and abandon civilised Athens for a sylvan world bathed in the light of a feminine moon, a wood that is punningly equivalent to madness. Not true madness of course but a special form of it – love madness, moon madness.

The idea of foreclosure seems to smuggle back into the argument the notion of binary opposites that was ousted earlier, simply substituting sanity/madness, Oedipus/psychosis and symbolic/imaginary for the more conventional culture/nature, order/disorder, and so on. But that is not quite the case, because Hermia and Lysander have not conclusively rejected the symbolic: Hermia has until Theseus' wedding day to make her choice. If her agreeing to this deferral implies at least a temporary submission to the symbolic mode, her agreeing to Lysander's plan to elope implies a recoiling from it. It would seem, then, that the interim in the wood is a liminal period, during which the lovers are straddling the boundary line between the cultural symbolic and the natural imaginary. Wode they may be, but only north-north-west. Even so, in that direction lie hobgoblins aplenty – or at least one hobgoblin who takes many shapes.

For the schizophrenic, foreclosure means that the hobgoblin imaginary reappears with the frightening immediacy of childhood. The experience is described by Robert Graves in his poem 'The Cool Web', where children, because they lack the verbal sophistication to tell

> how hot the day is,
> How hot the scent is of the summer rose,
> How dreadful the black wastes of evening sky,
> How dreadful the tall soldiers drumming by

must suffer the inexpressible onslaughts of an imaginary more closely in touch with the real. We adults, on the other hand, are ensconced within the symbolic and hence buffered against these terrors. But if we were to throw off language

> Before our death, instead of when death comes,
> Facing the wide glare of the children's day,
> Facing the rose, the dark sky and the drums,
> We [should] go mad no doubt and die that way.

The storm-bound Lear does just this on the cold heath, throwing off language and the rest of culture's warm clothing, only to scald madly on a wheel of fire.

In Shakespeare's youth the hot scent of the rose, the dreadful black wastes of night, and the tall soldiers drumming by were translated for children into the approved demons of the day. In 1584 Reginald Scot catalogued most of them:

> But in our childhood our mothers maids have so terrified us with an ouglie divell having hornes on his head, like a dog, clawes like a beare, a skin like a Niger, and a voice roring like a lion, whereby we start and are afraid when we heare one crie Bough: and they have so fraied us with

bull beggers, spirits, witches, urchens, elves, hags, fairies, satyrs, pans, faunes, sylens, kit with the consticke, tritons, centaurs, dwarfes, giants, imps, calcars, conjurors, nymphes, changlings, *Incubus*, Robin good-fellowe, the spoorne, the mare, the man in the oke, the hell waine, the fierdrake, the puckle, Tom thombe, hob gobblin, Tom tumbler, boneles, and such other bugs, that we are afraid of our owne shadowes: and then a polled sheepe is a perillous beast, and manie times is taken for our fathers soule, speciallie in a churchyard, where a right hardie man heretofore scant durst passe by night, but his haire would stand upright. (Bullough 1957: 396)

And to the perilous polled sheep taken for our father's soul Scot might have added, as Shakespeare does, a bush supposed a bear and a bottomless dream supposed a tryst with a fairy queen – not to mention an audience willingly supposing the wayward impulses of a lover's mind to be Robin Goodfellow armed with a vial of flower juice.

As I have described it, foreclosure seems more decisive and categorical than it is, as if a single No to Oedipus were a satanic *non serviam* that sent one plunging irrevocably all the way to pandemonium. But in reality, I am told, and do in part believe it, foreclosure comes on gradually and need not entail a total fall from symbolic grace. In fact, language is often the schizophrenic's most precious possession. Unfortunately it possesses him more than he possesses it. We all must endure slips of the tongue, embarrassing *double entendres*, and dream distortions as language plays Edgar Bergen to our Charlie McCarthy, but for the schizophrenic these metamorphose into voices carved out of thin air, byzantine delusional systems, and hebephrenic word salads that are in no one's recipe book. For most of us the real is symbolic, which is lucky for us, as the children in Graves' poem testify. But for schizophrenics the symbolic is real, which is unlucky for them, as Lear, his mind aflame, testifies.

One way language goes awry for schizophrenics, as it does for Graves' children and Shakespeare's moon-mad characters in the wood, is by endowing rhetorical figures with an alarming reality. 'Love at first sight' is only a metaphor in Athens, but in the wood, when Puck applies the flower juices, it unmetaphors itself with astonishing effect.[9] Similarly, in Athens Helena speaks metaphorically of a blind Cupid, but in the wood her metaphors come alive in Oberon's story about once seeing, 'Flying between the cold moon and the earth', an armed Cupid who loosed his love-shaft at a fair vestal, only to have it quenched by the chaste beams of the moon, miss the imperial votaress, and fall harmlessly upon a little western flower, which it transformed from milk-white to passionate purple (ii.i.155–69). Here is the origin of love's sylvan contretemps, as though Cupid's bad marksmanship were passed on to Puck, causing him to miss Demetrius and hit Lysander instead with the flower juice. In fact, Oberon's entire speech moves by a kind of blind metonymy in which the contiguous is contagious. Its action originates in the Orphic magnetism of a mermaid's singing, to hear which 'certain stars shot madly from their spheres', thereby inaugurating an aerial domino-effect proceeding from flying stars to flying Cupid to flying arrow and ultimately to a flying Puck, who is about to 'put a girdle round about the earth' to fetch the flower that has absorbed the seductiveness of the mermaid's singing.[10] The young men, wounded in turn by the flower's juice, shoot from their spheres quite as madly as the stars did, in pursuit of a union with the beloved whose purest representation is a concord of sweet sounds. The erratic movement towards this consonance is marked first by Bottom's 'I have a reasonable good ear in music. Let's have the tongs and the bones' (IV.i.28–9); then by the awakened Titania's call for 'Music, ho! Music, such as charmeth sleep' (82); then by the harmonies, if not of mermaids singing, at least of Theseus' hounds baying, which awakens the lovers now coupled in 'gentle concord' (IV.i.142); and finally of the song at the very end of the play that accompanies the blessings bestowed by the fairies wending their way through palace and theatre.

As a kind of generative first cause, Oberon's speech sets the stage for a series of literalised metaphors and metonymies in the wood. Puck's first mistake with the flower juice, for instance, combines the two figures, in keeping with Lacan's notion that unconscious desire (which is surely what Puck represents) can confuse one appearance with another that is metaphorically similar to it, as Lysander is to Demetrius, or with one that is metonymically contiguous with it, as the two men are in the wood. For the lovers, Athenian metaphors become sylvan realities. Helena's wish to be Hermia comes true in all but bodily fact in the wood, while Demetrius' wish to be Lysander and possess Hermia's love is realised roundaboutly when the doting Lysander ends up wishing in effect to be Demetrius by possessing Helena's love. Here is true moon madness. For the dazed Lysander to look in Helena's eyes and see reflected there a lovesick rival of Demetrius is lunacy indeed – or else metaphoric similarity gone mad, for his interchangeability with Demetrius was implicit in his insistence in Athens that they were virtually identical (I.i.99–102).

It seems the symbolic can be forcluded but not entirely annulled. The lovers postpone and flee from the tyrannic 'sentence' of Athenian law, only to find in the woods that perfectly ordinary words, as if released from their bondage to law, assert their own dominion. Helena's name, separated from that of the mythic maid of irresistible beauty by no more than a final 'a', is no great matter in Athens, where the name of Hermia alone holds sway.

But in the woods a syllable here or there is momentous indeed. Thus when the flower-eyed Demetrius subtracts an 'a' by crying as he awakes 'O Helen', the previously hateful Helena instantly metamorphoses into the face that once launched a thousand ships and now a small host of epithets and adjectives: 'O Helen, goddess, nymph, perfect, divine!' (III.ii.137). Bottom, on the other hand, does not suffer a change of name but a literalisation of it. He, who in Athens was an ass in name and metonym only, becomes in the wood an ass in fact. (A discussion of the metonymic unmetaphorising of Bottom must be deferred to the following chapter.)

Finally, in Athens Hermia's chiding joke about 'all the vows that ever men have broke, / In number more than ever women spoke' lightly expresses a fear that Lysander could become a break-vow like Demetrius (I.i.175–6). In the wood, when she asks him to lie further off, Lysander's sophistical exoneration of himself takes up the subject of her fears. Beshrew him if he meant country matters when he proposed lying together; he was speaking figuratively:

Two bosoms interchanged with an oath –
So then two bosoms and a single troth.
Then by your side no bed-room me deny,
For lying so, Hermia, I do not lie.
(II.ii.49–52)

Here again figurative language takes on a formidable literalness. In his witty exoneration of himself, Lysander beats a hasty retreat from nature to the symbolic: not his and Hermia's bodies but their oath and plighted troth will unite the two. In the puns of his last line, however, words rebel and play with him as much as he with them. Suddenly, that is, the 'lie' that has all along remained concealed in 'Lysander' stands out clearly. In name only, of course. Yet a little later, while Hermia is dreaming her terrifying dream of a Lysander whose forked tongue is figured as a serpent worming its way into her heart while he himself sits at a cool remove and observes the effect, the real Lysander is in the very process of breaking his vows to her. The truth in the dream and the lie in the name emerge simultaneously, thus realising Hermia's earlier fears.[11] The wood only imparts a wild literalness to symbolic processes already more tamely present or but barely concealed in Athens.

NAGUAL NATURE

The lost lovers are spared the bugs and goblins Elizabethans were coached to imagine, and even though Scot has fairies on his list and the wood is alive with them, the lovers see no fairies either. Nor, despite Oberon's references to 'lion, bear, or wolf, or bull' (ii.i.180), do they see what one might expect in a forest – a wild animal, or even, for that matter, a wild man like Bremo, hairy and cannibalistic, a reincarnation of the *homo sylvestris* of medieval romance (Bernheimer 1952), who stomped the stage in *Mucedorus* a few years before Shakespeare's play (around 1589). Encounters with the genuinely wild were on the wane in the late sixteenth century and certainly in Shakespeare, for whom nature is usually a sanctuary from the corruptions of the court and whose only wild man, Caliban, occupies an island, not a forest (Marienstras 1985: 15). The wildness encountered by the lovers in *A Midsummer Night's Dream* is out-there only as a projection from in-here. What they see are their own anxieties and desires projected and metaphorised in animal form. In fact, judging from the number of animal images employed, the journey from Athens into the wood appears to be a psychological journey from the lovers' cultural nature into what the Tzotzil Indians of Chiapas, Mexico, call *nagual* or animal nature. According to the German anthropologist Hans Peter Duerr,

> Humans rarely manage to see their own *nagual* nature, and in German fairy-tales encountering one's *alter ego* often means death. That is quite plausible. For whoever sees his *other* ego, has let go of his familiar one. You might say, his everyday personality 'died', it dissolved in order to make room for another part of his self. (Duerr 1985: 65)

Critics have been slow to recognise the influence of the Tzotzil Indians on Shakespeare; however, in Apuleius' *The Golden Ass*, usually held to be a source for *A Midsummer Night's Dream*, the notion of a *nagual* nature in humans is obvious. At least it was obvious to Edward Topsell, whose comments forecast Duerr's remarks above:

> Apuleius in his eleven bookes of his golden Asse taketh that beast for an Emblem, to note the manners of mankind; how some by youthful pleasures become beasts, and afterward by timely repentant old age are reformed men againe. Some are in their lives Wolves; some Foxes, some Swine, some Asses. . . . This world is unto them an enchanted cup of Circes, wherein they drinke up a potion of oblivion, error and ignorance; afterwards brutizing in their whole life, till they taste the Roses of true science and grace enlightening their minds. (Rowland 1974: 23)

Topsell's potion of 'oblivion, error and ignorance' substitutes for death in Duerr's account. Behind both lies the notion that to integrate the personality and become fully civilised we must experience a return of our

repressed animal nature and come to terms with it; or as Plato's metaphor
has it, keeping the psyche's chariot in the middle of the road requires us to
rein in and reign over the black horse as well as the white one. Thus
medieval knights are obliged to leave the court and overcome feral men
and animals in the wilderness (Bernheimer 1952: 122), and heroes of
fairy-tales, of which *The Golden Ass* is a kind of long bawdy version, are
magically transformed into animals and rehumanised for the better later on
(Bettelheim 1975: 76–83). Less optimistically, Swift's Gulliver and Wells'
Edward Prendick may return from Houyhnhnmland or the island of
Doctor Moreau with their humanity still in question, and sophisticated
adventurers like Dr Jekyll or victims like Gregor Samsa may go through a
bestial glass darkly and never return again.[12] Bottom falls somewhere
in between, experiencing a physical transformation that does not 'take'
intellectually, and therefore in a sense is not experienced at all. He
acknowledges a marvellous hairiness about the face and an uncommon
itchiness of the pelt, but 'oblivion, error and ignorance' obviate any
revelations on his part about inward asininities. His confused recollection
of his dream is hardly what Topsell meant about tasting the roses of true
science and the enlightenment of grace.

Within the cultural imaginary, wild animals and monsters often exist to
define what humans fear they are or may become and therefore must insist
they are not and never will be. Reginald Scot's catalogue documents the
fear and distances its objects; his myriad apparitions are all frighteningly
but also safely out-there, even if no further than the bedroom closet. But
what was out-there usually was thought to originate in-here. In *The Sicke
Womans Private Looking-Glasse* (1636), John Sadler said that monsters were
caused either divinely or naturally; the divine cause 'proceeds from the
permissive will of God, suffering parents to bring forth such abominations,
for their filthie and corrupt affections which are let loose unto wickednesse,
like brute beasts that have no understanding' (Sadler 1636: 133). Inward
brutishness will out, most monstrously.[13] The lion in the woods outside
Babylon is certainly out-there too, but he is also reflected inwardly, in that
passionately untamed part of Pyramus and Thisbe that defies cultural walls
and patriarchal prohibitions. Neglect reason in favour of desire, as they do,
and the leonine imagination will leap to disastrous conclusions. Not only
may Helen's beauty take up residence in a gypsy's brow, but in the
night, imagining some fear, how easy is a bloody mantle supposed a dead
Thisbe.

The Athenian lovers meet no mousing lions in the wood; yet merely to
adventure for love is to risk death. 'Stay, though thou kill me, sweet
Demetrius', begs Helena (ii.ii.84); and Hermia, awakening from a
nightmare in which she thought herself killed by a serpent (ii.ii.145–50),

swears to Lysander 'Either death or you I'll find immediately' (156). Similarly, but less physically, Helena must die to become for Demetrius

> . . . your spaniel; and, Demetrius,
> The more you beat me, I will fawn on you.
> Use me but as your spaniel, spurn me, strike me,
> Neglect me, lose me; only give me leave,
> Unworthy as I am, to follow you.
> What worser place can I beg in your love –
> And yet a place of high respect with me –
> Than to be used as you use your dog?
> (II.i.203–10)

So must Hermia die to become for Lysander 'thou cat, thou burr! Vile thing, let loose, / Or I will shake thee from me like a serpent!' (III.ii.260–1)? Granted there is a difference between metamorphosis and metaphor, between Titania's seeing Bottom with an ass's head on his shoulders and Hermia's calling Demetrius a dog, a cur, a worm and an adder (III.ii.65, 71). Only Bottom is literal-minded enough to unmetaphor a metaphor and become, with Puck's aid, an ass. And only Puck is figurative enough to take any animal shape he likes without losing his fairy identity, without 'dying':

> I'll follow you, I'll lead you about a round,
> Through bog, through bush, through brake, through brier;
> Sometime a horse I'll be, sometime a hound,
> A hog, a headless bear, sometime a fire;
> And neigh, and bark, and grunt, and roar, and burn,
> Like horse, hound, hog, bear, fire, at every turn.
> (III.i.101–6)

Yet death does occur, albeit metaphorically. As Jan Kott notes:

> 'Death' and 'dead' are uttered twenty-eight times; 'dying' and 'die' occur fourteen times. The field of 'death' appears in nearly fifty verses of *A Midsummer Night's Dream* and is distributed almost evenly among the events in the forest and the play at Theseus' wedding. The frequency of 'kill' and 'killing' is thirteen, and 'sick' and 'sickness' occur six times. (1987: 55)

In keeping with this, insofar as the lovers' *nagual* nature is exposed, they temporarily lose the symbolic immortality of culture and find themselves lost in a liminal zone between life and death. *Pyramus and Thisbe* parodies this experience; the lovers' flight from the oppressiveness but also the protectiveness of patriarchy takes them into a wood where the roaming imagination, more wild and dangerous than lions, brings real death. But that is because *Pyramus and Thisbe* is a woeful tragedy. For the lovers in the wood outside Athens death takes a more reassuring metaphoric form, as sleep. On Oberon's orders, Puck first leads the sword-waving young men harmlessly astray until, instead of killing one another, they are both conquered by 'death-counterfeiting sleep' (III.ii.364), and then later he casts a final spell over everyone: 'strike more dead / Than common sleep of all these five the sense' (IV.i.80–1).

This casting of the lovers into a death-like sleep prepares us of course for the fairy-tale conclusion, when all start up from sleep as if reborn again, savouring on their lips, no doubt, a taste of the roses of true science and enlightening grace. Let us consider this awakening.

THE WOOD AND THE HUNT

If the journey into one's *nagual* nature is liminal, the scene where it takes place, the wood, is too. It is called the 'palace wood' (I.ii.92), and is evidently neither city nor wilderness but something in between. This ambiguity also characterised the forests of Shakespeare's time. A Tudor 'forest' was not simply a timbered wilderness but, as the jurist John Manwood carefully defined it in 1592, it was 'a certain Territory of wooddy grounds and fruitful pastures, priviledged for wild beasts and fowls of Forest, Chase and Warren, to rest and abide in, in the safe protection of the King, for his princely delight and pleasure' (Marienstras 1985: 18). A forest proper is a kind of sylvan zone between the civilised and the wild, and thus the 'palace wood' in *A Midsummer Night's Dream* occupies a space between orderly law-governed Athens and the true wilderness beyond, where Amazons, centaurs, cyclops, satyrs and other monsters more fearful than donkey-headed weavers savage all who come within their compass.

As a zone between wilderness and civilisation, the wood is geographically analogous to the liminal period between sleep and waking life, that blurry period when wild dreams are not quite gone and tame realities not quite materialised. The door of consciousness thus ajar, this is the time, according to tradition, when demons, fairies and other kinds of spirits appear (De Becker 1968: 152, 211) – perhaps at the brink of dawn when the wood stirs and awakening rustics rub their eyes as they glimpse flocks of fairies running 'from the presence of the sun, / Following darkness like a dream' (V.i.380–1). In this half-light, one would expect the moment of the lovers' awakening to carry special significance, which is just what Harry Morris finds:

> When Theseus comes upon the sleepers, although he is accompanied by Hippolyta, Egeus, 'and all his train', any one of whom might bend down, gently to nudge the youths awake, he rouses them in an unusual manner: 'Go, bid the huntsmen wake them with their horns' (iv.i.137). Both Quarto and Folio indicate *'They all start up'* as though trumpets have announced judgment day, and the first words spoken by one of them are, 'Pardon, my lord'. (1985: 250)

Although Morris interprets this allegorically, as the trump of doom, the use of horns to awaken the lovers fits quite naturally into the context of the royal hunt and bespeaks a judgment, to be sure, but of a more secular sort. It has to do with the odd status of the lovers in the forest. In flight from Theseus' judgment, Lysander and Hermia are outlaws, and as outlaws within the forest they are especially vulnerable. For an Elizabethan fugitive who entered the forest forfeited the protection of common law, which required a warrant for his apprehension. Inside the forest and outside the law, he could be hunted, seized and even killed by a forester provided, as Manwood put it, 'after hue and cry made to him, to stand unto the peace, [he] will not yield himself, but doe flie or resist' (Marienstras 1985: 27). Thus a fugitive inside the forest was in the dangerous position of a wild animal outside it. As a result he had to weigh the risks of hiding in the thickets of the law or in those of the wood.

Not that the lovers are criminals on the loose, but they are fugitives from the law, as is clear when Lysander confesses their flight upon awakening and Egeus begs, 'the law, the law, upon his head' (iv.i.154). Lysander's appeal to Theseus, 'Pardon, my lord', is especially appropriate in the forest because the forest was emblematic of royal authority. A wilderness became a forest, a sanctuary for animals,[14] only when defined as such by the monarch. Moreover, as Richard Marienstras has shown, the king's power to tame wild places and animals, to establish forests, was a domestic version of his power to tame 'wild' countries and peoples – the Irish, for instance, or the Indians.[15] This royal power was somehow natural and cultural at the same time: a power to create culture by brute force. Thus in his 'Trew Law of Free Monarchies' (1598) James I claimed that because Scotland had been conquered by Fergus, and England by William the Conqueror, before a parliament existed, 'it follows, of necessity, that the kings were the authors and makers of the laws and not the laws of the kings' (Marienstras 1985: 24). William the Conqueror, it seems, hunted wild Saxons in the wilderness of England and tamed both them and it by the natural law of force, by which right he subsequently carved out royal forests within which his word alone held sway. Citing the twelfth-century writer Richard Fitz Nigel, Manwood opined that 'offenders in the Forests, for their offences are subject unto the only Judgement and determination of the King' (Marienstras 1985: 23). In this light the judgment signalled by the foresters' horns is delivered not allegorically by the Lord of Hosts but quite realistically by Theseus, lord of the forest.

This would imply that the lovers are poachers who have encroached on the sanctuary of the royal forest. What they have been hunting, as part of the long tradition of the love chase, is one another.

> The hunt of love occurs at least as early as Plato's *Sophist* where the hunt provides an overriding metaphor: human affairs become narrow subdivisions of a great pursuit. All men prey upon one another in diverse ways – through war, tyranny, piracy, oratory, law, and conversation. Love, finally, emerges as one category of the private, persuasive land hunt. 'Have you never seen the ways lovers hunt each other?' is the query rhetorically raised. (Thiébaux 1974: 89)

In the Athenian wood, as we have seen, the lovers' arrowing looks have darted this way and that, glancing mostly off tree trunks; but occasionally, taking Sartrian predatory form, they have impaled their quarry too, reducing them to dogs, cats, serpents, adders, worms and so forth. Everyone has been hunter and hunted in both the loving and the hateful sense. This kind of ambiguous status also plagued Elizabethan poachers in the forest: if they were seen, 'hue and cry' was made, as Manwood says – and horns too were sounded according to another authority (Marienstras 1985: 27) – and then the hunter became the hunted. What, then, is the status of the awakening lovers when, to the accompaniment of shouts and horns, '*They all start up*'? In this context, they start up either like hunted animals in the royal forest or like fugitives who have invaded the monarch's grounds.

At best of course the lovers are but metaphoric animals, not the kind Theseus was preparing to hunt when he stumbled on to them. Which of course makes us wonder just what kind he *was* preparing to hunt. Normally we would expect him to be hunting the hart, traditionally the royal game, especially in literature; but the only animal mentioned, by Hippolyta, is the bear:

> I was with Hercules and Cadmus once,
> When in a wood of Crete they bayed the bear
> With hounds of Sparta.
>
> (iv.i.111–13)

To be sure, this was in Crete, not in a wood outside Athens, yet when Theseus quickly claims that his hounds too 'are bred out of the Spartan kind' the two hunts are linked together. In Elizabethan England the bear did not usually appear among the huntable animals listed as beasts of the forest, beasts of the chase, or beasts of the warren. On the other hand, George Turbervile devotes two chapters to the bear in his *The Noble Art of Venerie or Hunting* (1575). So the bear seems a legitimate candidate to be hunted in this scene, indeed with some danger to Puck, who threatens to transform himself into a bear (III.i.104), and to Helena, who says she is as ugly as one (II.ii.94).

However, the bear to be hunted is no more real than the hounds who hunt it. The hounds Theseus describes (IV.i.118–24) dissolve from realistic animals into allegorical function, which is to provide with their belling voices a *concordia discors* that aptly reverbs the social harmony of the sleeping lovers. Like the hounds, the bear may also play an allegorical role, in which case we should look to folklore and allegorised bestiaries for its possible significance – as Marienstras has done:

> Quite apart from the role played by the bear in popular English spectacles ever since at least the reign of Henry II, during the Middle Ages this creature represented concupiscence or lust. In European folklore it was a symbol of male sexuality; in some stories, bears violate women or fornicate with others who are consenting. The bear also symbolises brute force, cunning and anger. It is connected with rituals associated with the end of winter. (1985: 203)

In 1607 Edward Topsell agreed that the 'bear is of a most venerous and lustful disposition' – and not merely male bears, for 'Night and day, the females, with most ardent, inflamed desires, do provoke the males to copulation, and for this cause at that time they are most fierce and angry' (1981: 22). Moreover, Topsell follows medieval bestiaries in pointing out a feature of the bear's amorising that makes it a likely symbol of human sexuality: 'The manner of their copulation is like a man's, the male moving himself upon the belly of the female, which lies on the earth flat upon her back, and they embrace each other with their forefeet' (1981: 22).

In this figurative light a hunt aimed at 'baying the bear' would seek to kill or tame lechery, an appropriate enough intention on the morning of the day the three couples submit their sexual impulses to the rule of marriage. More broadly still, 'to bay the bear', Kirby Farrell says, 'is to disarm the malevolence which prowls the heart as well as the overtly alien wood. Through the music of his hounds Theseus would assure his beloved of his gentle power – "such sweet thunder" – in the territory of passion' (1976: 101).

A similar interpretation emerges if we focus not on the animal hunted but on the hunting animals – Theseus' dogs. For if we look at Theseus' description of his 'hounds bred out of the Spartan kind' we see, a bit beyond them, the dogs of Actaeon, catalogued in such obsessive detail in Golding's Ovid (Rouse, 1966, III: 245–71), beginning with Blackfoot and Stalker

('This latter was a hound of *Crete*, the other was of *Spart*'). When the hounds turn on Actaeon in his stag-shape, Ovid has him cry, 'I am *Acteon*: know your Lord and Mayster sirs I pray' (275). But the dogs do not know their lord and master, and what this means, to the properly schooled reader of Ovid, has little to do with dogs but a lot to do with 'affections'. How one becomes a properly schooled reader of Ovid is dictated by Golding in his introductory *Epistle*, a brief primer on the virtues of allegorical interpretation. To 'bring ageine the darkened truth to light', Golding advises, we must draw aside the lies and fables with which the poet has curtained his true subject (*Epistle*: 537–40). That subject almost always features a contest between higher reason and lower affections:

> For as there is no creature more divine than man as long
> As reason hath the sovereintie and standeth firme and strong:
> So is there none more beastly, vyle, and develish, than is hee,
> If reason giving over, by affection mated be.
>
> (565–8)

Here is Actaeon to the life. Or rather to the death; for nothing will make one's life more 'beastly, vyle, and develish' – and 'brief', Hobbes would add – than catching a glimpse of Diana at her bath. In this rash moment Actaeon lets slip the dogs of his own desire and thus bestialises himself even before Diana does so in revenge. That this is a proper reading is attested to by Orsino in *Twelfth Night*, who says that no sooner did he spy the beauteous Olivia than

> That instant was I turned into a hart;
> And my desires, like fell and cruel hounds,
> E'er since pursue me.
>
> (I.i.21–3)

The object of all this is to demonstrate that unlike Actaeon Theseus is Lord and Mayster over animality. Indeed at this point he seems the very emblem of royal authority and power. Before him lies his forest: wilderness brought under the rule and definition of the king ('At the Duke's oak we meet', Quince announced earlier (I.ii.101)). Around his feet cavort his dogs, not clamouring for his flesh like those of Actaeon but chorusing cheek to jowl in harmonic obedience. At his side stands the Amazonian queen who hunted with Hercules and Cadmus in Crete and was Diana's votary, but who is now his bride-to-be, even as her story about Spartan hounds marries with his description of his dogs' even sweeter thunder. And finally, on the ground lie his subjects, the lovers, in whom nighttime desires both fell and cruel have subsided at dawn, leaving in their place love, amity and a renewed prospect of marriage. Clearly reason is soverein and standeth firme and strong in the person of Theseus, and wildness and animality have been brought to heel in his Amazonian bride and the lovers as well.[16]

That being so, what more proper occasion and place than this for the regal duke to proclaim the supremacy of royal judgment and the irrelevancy of Egeus' cries for 'the law, the law'? That judgment ratifies Oberon's revisions of love, marks an official end to the liminal wodeness of the wood, and, in company with Theseus' speech on reason at the beginning of the next act, forms a partition separating animal from human, dream from reality, night from day, and fairies from Athens. Yet a partition is itself a liminal entity, which implies that these things may not be as clearly divided as Theseus thinks.

PUCK'S SWEEPING

The notion of a partition returns us to Puck's domestic labours at Theseus' limen. What we see now is that he is engaged in an act that summarises and highlights the entire action of the play. Just as the play has featured the wresting of a new order out of the blurred disorder of the forest, so his sweeping out of dirt is a purificatory act of order, appropriately taking place at a threshold, where those who are about to enter traditionally purify themselves, or at least remove their shoes as in Japan. Sweeping dust away leaves a palace that is both clean and neatly divided from the outside, one that contains only what is proper to it.[17] At the same time it is the preliminary purgative phase of a brief ritual of blessing. Puck sweeps away dirt, and Oberon and Titania sweep away 'the blots of Nature's hand': moles and hare-lips, scars and marks prodigious (v.i.407–8). Palace dust dispensed with, the field-dew of fairyland can now consecrate, so that 'the issue there create / Ever shall be fortunate. / So shall all the couples three / Ever true in loving be'.

By the same token, the triple marriage marks the purifying and ordering of Athenian society. The anomalous Amazon is now an Athenian duchess, the roving Theseus a married duke, the recalcitrant Hermia a loving wife, and the spotted Demetrius a devoted husband. With the dirt of defiance, jealousy and hatred swept out of the collective psyche, everyone is safely tucked away under the same palatial and societal roof. Love's wild force, erratic as lightning in the collied night, is now grounded by Athenian ritual. For a few moments the fears that ghosted through the forest reappear as roaring lions, howling wolves and wide-gaping graves in Puck's song-like speech. But Puck's quatrains tame these threats of death; and as the fairies, who 'Now are frolic', wend their way through each several chamber of the palace, scattering talismanic field-dew as they go, their dancing traces a magic circle that keeps life's adversities at a safe remove, and their song reflects the harmonies of married life restored in fairyland and newly wrought in Athens.

Thus Puck's door emblematises the openness and closedness that mark the end of the play. It opens, like the last act, to admit the workmen and the lovers freely into the festive royal presence – and the fairies covertly. And it closes to keep hostile influences outside. The baying of Theseus' hounds, converted into social harmonies, drives away all symbolic bears, and if 'the hungry lion roars', as Puck declares, it does so far off and unheard. Even Egeus is no longer around to growl about the law. As a result *A Midsummer Night's Dream* ends more benignly perhaps than any other Shakespearian play – though less benignly than is sometimes claimed.[18]

This royal progress of the fairies through palace and theatre blesses the audience too, incorporating us for a few minutes into *A Midsummer Night's Dream*, now become the dream of a harmonic society. For the performance of the play enacts all three phases of Van Gennep's transitional rite, separating us from the real world as we enter a liminal world of imagination, there to become, by virtue of our shared imaginative experience, transformed from random individuals into an audience.[19] While this blessing is taking place, however, Puck introduces a discordant note by carrying his liminal lustrations to a new level. Standing as Epilogue at the back door of the play, at the border between fictional Athens and real London, he lightly suggests that we take Shakespeare's title literally and dismiss our experience as 'no more yielding than a dream'. In effect he invites us to sweep this dusty play out of reason's palace as briskly as Theseus does *Pyramus and Thisbe*: 'But, come, your Bergomask. Let your epilogue alone' (v.i.356–7).

This should remind us of a great gap in my argument, the fact that I have said nothing about *Pyramus and Thisbe*, which intervenes, which indeed constitutes an interlude, between the happy resolution of the forest experience, subsequently confirmed by multiple marriage, and the equally happy moment when the newly-weds depart for bed and the begetting, Oberon assures us, of bevies of unblemished children. In design a tragedy but in performance a farce, its generic integrity undermined by its own self-description as 'very tragical mirth', *Pyramus and Thisbe* merits Theseus' quizzical comment, 'How shall we find the concord of this discord?' (v.i.60). Since Theseus is referring back to the *concordia discors* that marked the reconciliations of the lovers, his remark suggests that despite its marriages and festive airs *A Midsummer Night's Dream* cannot lay claim to a perfectly happy ending until it comes to terms with the discordancies of *Pyramus and Thisbe.* Let us then move in that direction.

· 5 ·

Names and Translations

At the end of Act 4 we witness Theseus' surprising willingness to renounce the law and incorporate the wild workings of love into the symbolic. His behaviour here seems contingent on his having exorcised the demons of his own pre-marital doubt. In what I have called 'Theseus' dream', the duke imagines a fairy drama in which Oberon's reassertion of mastery over the rebellious Titania assuages his own anxieties about making the Amazonian queen his bride. The sure sign of his psychic health is his ability to cast out of consciousness the fairy fantasies on which he has relied. He never will believe these fairy toys. That is an admirable exercise of reason; but he goes further, to indict not merely the fanciful products of imagination, useful as they may have been to him, but the imagination itself, useful to all of us. For although madmen will gladly part with their devils, where would lovers be without the ability to transform a brow of Egypt into Helen of Troy, and where would we all be if poets, not to mention the poet in each of us, were restricted to hard fact? Theseus deals with strange differences – fairies, fantasy, imaginings – by either denying them altogether or acknow-ledging them with condescension; that is, either by keeping differences outside the palace of reason or by letting them in through the servants' entrance. From before Plato to the present, the fear of difference has been dealt with by western reason and culture in this Theseus-like way – by banishing it outside or by enveloping and subordinating it – as post-modernism has repeatedly shown with respect to women, races, ethnic groups, the mad, criminals, other species and so on. As a result, difference is not permitted to express itself on its own terms (and of course one wonders how it could).

This situation is writ small in metaphor. To escape the prison-house of language, we venture into a wilderness beyond the borders of the dictionary and, if we are lucky, get a glimpse of something out there for which language lacks a name. But since this wild 'other', fleeing darkness like a dream, is too elusive to capture, our only recourse is to glance from it to the dictionary and back again, eyes rolling in a fine poetic frenzy, until we discern a likeness, however remote. 'Ah', we may say, if our name is Shakespeare, 'this strange fantasia of desire is like a fairy-tale.' But what a falling off was there! To imagine a fantasy, a midsummer night's dream, as a fairy-tale may be the best way to describe what we have experienced, but the metaphor familiarises strangeness (everyone knows about fairy-tales) and thus loses precisely what we sought to express. If a robin redbreast in a cage puts all nature in a rage, as Blake declared, it is because the caged creature is a robin redbreast in name only, all its radical differences having been left behind when it was thrust inside. Thus metaphor, a cage for unnamed wild ideas, has so often been accused of being a lie because it pretends to tell a propositional truth. In fact, however, this pretence is so flagrant that metaphor becomes honest by reversion; it announces itself as a lie by declaring that the likeness it lights up is like that of the new moon, only a thin slice of the difference it leaves in darkness.

The dissatisfaction this engenders is familiar to Bottom. For when he awakens in the wood, on the limen of consciousness, his mind is rather like Puck's door, both open to the fast-fading world of fairyland and closed against it. In his famously confused speech about it, his rare vision suffers severely from its transformation into language:

> I have had a most rare vision. I have had a dream, past the wit of man to say what dream it was. Man is but an ass, if he go about to expound this dream. Methought I was – there is no man can tell what. Methought I was – and methought I had – but man is but a patched fool, if he will offer to say what methought I had. The eye of man hath not heard, the ear of man hath not seen, man's hand is not able to taste, his tongue to conceive, nor his heart to report, what my dream was. (IV.i.203–12)

Bottom seeks to translate an experience that does not readily yield itself to language. In fact he is attempting to translate a 'translation', the term Quince used on encountering his metamorphosed friend: 'Bless thee, Bottom, bless thee! Thou art translated' (III.i.113). Clearly it is easier to *be* translated than to translate, especially, as Fredric Jameson attests, when the matter one seeks to translate is dreams:

Anyone who has ever tried to recount a dream to someone else is in a position to measure the immense gap, the qualitative incommensurability, between the vivid memory of the dream and the dull, impoverished words which are all we can find to convey it: yet this incommensurability, between the particular and the universal, between the *vécu* and language itself, is one in which we dwell all our lives, and it is from it that all works of literature and culture necessarily emerge. (Jameson 1982: 338–9)

These speeches by Bottom and Jameson (with apologies to Mr Jameson) occupy a familiar place in discourse, the 'inexpressibility topos', as Ernst Robert Curtius calls it (1953: 159–62). Writers from Homer to Hemingway have lamented the feebleness of language to phrase subjects this godlike (one's emperor), this beautiful (one's beloved) or this profound (one's own thoughts). Dreams especially defy translation, whether the dreamer is the ordinary variety, like the newly awakened Bottom, big with idea and little with words, or, more grandly, a platonic artist trying to envision the shadowy abstractions flickering in the cave of consciousness, or a medieval icon-maker giving Christianity's collective dream a local habitation on a cathedral wall, or a Petrarchan poet lamenting the distance between the lovely Laura and his own panting phrases.

The traditional medium for translating mysteries and dreams is art. Bottom himself, registering the increasing distance between himself and fairyland, seeks recourse in balladry:

> I will get Peter Quince to write a ballad of this dream. It shall be called 'Bottom's Dream', because it hath no bottom; and I will sing it in the latter end of a play, before the Duke. Peradventure, to make it the more gracious, I shall sing it at her death. (iv.i.212–17)

Bottom is surely right to call on the poet Peter Quince for a ballad about dreams and fairies, at least in the opinion of Bottom's proposed audience Duke Theseus. For in the duke's famous speech on imagination, he ranks poets high among those who are afflicted by Plato's *furors* and suggests that 'antic fables' and 'fairy toys' are about the best one can hope for from them. He speaks almost as though he had overheard Bottom's musings on his dream, because he construes the act of poetic creation to be a metamorphic affair in which fancy's wild flights are caged in words:

> The poet's eye, in a fine frenzy rolling,
> Doth glance from heaven to earth, from earth to heaven;
> And, as imagination bodies forth

The forms of things unknown, the poet's pen
Turns them to shapes and gives to airy nothing
A local habitation and a name.

(v.i.12–17)

Moulding airy nothing into bodies and shapes that can occupy a local habitation is a hard kind of naming, one that seems guaranteed to lose more than it gains, as the ballad of 'Bottom's Dream' seems sure to do also. In fact, 'Bottom's Dream' never materialises. But then how could it? Bottom cannot even define it for himself, let alone tell Peter Quince about it – any more than rhapsodes and poets can tell you about the things they name, according to Plato. And yet in all this talk about translating dreams and airy nothing, in a play that calls itself a dream and presents us with the airy nothingness of fairyland, perhaps Shakespeare is telling us a good deal – not about what he has translated but about the process of translating or naming itself. For the inexpressibility topos only makes explicit a fact that is implicit in all translative discourse, the loss of the referent. Thus Barbara Freedman cites Freud's conviction that dreams can never be reconstructed; all that is available for study is the dreamwork, the deflective processes of mediation itself (Freedman 1991: 178). Shakespeare seems to be doing something like that in *A Midsummer Night's Dream*, except that his interest is less in dreamwork than in playwork, or in playwork as dreamwork, as we might suspect from the fact that Bottom's 'dream' occurs during the rehearsal of *Pyramus and Thisbe* just as he is attempting to translate himself from Bottom into Pyramus. Bottom exits from Athens and makes an entrance as Pyramus in a play that disappears into a dream that is part of a larger play that is called a dream.

Shakespeare's study of translation, mediation and naming in dream/ drama glances at a great many aspects of the play. Translative turns and changes, after all, are just what you would expect in a wood dominated by the spirit(s) of Ovid's *Metamorphoses* and given to Van Gennep's rites of passage. Tropes are themselves miniature rites of passage in which things unknown cross the limen of the symbolic and enter the local habitation of discourse. These translations take place most interestingly, it seems to me, in Theseus' speech about poetic naming, in the ambiguity of the fairies, in Bottom's metamorphosis, in the performance of *Pyramus and Thisbe*, and in the Epilogue. These will be discussed, mostly in that order, in this and the following two chapters. First, however, let me talk a bit about names and naming, starting where the King of Hearts says one should start, at the beginning.

BAPTISMS

The very beginning, the first translation of airy nothing into a material something, took place when Jehovah spoke the world into being *ex nihilo*. Had it not already been recorded, Bottom would no doubt get Peter Quince to make an epic of this and call it 'Jehovah's Dream'. Jehovah found a local habitation for his dream, but it is not clear whether he explicitly named anything, even Adam, who just seems to *be* Adam. But Adam himself is a name-giver, and God is curious about the names he will give each of the animals paraded before him. According to Agrippa, this naming proceeded according to sound cratylic principles:

> Adam, therefore, that gave the first names to things, knowing the influences of the Heavens and properties of all things, gave them all names according to their natures, as it is written in Genesis, where God brought all things that he had created before Adam, that he should name them; and as he named any thing, so the name of it was; which names, indeed, contain in them wonderful powers of the things signified. (Agrippa 1974: 212–13)

Adam himself declares that Eve 'shall be called Woman because she was taken out of Man' (*Genesis* 2: 23), thereby confirming her ancillary status and suggesting that Adam's original sin, or at least fatal weakness, was his lamentable desire for female supplementation.[1] In any case, Adam took possession of both animals and woman by naming them, by transforming nature from the real into the symbolic in the approving presence of God the Father. Even in postlapsarian times humans are not fully human until they can get their names listed in the symbolic register at least twice. First (though it normally comes second), the child must concede to, or embrace, the authority of *le nom du père*, which, as we saw so vividly at the opening of *A Midsummer Night's Dream*, stands in for a paternalistic language.[2] Although this threshold experience is normally part of the oedipal resolution, in the opening scene it is displaced from childhood to the occasion of adolescent marriage and dramatised as an affair of the patriarchal state. Hermia and Lysander are inexpressible signifieds refusing to accept the signifiers prescribed for them in the symbolic, forced to regressive flight into an imaginary wood, where they encounter the symbolic of fairyland governed by Oberon and erratically mediated by Puck. Eventually, awakened by Theseus, they discover that for some mysterious reason the social vocabulary now has a name to accommodate their private meaning.

But well before a child encounters *le nom du père* – even well before it encounters the world at birth – it acquires a name of its own. As Lacan says:

> Everything begins with the possibility of naming, which is both destructive of the thing and allows the passage of the thing onto the symbolic plane, thanks to which the truly human register comes into its own. It is from that point on that, in a more and more complicated manner, the embodiment of the symbolic within imaginary experience takes place. The symbolic will shape all those inflections which, in the life of the adult, the imaginary commitment, the original captation, can take on. (Lacan 1988: 219)

At the 'passage of the thing onto the symbolic plane' – Hegel's famous *Aufhebung* or sublation – the real and the symbolic part company, with the real 'lost' like the mother of Freud's grandson and the symbolic 'found' as in the substitutive game of lost and found the boy played. I say 'lost', but Lacan speaks of destruction, and Hegel perversely thinks of it as a murder, in which the real object (his example is a dog) is simultaneously killed off in the flesh and resurrected symbolically (Kojève 1969: 140–1).[3] The urge to associate the advent of symbolism with death and violence seems irresistible; thus Maurice Blanchot extends the murder from dogs to humans:

> Of course my language does not kill anyone. And yet: when I say, 'This woman', real death has been announced and is already present in my language; my language means that this person, who is here right now, can be detached from herself, removed from her existence and her presence and suddenly plunged into a nothingness in which there is no existence or presence; my language essentially signifies the possibility of this destruction; it is a constant, bold allusion to such an event. (Blanchot 1981: 42)

Less violently construed, the act of naming confers on the object/person a symbolic identity independent of its reality, thus entailing what could be metaphorically called an erasure of the real. The ordinary hedge-flower that maidens call 'love-in-idleness', according to Oberon (ii.i.168), first grows more interesting in Lyte's *New Herbal* (1578) as he translates its Latin names into 'Pances, Loue in idlenes, and Hartes ease' (149); then begins to bloom in Gerard's *Herball* (1597) as 'Harts ease, Pansies, Liue in Idleness, Cull me to you, and three faces in one hood' (705); and positively flourishes in the catalogue of a Dr Prior: 'Herb Trinity, Fancy, Flamy, Kiss me, Cull me or Cuddle me to you, Tickle my fancy, Kiss me ere I rise, Jump up and kiss me, Kiss me at the garden gate, Pink of my John, etc.' (Furness

1963: 74). Amorous, fiery, medicinal, seductive, colourful: who would have thought the plain little hedge-flower had all this in her? But in herself she has not; she only springs to such varied life in symbolic gardens whose anthropomorphic luxuriance obscures – or chokes out, withers, kills or destroys – the individually real flowers.[4]

The notion of death or nihilation does become appropriate in the opening scene of *A Midsummer Night's Dream* when Hermia refuses to honour *le nom du père* and become a commodity on the marital exchange. Naming is here to be performed by the ritual of wedding, which would supply an unknown girl, merely the daughter of Egeus, with a public habitation and a name as the wife of Demetrius. This entering of her new identity in the social register would entail an erasure of the real, whomever she married, because she would be obliged to assume the name of her husband. Not that Hermia has not already got a name, but that cultural relocations are re-namings. Hence the process here is less a case of the unnamed entering the symbolic order than of a metaphoric transfer of names within the symbolic. As a metaphor slides the meaning of one word under another, so a wedding causes the signified of the bride to slide under the signifier of the groom, eclipsing her past identity.[5]

Hermia's past identity will be eclipsed if she weds Demetrius, but Hermia herself will be eclipsed if she does not. The threat of death applies, oddly enough, as much to Egeus as to Hermia. For her marriage will confirm the fact that, as a daughter, she cannot perpetuate the family name. In this respect daughters are as sinister as bastards; they 'kill' their fathers by depriving them of the symbolic immortality vested in their names. This prospect acquires prominence here by virtue of the absence, not only of mothers, but also of sons and brothers; the loss of Hermia would be less painful if Egeus had a son to preserve his name. Thus he as well as Hermia will suffer a certain eclipse of identity when she marries. But just what that eclipse will be is yet to be known. During the three days before her decision must be made, Hermia is suspended between various incompatible identities associated with marriage, since she must become bride either to Demetrius, Christ or Death. Moreover, inasmuch as the identities of Lysander and Demetrius are dependent on hers, and Helena's is dependent on Demetrius', all the lovers await their definitive baptism at the societal font.

Baptism accords with one's impression that in withdrawing to the forest the lovers are in some degree regressing to childhood. When Helena reports that 'Love is said to be a child' (I.i.238) our uncertainty whether she means the boy Cupid or the effects he produces on lovers is appropriate, for in this play Cupid's darts render lovers, if not exactly childlike, certainly childish. On the women's side, Helena's nostalgic evocation of her and

Hermia's schoolgirl friendship (iii.ii.201–19) makes their present dispute seem less the quarrelling of adults than the spiteful squabbling of children (iii.ii.282 ff.). So too with the challenging and counter-challenging of the contentious young men, which Puck degrades through mimicry to the level of a spanking:

> Come, recreant, come, thou child,
> I'll whip thee with a rod. He is defiled
> That draws a sword on thee.
>
> (iii.ii.409–11)

This lends another aspect to the awakening of the lovers at the end of Act 4, insofar as they do so like children roused by the parental figures of Theseus and Hippolyta. Demetrius speaks for all of their erratic fancies when he describes his faded love for Hermia as 'the remembrance of an idle gaud / Which in my childhood I did dote upon' (iv.i.166–7). From this standpoint, the wood is a liminal territory on the border between childhood and adulthood, and the lovers can make the transition only by experiencing the childishness of dotage *en route* to the maturities of true love.

Of course while Love, in the form of Puck, is reducing these lovers to children, Titania is doing the same with Bottom (Huston 1981: 106–7; Dunn 1988: 22). For if Bottom in some degree supplants Oberon in Titania's bower, he more obviously supplants the changeling child she has doted on and sought to keep. Hence he is catered to by elves, fed, petted, cooed and embraced to sleep by Titania, and ultimately rejected by her as a bad dream even as she must reject the dream of keeping the changeling child for ever. Whereas the proof of Titania's cure is suggested by her dismissal of the past – she expresses no interest in ballads called 'Titania's Dream' and never again mentions the changeling – poor Bottom, ejected from the dream bower of childhood a second time, is left to nurse his waning memories on reality's cold hillside. From this standpoint the dislocations of his waking speech suggest the liminal confusions of a child passing from the imaginary into the symbolic, although Bottom is so steadfastly himself that he seems neither imaginary nor symbolic, only real. However, that is a subject that needs coming back to.

NAMES

Normally, when our identity is threatened, we are likely to retreat to what we regard as our most private property, our proper names. Whoever may utter it, my name refers to no one but me,[6] whereas the pronoun 'I', which seems so intimately mine on my lips, betrays my affections the moment someone else utters it. Then, in a verbal version of Sartre's proprietary look, I am converted into a 'you', a distanced other on the periphery of someone else's 'I'-centred world. Shifters like 'I' and 'you' are good examples of the elusiveness of desire and identity in the symbolic. Longing for a defined and stable self, we find ourselves perpetually proposing marriage to an incorrigibly promiscuous 'I'. No wonder Shakespeare's male characters cling to their proper names (while suppressing those of their wives) and trace their genealogies anxiously. No wonder Hamlet doffs all assumed identities in the graveyard and proclaims with an air of relief and challenge, 'This is I, Hamlet, the Dane!' or Webster's heroine cries, 'I am Duchess of Malfi still!'

Trumpeting an identity is not an option for the changeling child, who is neither endowed with a name by the poet's pen nor bodied forth on stage by an actor, so that for the audience he remains a 'thing unknown'. This is in keeping with the fairy preference for making off with unchristened infants, who are more vulnerable than others because they have not been ritually stamped as the property of a Christian society (Briggs 1967: 115). Even at the end of the play, when his new status as Oberon's squire has been established, the changeling remains invisible, apparently a dismissible cipher in the marital dispute. On the other hand, most of the lesser fairies – Cobweb, Peasblossom, Mustardseed, Moth – seem inextricably bound to their names. Plato's Cratylus must have played godfather at their baptism, or perhaps Paracelsus, since their names are cultural extensions of the Paracelsian theory of 'signatures' – the belief that plants, herbs and minerals were inscribed with a code indicating their nature and use. In Shakespeare's fairies these 'natural' signatures or indices become self-defining metonymic names, to which Bottom alone among humans has access, perhaps because he is himself something of a 'natural'. In any event, nature and culture are so seamlessly interwoven in the fairies and their names that, as Keir Elam neatly puts it, 'each *nomen* is also immediately and magically a *numen*' (Elam 1984: 136).

Most of the workmen's names – Quince, Snout, Bottom, Flute, Snug – are similarly metonymic, linking them to the objects of their trade, to the human body, and to nature (Sewell 1960: 127–33). Technically, 'quince' refers to the 'quines' or 'quoins' (wooden wedges) a carpenter had need of, 'snout' to the nozzles a tinker would repair, 'bottom' to the core of the skein a weaver winds his yarn on, 'flute' to the flutings of the church-organs a bellows-mender would sometimes mend, and 'snug' to the kind of fit a joiner would aspire to. Starveling's name is non-technical, but in its reference to the proverbial thinness of tailors (it took 'nine tailors to make a man') it points to a metonymic corporealisation that also characterises

Snout, Bottom, and, in the bawdy sense, 'Peter' Quince most obviously, but also Flute, who qualifies to play Thisbe because of the trilling exhalations from his own thoracic bellows, and Snug, which implies a cosy bodily warmth and security. Finally, 'quince' also refers to both fruit and tree, 'snout' has obvious animal implications, and bottoms and snuggling are not restricted to humans. When their names combine artful labour, human and animal bodies, and nature like this, the term 'mechanicals' seems a misnomer for the workmen.

Thus the identities of the fairies and workmen are securely grounded in the everyday world. Invisible filaments bind Cobweb to cobweb; green tendrils link Peasblossom to his flowery kin; and yarn, flesh and metonym connect Bottom to the implement of his trade, to the implement of his sitting down, and to his asinine character. No wonder Bottom remains unalterably himself even in the bower of a fairy queen! The aristocrats, on the other hand, seem more vulnerable, since their names are disconnected from external objects and derive instead from literary texts – North's Plutarch, Chaucer's *Knight's Tale*, Ovid's *Metamorphoses*, *Huon de Burdeux*, anonymous Greek myths. As a result, although the play begins in Athens, the appearance of a Warwickshire wood inhabited by rural English workmen and fairies makes Theseus' palace seem unreal and Athenian ladies and gentlemen out of place (Barton 1974: 218). It is hardly surprising that a good Anglo-Gaelic hobgoblin like Puck should confuse a couple of classical Greeks like Demetrius and Lysander, and hence give the whirligig of fantasy its first spin. Unlike sylvan creatures and plants, which declare themselves openly, humans cannot be identified by natural signs. Lysander and Demetrius were so alike in Athens – 'as well derived', 'well possessed', 'fortunes every way as fairly ranked' (i.i.99–101) – that they rival the twin sons of Aegeon in *A Comedy of Errors*, 'the one so like the other / As could not be distinguished but by names' (i.i.51–2). But the names they are known by in Athens are of no help to Puck in the wood.

For that matter, they are not much help to the Athenians themselves, since no matter how constant their names may be, the bearers of those names become more and more indefinable. Thus as things fall apart and identities waver, the lovers cling to names. When Lysander raises the spectre of licentious nature by proposing to sleep with or beside Hermia (ii.ii.35 ff.), she addresses him by name three times, as if to invoke and bind him to his civilised Athenian identity. Seeking to exonerate himself by punning on the word 'lie', he merely succeeds in stripping the film of familiarity from his name and revealing its hidden signifier. A lover whose name is composed of and around a lie seems doomed to betray his beloved; and it is not long before Lysander, with Puck's help, lives up to his name by abandoning Hermia and assuming a new identity as the lover of Helena. In keeping with his having become a reification of his name, Lysander is now inspired to do away with his rival Demetrius syllable by syllable: 'Where is Demetrius? O, how fit a word / Is that vile name to perish on my sword!' (106–7). The scene ends with Lysander pursuing Helena and with Hermia awaking from her nightmare crying, 'Lysander! What, removed? Lysander! Lord! / What, out of hearing? Gone? No sound, no word?' (ii.ii.151–2).

Confusion begets further frustration in Act 3 Scene 2, and the calling of familiar names yields to name-calling. Hermia attacks Demetrius, 'Out, dog! Out, cur!' (65), only to be attacked herself by Lysander, 'thou cat, thou burr! Vile thing . . . Out, tawny Tartar, out! / Out, loathed med'cine! O hated potion, hence!' (260 ff.). She protests 'Am not I Hermia, are not you Lysander?' but then turns on Helena – 'You juggler! You canker-blossom! / You thief of love!' – who in turn first reproves her for forgetting their youthful friendship and then, goaded further, replies in kind, 'You counterfeit, you puppet, you!' (iii.ii.260–88). The episode ends with the young men dispossessed of their identities by the mimetic Puck, who leads them through illusions into the exhausted sleep from which Theseus will later awaken everyone.

This is all somewhat analogous to the famous incident recorded by Lévi-Strauss in *Tristes Tropiques* in which the superficial names of the Nambikwara girls dissolved when they spitefully revealed one another's secret names (1973: 278–9, 296–7).[7] In the wood of *A Midsummer Night's Dream* it is Puck who unwittingly exposes the secret and somewhat repellent identities of the lovers – identities that seem to have been repressed or only dimly discernible in Athens. Before Hermia and Helena enter the wood, their friendship is strained but still intact; once there, it yields to vituperation and even physical attack (iii.ii.298). Similarly, the Athenian competition between Lysander and Demetrius escalates murderously in the forest. Violence becomes endemic. Demetrius threatens Helena with death, and Hermia attacks her physically; Hermia dreams that a snake-like Lysander is eating her heart or at least that he is permitting a snake to do so; and the two young men would gladly kill one another if not diverted by Puck. In a sense, 'the forms of things unknown' in Athens, things suppressed and unconscious, find a local habitation in the wood and become named, although this naming takes distorted shapes in hyperbole, metaphor, metonymy and pun. The most distorted shape of all occurs when Bottom's asininity in Athens gets named in the wood by his translation. It behoves us then to consider Bottom's metamorphosis more closely. But first we need to consider Theseus' notions about poetic translation.

FIGURING FAIRIES

When Bottom reflects on his dream, his thoughts drift towards literature as the ideal liaison between inward feelings and outward audience. Properly titled and couched in Peter Quince's finest language, his elusive experience will be fit for its audience. But will his audience be fit for it? The audience Bottom has in mind for his ballad is an unpromising one, since Theseus seems as inherently sceptical of dreams and fairies as Mercutio in *Romeo and Juliet*. In fact, the famous speech in which he expresses his doubts (v.i.2–22) is so much more germane to Bottom's experience than it is to the lovers' that one almost wonders whether Bottom and Quince caught the duke in the dressing room between Acts 4 and 5 and recited the first draft of 'Bottom's Dream' to him. However it may be with Theseus, Shakespeare may well have composed the duke's speech with Bottom's monologue still sounding in his imagination, which is perhaps why the speech begins by debunking 'fairy toys' (of which only Bottom could have spoken) and moves on to describe the rather erratic collaboration of the poet's eye, his imagination and his pen as they, like Bottom and Quince, seek a literary habitation and a name for things unknown.

Things unknown, or previously unexpressed, or inexpressible directly, usually find lodgings in tropes. Thus Theseus' speech metaphorically equates lunatic, lover and poet in terms of imaginative invention. All are subsumed under a notion of 'transport' that derives ultimately from the four *furors* of Plato, who, like Theseus, scoffed at poets while helping himself to their devices: 'For the poet is an airy thing, a winged and a holy thing; and he cannot make poetry until he becomes inspired and goes out of his senses and no mind is left in him' (*Ion* 534c). Getting himself transported to inspirational altitudes, however, is but half the poet's task; he must also get down again, and that means endowing inspiration with a certain body and weight. In his own speech Theseus is embodying an inspired, albeit satirical, conception of the mysteries of poetic creation in a metaphor about the bodying forth of airy nothing.[8] His metaphor takes metaphor itself for its subject, insofar as the etymological 'carrying over' or 'transporting' attributed to metaphor operations is reflected in his description of ideas being conveyed from heaven to imagination to the scribbled page. Similarly, the 'turning' action of trope is called forth by Theseus' reference to the 'poet's pen' that 'Turns [imagined forms] to shapes'. Indeed, as it gives cursive shape to signifiers on the page, this pen tropes figures of sense as well, giving a twist of meaning, for instance, to 'pen' itself by making it a metonym for both the poet and the act of writing.

As this last example indicates, the central metaphor of embodiment is complicated by metonymy, even in its most basic action of 'carrying over'. Etymologically, metonymy consists in a 'transfer of name', and what Theseus describes is a series of transfers, from heaven to earth, from earth to imagination, from imagination to pen, from pen to paper and name. This poetic process is suggestively similar to the series of events that brought desire into the wood, as Oberon explained earlier (II.i.155–72) – the dart of Eros, deflected from its queenly target, 'fell upon a little western flower' which now has the capacity to fall upon lovers' eyes and 'make or man or woman madly dote'. This flight of Eros' dart is a metonymic process based on contiguity and infection, and the echo of this process in Theseus' speech suggests how metaphor is infected and perhaps corrupted by metonymic desire. That is, metaphoric recognition, the likeness registered by the poet's eye as it roves comparatively between heaven and earth, is a kind of static seeing at a distance. Metonymy endows metaphor with the desire to transfer this likeness by means of the imagination and the pen on to the scripted page. However, the process of transferral entails a fall from metaphoric grace as the ethereal is corporealised; what is 'carried over' is necessarily 'carried down', rather as the idealised image of the beloved in dotage must eventually suffer a disillusioning loss of grace in its descent to quotidian familiarity.

This equation of poetic and erotic desire will be made much more memorably in *Pyramus and Thisbe*, as I hope to demonstrate in the following chapter. More immediately, we see Theseus' scorn of poetry becoming wonderful poetry itself through his own reliance on poetic tropes, as if all language were inescapably coloured by figuration. If so, then cool reason and the overheated imagination differ not in categorical kind but only in thermometric degrees. The prohibitive business of reason is to maintain differences, classically between 'A' and 'not-A', especially when 'A' represents that which is legitimate and 'not-A' that which is not – or, as Theseus puts it in his speech, the difference between fact and fairies, bushes and bears, and sane reality and the mad imaginings of lovers, madmen and poets. But the transgressive passion of tropes is to find a way through or around those partitioning differences and, as all lovers hope to do, effect a union. In that event, some monstrous couplings of 'A' and 'not-A' may take place, albeit not without a certain *jouissance* of the text. A word-dominated play like *Love's Labour's Lost* would no doubt explore this issue verbally, but because *A Midsummer Night's Dream* specialises in eyes and things visible, textual matters assume a corporeal aspect, most obviously in the metamorphosis of Bottom but also in the more subtle translations of the lovers in the wood and of hobgoblins, elves and fairies in fairyland.

The fairies constitute a classic instance of the union of 'As' and 'not-As', despite Theseus' insistence on keeping fairyland distinct from the world of hard Athenian fact. When he dismisses fairies as fanciful figurations on a par with Hellenic gypsies, madmen's devils and poets' musings, his critique would be more telling if the fairies themselves had not already anticipated his scepticism and confounded his categories. Take, for instance, Titania's long speech citing the disastrous effects on nature of her and Oberon's quarrelling. She makes a point of cause and consequence. '*Therefore* the winds, piping to us in vain', she says, have sucked up from the sea contagious fogs, converted them into rainfall, and flooded the land. 'The ox hath *therefore* stretched his yoke in vain', for nothing can grow; and '*Therefore* the moon, the governess of floods, / Pale in her anger, washes all the air, / That rheumatic diseases do abound'. All nature is afflicted. 'And this same progeny of evils', she sums up,

<blockquote>

comes
From our debate, from our dissension;
We are their parents and original.
(II.i.81–117)
</blockquote>

All of these 'therefores' mark Titania as fairyland's Aristotle of causation, except of course that she turns cause and effect metonymically backwards, reversing the process whereby the rustic imagination, confronted by inexplicable disorders in nature, is obliged to concoct an explanation out of fairy folklore.[9] If she were to pause occasionally, smile at the audience, and mouth the words 'So they say', the truth would out, and her last sentence would make its ironic implications explicit: 'All these parent and original disorders, aided by the midwife of naïve country imagination, have given birth to the story about our debate and dissension.'[10]

Titania's speech violates Theseus' distinction between the 'A' of cool reason and the 'not-A' of hot imagination, for in rustic usage the fairy-conceiving imagination acts in the interest of cause-seeking reason. It is as if reason, invaded by the virus of desire, seeks the satisfaction of an explanatory cause with all the passion of a lover seeking union with his beloved. Titania then *is* an Aristotle of causation. For she tells us that when the rustics' search for a reasonable cause of unnatural disasters arrives at a blank, they fill in that blank with fairies, which is not so very different from Aristotle searching backwards from one moved object to its mover, until finally he comes to a blank and fills it with, if not fairies, an Unmoved Mover. When reason cannot find a local habitation and a name on its own, imagination will find them for it.

Earlier and somewhat less grandly, Puck tells the same tale when he acknowledges to an unnamed Fairy that he is indeed the merry wanderer of the night who is gifted with such formidable mimetic talents that, unlike Bottom, he not merely wants to play all parts, but can do so:

I jest to Oberon, and make him smile,
When I a fat and bean-fed horse beguile,
Neighing in likeness of a filly foal;
And sometime lurk I in a gossip's bowl,
In very likeness of a roasted crab;
And when she drinks, against her lips I bob,
And on her withered dewlap pour the ale.
The wisest aunt, telling the saddest tale,
Sometime for three-foot stool mistaketh me;
Then slip I from her bum, down topples she,
And 'tailor' cries, and falls into a cough;
And then the whole quire hold their hips and loff,
And waxen in their mirth and neeze and swear
A merrier hour was never wasted there.

(II.i.44–57)

Puck gives anamorphism a reverse twist: instead of seeing something previously indistinguishable, the audience must now unsee something that is palpably apparent. From a straight-on view Puck is clearly a mimetic genius, the perfect embodiment of the Keatsian artistic imagination that can invest itself in anything it chooses. But the more impressive his talents as actor, mischief-maker and court jester become, the more dubious he seems. He fades before our eyes, leaving not so much as an anamorphic blur to mark his place. As a result, like the viewers of Holbein's painting who think themselves in visual control of the occasion, or like Sartre's voyeur at the keyhole, we suddenly find ourselves more seen than seeing. It is a bit of an embarrassment, because our condescending suspension of disbelief in Robin Goodfellows is now puckishly equated with the superstitious credulity of country folk. If we had a mirror, we would see an image of ourselves looking very much like a composite photograph of a farmer uncolted, a gossip un-aled and an aunt unseated. Thus if the whole quire now hold their hips and loff, it is not only at their unfortunate quiremates but at us as well.

Clearly Puck is a master translator; he can be himself if he chooses or anything else, metamorphosing 'into' or 'out of' at will. From the rustics' perspective, it is always 'out of', since like MacCavity the cat, he is never to be found at the scene of the crime. The pity is that when he translates himself into a filly foal or a roasted crab-apple, his fairy form disappears entirely. In that there is an infinite loss. For who would trade Robin Goodfellow in the airy flesh for unruly crab-apples and joint-stools, or even for a hog or a fire? Yet these are the only shapes in which Puck can appear to ordinary mortals, certainly to sceptical ones like Theseus.

As an artist specialising in diminished things, then, Puck bodies forth the form of one airy unknown, himself, by disappearing as a fairy and appearing as a real object or animal in the rustic world. Fortunately, this procedure can be turned inside-out like a cheveril glove, provided we have a glover's son for a playwright. For Shakespeare quite literally bodies forth on stage, in the corporeal shape of an actor, the airy nothing of which Puck is composed in rustic dreams and superstitions.[11] Here too would seem to be an infinite loss. For surely the actor who seeks to translate Puck into theatrical reality, however flighty he may be, can only pale beside a creature who in our imaginations can girdle the earth in forty minutes. However, to lament what is lost when Puck falls from our bookish imagination to the stage, as romantic critics often did, is too easy. Puck himself challenges us to greater feats of imagination than conjuring up a miniature aerial spcedster as we read the text. For he insists that in the theatre he simultaneously is and is not present – that he is always precisely where he claims not to be, right in front of us, and never where our eyes tell us he is, right in front of us. Fairies can manage that sort of thing, but only with the aid of the audience's theatrical imagination. Witness (and unwitness) Oberon when, readying himself to eavesdrop on the lovers, he announces to the audience, 'I am invisible' (II.i.186). And so he is – and is not. These visibly invisible fairies lie like metaphors, and tell the truth like metaphors. 'There is no Oberon', declares W. D. Snodgrass (1975: 209), 'and Titania is his consort.'

Titania, thanks to Puck, is Bottom's consort too. For if Puck is primarily an actor, Bottom releases the artist in him, the sculptor whose raw material is the human body, or the animal body, or in Bottom's case a bit of both.

TRANSLATING BOTTOM

I said earlier that Shakespeare explores the nature of theatrical representation by corporealising tropes. 'Translation' is a good word for this, because it combines the notion of physical metamorphosis with those of 'turning' and 'transferring' associated with tropes, especially metaphor and metonymy. But Peter Quince supplies a better word when he says that to represent Moonshine one of the players 'must come in with a bush of thorns and a lantern, and say he comes to disfigure, or to present, the person of Moonshine' (III.i.55–7). By 'disfigure' Quince means, of course, 'figure', and by 'present', 'represent'. Nevertheless, Quince's malappropriateness generates meanings wonderfully appropriate to Shakespeare's business – that is, stage business. In the first place, it equates figuring with marring (and illustrates it too, insofar as Quince's attempt to say 'figure' is 'disfigured'). This is the kind of mistake that speaks the truth, reminding us that the act of figuration has always been thought of as a violation of plain speech and hence characterised by metaphors of defacement and deviation, of troping, twisting and wrenching, of illegal transport or smuggling, and of course of lying. In the second place, as Schlegel first observed, to dis-figure is to 'un-trope' or unmetaphor,[12] hence para-doxically to erase disfigurement and defacement by returning speech to its plain good looks again. For Quince, this means 'to present' on stage and thus implies a translation of verbal tropes into the material stuff of theatre, most indispensably into bodies that stand (and fall and run and speak) for other bodies.

Bottom himself is a palpable gross instance of Quince's disfiguring, since in his translated form he is not so much an animal as a metaphor fleshed out in animal form – a metaphor unmetaphored and as a result monstrously disfigured. However, this is only to be expected, since to dis-figure even the most familiar figure is to give birth to a monster – a warrior with the heart of a lion, a chair with arms, a clock with a face. Because poets can provide even stranger concoctions, such as Campion's young lady with a garden in her face or Eliot's yellow smoke that rubs its muzzle on the window panes, one can understand why in 1670 Samuel Parker pro-posed an Act of Parliament forbidding what Samuel Johnson was to call 'heterogeneous ideas yoked by violence together'. And yet it is just such heterogeneity that best illustrates the workings of metaphor, and Bottom is heterogeneity itself.

To see Bottom's special virtues in respect of translation, we can compare him to a more perfect example – Gregor Samsa's metamorphosis in Kafka's famous short story of that name. The troping of Gregor's body is completely accomplished in the opening line of the story: 'When Gregor Samsa woke up one morning from unsettling dreams, he found himself changed in his bed into a monstrous insect.' Unlike Bottom, Gregor has already awakened from unsettling dreams; there is no return to human shape for him. Hence we never know what his human body was like. Bottom is more complicated. He resembles what Hofstadter and Moser, studying verbal mistakes in the interests of cognitive science, call 'malaphor', a neologism that illustrates its own definition: 'the seamless blending of two (or more) stock phrases (or even just words) into a single new phrase (or word)' – that is, either a portmanteau word, as in 'She had a nice *aurora* of perfume around her', or a portmanteau phrase, as in 'We'll burn those bridges when we come to them' or 'You hit the nail right on the nose' (1989: 196–200). The virtue of a malaphor, they observe, is that by exhibiting bits and pieces of the phrases that went into it, [it reveals] some of its birth pangs. When a suitable word or phrase is effortlessly retrieved from memory, it is like a well-executed magic trick: it gives up no information about how it was carried out, and thus remains magical and impenetrable. In a malaphor, on the other hand, you see not only the miraculous appearance of a rabbit, but also perhaps a tip of the rabbit's ear protruding from underneath the table, a bit of glue, or a hint of a trap door in the tabletop. (1989: 197)

Gregor Samsa's transformation into an insect is just such a well-executed and hence impenetrable magic trick. If we think of the insect as a metaphor for Gregor, then the human signified (the Gregor we never see in human form) has become totally identified with, has disappeared into, its insect signifier.[13] Metamorphosis is thus an unmetaphoring movement beyond metaphor, a fusion of signifier and signified brought about by suppressing the demurrer of difference implicit in metaphoric assertions of identity.[14] Signification and reference condense into a material object that is simply itself, an impenetrable blank wall, the very perfection of a wall.

In Bottom's case, however, the wall has a cranny in it, because the metamorphic process is arrested before Bottom is entirely animalised. How much of Bottom remains untranslated is up to the director,[15] but surely one part of him that cannot be translated into an ass is his bottom, which is already an ass (even though metaphorically that is precisely what *is* translated). That means that the magic is compromised not by 'a bit of glue, or a hint of a trap door in the tabletop', but by the presence of a human arse on a jackass. Monstrously disjoined, metaphor turns visibly malaphoric, caught in the very act of signification. The stage presents us with a corporeal illustration of the fact that meaning never exists apart from its material representation and that metaphoric meaning lies in neither the signified nor the signifier alone but is a kind of offspring of their union, a *tertium quid* arising like harmony from the interactive presence of both. Without his equine signifier Bottom would remain meaningless, a mute inglorious signified; but if he were expressed by a signifier that simply substituted for him, as metaphor is often said to do, he would remain equally meaningless, a signified in eclipse, like an apple or joint-stool into which Puck has disappeared.

Another point made by this malaphoric metaphor is that it is by no means merely metaphoric. The classical metaphors used to define metaphor – as a 'carrying over', a 'substitution', a 'comparison', an 'analogy' and so forth – all imply a gap or division between signified and signifier. Metaphor thus features a doubling at a distance that contrasts with the often close physical contiguity that characterises metonymy and synecdoche.[16] However, by arresting Bottom in mid-metamorphosis, Shakespeare metonymises metaphor. In fact, he makes of Bottom a monstrous multitrope: not only a metaphor but also an incarnated pun on the word 'ass', a metonym featuring a bottom become a top, and a synecdoche in which a posterior part becomes, if not a whole, an even larger part than it was (and surely Bottom's bottom should have at all times a preposterous pre-eminence). The effect of this is to collapse metaphoric distance into metonymic and paronomastic proximity, so that the meaning of 'the human animal' is given a sharply literal and arresting turn. At first glance, Bottom's half-metamorphosis merely repeats the exploitation of animals elsewhere as metaphors for the lovers' degradation. But here the traffic in meaning goes both ways. Bonded bodily and figuratively, Bottom becomes ass-like, and asses become Bottom-like, a fusion of man and beast that, far from degrading either, proves almost as lovable for us as it does for Titania and the fairies.

As for Bottom: with his own steatopygous bottom sticking balkily out behind – a visible denial of total equine animality in favour of meta-phoricity[17] – he is, it would seem, a rather half-assed metaphor. But since that in a sense is what all metaphors are, we should applaud the forthrightness of Bottom's bottom and regard it as a fitting appurtenance to a weaver who is bumptiously kind, gentle, forthright, endearingly innocent and unselfconscious, and essentially untranslatable – asinine in some respects, no doubt, but uniquely Bottom too, and far more than an ass. Moreover, we might note that if Bottom's body protrudes from his asinine shape to announce his only half-translation, it does no more than the body of Theseus does in protruding from his Oberon shape. Bottom would have good reason to ask the duke, so smugly given to rational distinctions, which is the more monstrous, a beast-man or a fairy-man.

Mentioning Theseus gives rise to another point about Bottom's trans-lation and the duke's metaphor for poetic creation. For that metaphor depicts a unifying process in which the images registered by the poet's eye as it glances between earth and heaven are condensed into a body, and in some respects Bottom illustrates and in some respects he parodies this process. As for the parody, it is often suggested, for instance, that Bottom's awakening speech is something of a dark glass through which one can discern Christian truths about the transcendence of the 'natural man' by spiritual apprehensions of divine wisdom (Goddard 1951; R. F. Miller 1975; Hassel 1970; Rhoads 1985: 79–82).[18] This calls attention to the appropriateness, even the necessity, of metaphor in a dualistic universe in which the perfection of the deity (or of a fairy queen) so radically transcends its flawed and fallible creations. Such a hierarchy gives rise to medieval religious allegory with its stress on God's metaphoric difference from humankind. On the other hand, a metonymic approach to this relationship would stress contiguity and suggest that everything is somehow part of the supernatural whole; but it might also carry a disconcerting implication that the divine is not all that different from the profane. Perhaps that is partly why making metaphors has usually been regarded as superior to making metonyms. It requires a gift for discerning and winging your airy way towards distant resemblances – glancing back-and-forth between earth and heaven, as Theseus puts it – whereas to come up with a metonym you merely have to scout around in the immediate, highly imperfect neighbourhood. Thus from Aristotle to Jacobson and Lacan, metaphor has been held to be the stuff of poetry, and mere metonymy a matter of prose.[19] As mentioned above, Theseus' speech reflects these views by associating metonymy with the corruptive transiency of desire as it translates altitudinous metaphoric visions downward into 'bodies' that the poet's pen conveys into language and on to the page to create the pleasures of the text.

Bottom's translation repeats this process in burlesque form and with a light glance at neoplatonism. That is, any echo of Paul's letter to the Corinthians or of the writings of Ficino or Castiglione about casting off the body *en route* to an encounter with divine love is here turned into a bottom-side-up parody. There is no doubt a great distance between the profane Bottom and the fairy queen, but his unwitting way of closing that distance is not through disembodiment. Instead of ascending the ladder of love from individual bodies to universal beauty in a spiritualising action, Bottom slips to its bottom-most rung and tumbles into self-engrossed corporeality. In a moment of regal hubris, Titania says that she will purge Bottom of his 'mortal grossness' so that he may 'like an airy spirit go' (III.i.154–5); but the next time we see him, his unaerated body is luxuriating in scratchings and yearning for bottles of hay, quite oblivious of Titania and the fairies except as instruments of his corporeal pleasures. In keeping with this, at his awakening he is wholly absorbed in the mystery of himself – 'Methought I was – and methought I had' – thus achieving, at a moment rich with the possibility of self-realisation, a *nosce teipsum* in reverse.

In a modern context of vision, Bottom's speech suggests an inversion of the mirror-state, that moment when the child infers the unity and coherence of its own body from its image in a mirror (or in a mirroring other person) – an act of creative bodying forth somewhat analogous to that in Theseus' metaphor. And insofar as Bottom substitutes for the changeling boy in Titania's bower, and is treated as a child (Huston 1981: 107; Dunn 1988: 22), he awakens in an appropriate state of childlike wonder. But instead of converting *le corps morcelé* of his psyche into a gestalt, his comic anti-anagnorisis mirrors his anatomical monstrousness in the bower by dwelling on the dislocations of body and sense: 'The eye . . . hath not heard, the ear . . . hath not seen, man's hand is not able to taste, his tongue to conceive, nor his heart to report, what my dream was'. Instead of going through the mirror phase, Bottom goes right through the mirror itself into fairyland and becomes *le corps morcelé*, from which dream he awakens with his body whole but his speech in bits and pieces.

In this respect, Bottom's awakening forecasts the disjointedness of bodies in the production of *Pyramus and Thisbe*, just as his translation stands as a grotesque paradigm for Peter Quince's bungled translation of 'Pyramus and Thisbe' and within it the arrested translations of Bottom into Pyramus, Flute into Thisbe, Snug into Lion, Starveling into Moon, and especially of Snout into Wall. No doubt, as with Bottom's dream, man is but an ass to go about to expound all these strange figurings and disfigurings, but at the risk of growing marvellous hairy about the face, let me take a closer look at *Pyramus and Thisbe* in the next chapter.

· 6 ·

Walls, Partitions and Performances

Liminal objects are points of transition, and a play featuring such objects
puts a premium on movement and metamorphosis, on passages from one
cultural state to another, albeit with a pause at the point of exit/entrance.
Liminality calls attention to the go-between get-between aspect of these
rites, which serve both to provide and to deny access. Both functions are
compressed into the paradoxical pause at the threshold, where the passer-
through takes on some of the inside-outness, open-shutness of Puck's door.
The paradox is less obvious in the case of Pyramus and Thisbe's wall, since
walls normally impede rather than promote passage. But this wall is an
exception because of its cranny, which permits the passage of squinting
looks and whispered declarations of love. The patriarchal wall shuts off and
divides, its secret cranny opens up and unites; and in some respects that summarises a principle at work throughout *A Midsummer Night's Dream*. Since in
an earlier chapter I gave priority to Puck's door, in this one it seems only fair
to give equal time to Pyramus and Thisbe's wall. Taking a cue from the
lovers, then, let us grope around the concept of wall in search of some chinks
and crannies opening on to larger issues of interest to Shakespeare.

OVIDIAN WALLS

The original location of some of these issues is Ovid's *Metamorphoses*,
where Shakespeare found the 'tedious brief scene of young Pyramus and

117

his Thisbe'. Walls loom large in Ovid's version of this tragic tale. The
scene, for instance, is Babylon, 'of whose huge walles so monstrous high
and thicke / The fame is given *Semyramis* for making them of bricke'
(Rouse, 1966 IV: 67–8). These brick walls divide civilized Babylon from
the fearful world of animals and barbarians outside. Inside, within Babylon
itself, stands the wall that divides the two nameless families, and within the
wall is its curiously subversive cranny: 'The wall that parted house from
house had riven therein a crany / Which shronke at making of the wall'
(83–4). Something there is in this shronken cranny that doesn't love a wall.
Something there is in the lovers too, who complain piteously to it:

O thou envious wall (they sayd,) why letst thou lovers thus?
What matter were it if that thou permitted both of us
In armes eche other to embrace? Or if thou thinke that this
Were overmuch, yet mightest thou at least make roume to kisse.
                                                              (91–4)

And so, despite a certain gratitude to its cranny, the lovers abandon the wall
in search of more immediate encounters. At the edge of the city they find a
larger and thicker wall with a larger and wider cranny, 'the City gate' (106),
through which they slip *en route* to their fatal meeting place at the tomb of
Ninus, former husband of Semiramis.[1]

Crannies are somewhat ambiguous; they serve the cause of love but also
lead to death, the hole in life's wall that all lovers locate sooner or later. As
this suggests, Ovid's use of crannied walls is highly symbolic. The wall
materialises a cultural taboo, the arbitrary patriarchal regulation of desire
(no reason is given for the parents' opposition); and the cranny ('This fault
not markt of any / Of many hundred yeares before' (84–5)) represents the
flaw in all cultural attempts to regulate desire. For desire – 'what doth not
love espie?' (85) – will always find a cranny somewhere, perhaps by natural
affinity, inasmuch as desire is itself inspired by a flaw in the psyche – an
incompleteness or want. A love based on a structural flaw does not augur
well; yet of course that is what love is always based on – and, for that matter,
language too, as Ovid suggests by having the lack that engenders desire in
the lovers engender also a need for signs. Prevented, that is, by the wall
from coming together bodily or even verbally at first, the lovers substitute a
private system of communication: 'No man was privie to their thoughts.
And for to serve their turne / In steade of talke they used signes' (80–1).

Whispers through a cranny are better than mute signs, but a direct
experience of the beloved's lips is better than both. Clearly, the solution is
to escape from walls and signs to an outside world where natural impulses
can range freely. Unfortunately, cultural restraints are not easily escaped;

the walls they flee from rise again in the likeness of the tomb of Ninus, itself both a material presence and a scene of absence. As a sign or trace, the tomb is an appropriate spot for Thisbe to leave her bloody mantle, a brief memorial of her passage, the meaning of which Pyramus so disastrously misinterprets.[2] The price of hermeneutic misprision in this case is death, which erects a final wall between the lovers. Yet even this wall is not impermeable, because as the grieving Thisbe observes, they who are twained by death – 'For death which only coulde alas a sunder part us twaine' (185) – are also they 'whome even death hath joynde in one' (190). The phallic sword that opens a route to Thisbe's heart also opens a cranny to and through death to a reunion with Pyramus.

The lovers' search for a way to express their love despite the presence of walls – a search that takes them from the silent 'signes' they used in public, to the whispers they used through the cranny, and finally to a meeting under the sign of Ninus – finds its apparent fulfilment in the metamorphic mulberry tree, which transforms all signs into a natural memorial. In Golding's memorable phrasing, as Pyramus dies, his blood,

> did spin on hie
> As when a Conduite pipe is crackt the water bursting out
> Doth shote itselfe a great way off and pierce the Ayre about,
> The leaves that were upon the tree besprincled with his blood
> Were died blacke. The roote also bestained as it stoode,
> A deepe darke purple colour upon the Berries cast.
>
> (147–52)

Fertilised thus by Pyramus' orgasmic dying, the mulberry tree annually converts a no-longer-living love into a fruitful ever-living sign of what has been lost. However, this metamorphosis of culture into nature is itself subject to a reverse metamorphosis, back into verbal signs. For this meaningful mulberry grows only within the orchards of Ovid's *Metamorphoses*. There the lovers find their textual tomb but also their ever-fructifying memorial.

And there too, if we switch our focus from the affairs of Pyramus and Thisbe to those of Ovid, we encounter still further walls. Or, more accurately, we encounter further 'partitions' – the term Demetrius uses in commenting on Snout's disjointed announcement of his role as Wall: 'It is the wittiest partition that ever I heard discourse, my lord' (v.i.166–7). A partition is a section within a discourse or treatise, a wall of words – a pretty good metaphor for Snout himself as he stands before his audience and presents his roughcast report on himself as Wall. Partition is a good term also for Ovid's tale of Pyramus and Thisbe, which carries the concept of walling-off still further by being an embedded tale, a partition within a

longer Ovidian story about Pentheus and Bacchus which begins near the
end of Book III (644) and concludes in mid-Book IV (513) when all of
Thebes is obliged to acknowledge Bacchus as its new god. In the interim,
however, the daughters of Minyas prove bastions of religious conservatism.
Refusing to attend a wild rite in honour of Bacchus, they keep at home,
weaving and telling stories – first of Pyramus and Thisbe, then of Mars and
Venus, Helius and Leuconoe, and finally Salmacis and Hermaphrodite. At
this point the sounds of unseen timbrels, flutes and horns mysteriously
float through Thebes, and an invisible but triumphant Bacchus takes his
revenge, putting an end to the defiant ladies' story-telling by turning them
all into bats.

Actually, Ovid's 'Pyramus and Thisbe' is merely one of a series of
embedded stories. The framing tale of Bacchus and Pentheus is itself a
recursive episode within the larger story of Cadmus and Thebes, which
occupies all of Book III and ends late in Book IV (742) with Cadmus
and his wife being turned into serpents. Thus 'Pyramus and Thisbe' is
partitioned off inside the *Metamorphoses* by at least two narrative walls,
which may explain why Shakespeare adopted the theatrical equivalent, a
play-within-a-play, and partitioned it off within *A Midsummer Night's
Dream*. Since this is one of the first inner-plays of his career, it should
reward closer examination.

TRANSLATIONS

Pyramus and Thisbe is partitioned off from the rest of *A Midsummer Night's
Dream* both fictively (life in Athens is real, life in Babylon is not) and
theatrically (as an inner-play). Yet the nature of a partition is to unite even
as it divides. Every wall has a cranny in it, whether it has one or not. The
very flagrancy of Wall in *Pyramus and Thisbe*, for instance, reminds us of
walls elsewhere in Theseus' Greece and Shakespeare's play. Everyone (but
especially Sheldon Zitner (1960)) has noted the division of the play into
different social classes (workmen and nobles), orders of reality (humans
and fairies), geographical locations (palace and forest), character groupings
(workmen, fairies, lovers, rulers), and roughly corresponding verbal styles
(prose, song and charm, rhymed couplets and blank verse). Theseus serves
as the master spokesman for all such divisive walls when he delivers his
sceptical speech at the beginning of Act 5 partitioning off fairies from
reality, and imagination from reason (v.i.2–22).

Despite Theseus, we can hardly help noting the frequent analogies and
parallels that belie the discreteness of these partitions. As Sidney Homan
says, 'Evidence abounds in the play to suggest that Theseus' dualism

obscures the unity and massive dimensions of the play's single world' (1981: 82). Despite Theseus, fairyland is very much like Athens, is indeed its exaggerated sylvan double, as the doubling of the four regal roles emphasises; and, by the same token, *Pyramus and Thisbe* doubles, by way of theatrical burlesque, the experience of the lovers in the palace wood. Again, the lovers themselves, even in their most divisive moments, are bathed by the same moonlight, governed by the same Oberon, and transfigured, they dimly recall afterwards, by the same dream reflected in the same story. Hippolyta serves as the master spokeswoman for all such crannied connections when she replies to Theseus' speech on reason by suggesting that the 'story of the night' and a collective transfiguration of minds together grow to something of great constancy, although accompanied by an aura of the 'strange and admirable' that teases the imagination and reminds us that, however wide the expressive crannies in our walls, something ineffably noumenal can never get through.[3]

Shakespeare could hardly help being aware of this dual aspect of verbal partitions. For him it would show most obviously in respect of what is lost and what is preserved by translation. Around the turn of the Christian era, Ovid translated an ancient Greek myth about Pyramus and Thisbe into Latin verse in *Metamorphoses*. In 1565–7 Arthur Golding translated Ovid into English narrative verse, and around 1595 Shakespeare translates both Ovid and Golding very loosely into *Romeo and Juliet* and very disjointedly into his own *Pyramus and Thisbe* (Rudd 1979; A. B. Taylor 1990; Martindale and Martindale 1990). As indicated above, merely to read Ovid's tale of Pyramus and Thisbe would suggest to Shakespeare the memorial nature of translation and the translative nature of memorials. All that remains of the experience of the Babylonian lovers is writ small on the berries of the mulberry tree and more largely on the leaves of Ovid's book, Golding's translation and Shakespeare's own adaptation, not to mention the works of Peter Quince. Yet to mention the works of Peter Quince is to emphasise what is lost in these translations, indeed in any translation.

PYRAMUS AND THISBE: PROLOGUE AND MOON

For Oberon, Titania, and especially Puck, no walls stand between theatre and fairyland; they do not merely pass back-and-forth unimpeded but are in both places at once. For Bottom, on the other hand, the wall between his dream and his waking consciousness is impenetrable and insurmountable. He hopes Peter Quince, the balladeer, will find a cranny in this wall, or drill one with his art, and fetch his dream through it into reality. Unfortunately the ballad by Peter Quince fails to appear. Fortunately, however, a play by

Peter Quince appears in its place, and we quickly see that, however he may fare as a balladeer, Quince's natural medium is the stage. For he and his players, especially Bottom himself, are strong on the here-and-now of matter, on what is present in presentations of reality. To portray the sad doings of the Babylonian lovers, they would bring Babylon itself into the theatre if they could – and so they should, because realism, after all, is such stuff as theatrical dreams are made on. Thus the Chorus in *Henry V*, before yielding to the constraints of a wooden 'O' and the histrionic limitations of the Chamberlain's Men, dreams of having 'A kingdom for a stage' and 'princes to act'. This Chorus is all one with the Bottom who cries, 'Look in the almanac. Find out moonshine, find out moonshine' (III.i.49–50), hoping to have the real thing to illuminate their production. He and his fellows place small faith in imagination, theirs or the audience's. They will bring reality itself on stage, and if they cannot do so entirely, they will at least construct theatrical scaffolding of the most explicit kind to support the audience's imagination: a prologue to outline the plot, costumes and props to identify the characters, speeches to identify the costumes and props, dialogue with built-in stage directions, and impromptu remarks to the audience to clarify the action.[4]

But if the workmen's staging invites, and receives, a mocking from its audience within the play, neither Shakespeare's audience nor his company should be quick to join in. After all, the Chamberlain's Men themselves assume an audience that cannot imagine a wood without green boughs scattered about, or a king without a crown, or young Grecian ladies without young English boys got up in female clothing. Indeed theatre exists as an institution because the imagination of its audiences wants more material stuff than words to work with – costumes and stage props and, most of all, human bodies to saw the air and tear passions to tatters. In Elsinore the players are advised to use all gently in this regard, but in Athens the mechanicals – whose trade requires them to work with such media as pots and pans, looms, bellows, needle and thread, hammers and nails – quite naturally insist on publicising the artful machinery of their performance. Whether they underestimate the imagination of the audience (and hence supply roughcast and lime to cement its conception of a wall) or over-estimate the power of their staging (and hence make Snug show his face beneath the lion's head to reassure the ladies), the result is a stress on the material presence of representation. Their ostentatious devices and precautions make most visible the transparent wall of theatrical artifice that offers us Pyramus-like theatregoers access to a Thisbe-like fictional world even as it divides us from it.[5]

Consider, for instance, Quince himself in the role of Prologue. In the opening section (v.i.108–17) he has as hard a time publicising the good intentions of his company as Bottom does expressing his dream. 'If we offend', he declares, 'it is with our good will':

> That you should think, we come not to offend,
> But with good will. To show our simple skill,
> That is the true beginning of our end.
> Consider, then, we come but in despite.
> We do not come, as minding to content you
> Our true intent. All for your delight
> We are not here. That you should here repent you,
> The actors are at hand; and, by their show,
> You shall know all that you are like to know.

This provokes a wry observation from Theseus: 'This fellow doth not stand [pause] upon points [punctuation]' (v.i.118). The nervous Quince 'stands' when he should not, and does not stand when he should; and as a result of these stops and starts his well-intended speech protesting innocent intent betrays him and says just the opposite.

Let me pause myself to point out that punctuation is a matter of partitioning, of creating walls within discourse. Even the spaces between words create thin pales of morphemic sense in an otherwise undifferentiated phonic flow. But just where those spaces are located is hard to tell, as we all know when listening to seemingly pauseless speech in an unfamiliar language – and sometimes, alas, to decidedly pauseless speech in our own language. Normally, therefore, discursive sense is deferred or rendered provisional until a mark of punctuation appears in the form of a breath taken, a voice lowered or raised or drawn out or cut short, at which point a phrase, clause, or sentence takes shape in our understanding. These pointings part the body of discourse and need to be done with some awareness of anatomy. 'Cut at the joints', Plato advises, but Quince makes joints where none exist, disarticulating the body of his speech into a *corps morcelé* analogous to Bottom's speech on awakening from his dream. But whereas Bottom's speech spoke of bodily functions – eyes hearing, ears seeing and so on – Quince's prologue announces itself as a verbal body. Its disjointedness foregrounds the material presence of language by freeing signifiers from signifieds and giving them a random life of their own, or, to keep to my major metaphor, by erecting a wall between signifier and signified by making and failing to make partitions where it should.

Quince's prologue is almost guaranteed to disconcert the rational Theseus by virtue of its inversion of logocentric and patriarchal hierarchies. In it, conscious meaning does not father forth a coherent body of words, imparting its spiritual imprint to secondary signs, as Theseus claimed Egeus did at Hermia's conception (i.i.47–51). On the contrary, Quince's unruly phrases render his intended meanings pointless. Yet not altogether pointless, either. If language acquires a will of its own, speaking through and for Quince the way the unconscious speaks through and for us in dreams and slips of the tongue, it creates not only a perversion of meaning but perhaps also a revelation of deeper feeling in the approved Freudian manner. Whatever Quince means, the words he *says* suggest that the urge to offend mingles with the desire to please, that the desire to please is secondary to the impulse to show off, and that the audience will indeed repent the fact that these actors are 'at hand' ('are present' but also 'are handicraft men', not real actors). 'Hard-handed men' desirous of winning the duke's favour would do well to suppress such ambivalent desires and fears, but here they come tumbling forth, to the amusement of the audience and the dismay of the breathless Quince.

I certainly do not mean to suggest that Quince and his fellows are concealing (or failing to conceal) deep resentments about performing for the duke. They are delighted to perform, and their consuming desire is to please by exhibiting their wonderful skills. But desire, unable to express itself directly, forced instead through the 'defiles of the signifier', as Lacan puts it, always takes a certain blemish from its passage, and suffers here a defiling disfigurement, if not a complete blockage.

Quince's failure properly to partition his prologue causes a parting between its signifiers and signifieds, the body and spirit of his speech. A more radical but less lengthy parting takes place when Robin Starveling undertakes Moon. His announcement that 'This lanthorn doth the horned moon present; / Myself the man in the moon do seem to be' (v.i.240–1) draws from Theseus an amused observation: 'This is the greatest error of all the rest. The man should be put into the lanthorn. How is it else the man in the moon?' Corporeal complications work a curious division in this Moon, rendering him analogous to a metonym, or more precisely a synecdoche, a strangely displaced synecdoche in which a part of the moon stands for the whole, but stands, unfortunately, outside the whole of which it is a part. Yet that is precisely what any synecdoche does: a detached part grotesquely substitutes for a whole, so that we have disembodied pieces of anatomy doing the world's work, as wittily instanced by Willard Espy (138):

'All hands on deck!' the captain cried;
    But he was wroth to find
That when the hands arrived on deck
    They left the men behind.

In Robin's case, it is hard to say whether we encounter a synecdochised body or an embodied synecdoche, whether a man dissolves into a trope or a trope metamorphoses into a man. In either case, we are left with a sense of the inextricability of body and sign, precisely when the two are most extricably parted.

Robin's dilemma grows worse when he attempts to brazen it out by declaring, 'All that I have to say is to tell you that the lanthorn is the moon, I, the man in the moon, this thorn-bush my thorn-bush, and this dog my dog'. This runs afoul of Demetrius: 'Why, all these should be in the lanthorn; for all of these are in the moon' (v.i.253–7). Poor Moon is now triply parted, with each part larger than the lanthorn it should be a part of. The effect is to call our attention to the 'part' played not only by Robin Starveling but also to the parts played by the actor playing him. For this part is parted too; the player must play not only the part of Robin but also the part played by Robin – that of a hopelessly parted Moon. Fortunately for the player, all of his body fits into both of his parts, and both of his parts come together in his body.

Before abandoning Moon I should note that his problem of incorporating parts into wholes is solved at another level by the peculiar pronunciation of the word 'lantern' as reflected in its being spelled 'lanthorn'. For the theatrical problem is no problem at all for verbal signs. This one neatly places 'thorn' (if not the thorn-bush itself) inside 'lanthorn' and fits 'horn' ('the horned moon') inside both thorn and lanthorn. This is reminiscent of one of Lacan's seminars when, to show how symbolic substitution works, he pointed out that he could bring elephants into the lecture room, despite the smallness of the door, merely by calling on the signifier 'elephant' (Lacan 1988: 178, 218). Not only could Lacan hale elephants into the lecture room, or at least into the imaginations of his audience but, he might have added, he could also achieve an effortless unity of identity among elephants in doing so, since the common noun erases all individual differences among pachyderms and leaves only what is 'common', a united concept. But as Robin Starveling discovers, the stage deals with bodies as well as concepts; and although the name of Moon unites its lunar components into a conceptual whole in the mind, it wields no such power over the unruly individual parts that stand outside it on the stage. Conceptually, nominally, Moon is perfectly at one with itself; theatrically, however, it is dangerously divided between Robin and the lantern. Moreover, if the lantern is a whole that cannot contain its parts, so is Robin, who, as both Moon and 'the man in the moon', is a whole with a part as large as himself – indeed, it is himself.

WALL

Robin Starveling's difficulty in stuffing random physical parts and divided wholes into a single representation of Moon suggests that finding a local habitation for the poet's bodyings forth is not always as easy as Theseus implies. It also suggests that Shakespeare may have been thinking about just such matters as he wrote a play in which fairies, nobles and workmen, forest and palace, classical Greece and Elizabethan England must all reside under a single theatrical roof. In fact *Pyramus and Thisbe* alone could have inspired his playful explorations of the part–whole issue, inasmuch as embedding a play within a play is rather like getting a man in the moon inside the moon when he is both. The grotesquerie I have been pointing out seems modelled on Bottom's half-metamorphosis in fairyland: as his bottom sticks out of his imbruted state, so Robin's body sticks out of the moon and Snug's face sticks out of his leonine costume. In fact, all of Peter Quince's players are like Bottom in being but half-translated, causing *Pyramus and Thisbe* itself to stick somewhat awkwardly out of *A Midsummer Night's Dream* and inviting the audience to perceive by way of contrast that the proper parallel to Shakespeare's play is not Bottom but Puck, who can fit himself into physical wholes or parts with undivided ease.

In his bizarre fashion Moon demonstrates that representation, flagrantly foregrounded, can become an impediment to itself, refusing access to its imaginative referents. Similarly, the actors Bottom and Flute eclipse the characters Pyramus and Thisbe as effectively as Moon eclipses the moon; and even Lion's one modest grunt drowns out a lion's roars. Between the audience and the tragic affairs of antique Babylon rises an uncrannied theatrical wall. This and the death of a dear friend would go near to make a man look sad, if it were not for the fact that what is lost to our view is compensated for by what is made present to our view – namely, wall or rather Wall. 'Wall' is Wall's cue; he is to enter now.

As I mentioned in the opening section of this chapter, the wall in Ovid's 'Pyramus and Thisbe' brings into focus the problem of representation because it is a sign as well as a structure: it stands for the prohibition of desire and its cranny for desire itself. Thus it incorporates the go-between get-between nature of mediation in general, as does Wall in *Pyramus and Thisbe*. Insofar as Wall also represents the prohibition of desire, he is a comic version of the patriarchal law of Athens that first stood between Hermia and Lysander and later came mysteriously down when Theseus set aside Egeus' demands. In the Peter Quince production, Wall comes down too, or makes an exit, but not before Shakespeare, taking a cue from Bottom's line about meeting in the wood to 'rehearse most obscenely' (i.ii.98–9), has exploited the ribald potentialities of Ovid's wall in ways that are summed up by Jan Lawson Hinely:

> The thwarted sexual development and frustration of the lovers blocked by this recalcitrant wall is bawdily suggested by a hodgepodge of vaginal, phallic, and anal allusions (Goldstein 1973; Gui 1952–3). The wall suggests both the female and male sexual organs. The phrases 'the crannied hole, or chink', 'the cranny', 'right and sinister'; . . . and Pyramus's address to 'Thou wall, O sweet and lovely wall, / Show me thy chink . . .' all allude to the female genitalia aspects of the wall (v.i.158–77). Thisbe, for her part, is unintentionally scatological when declaiming, 'My cherry lips have often kissed thy stones, / Thy stones with lime and hair knit up in thee', and 'I kiss the wall's hole, not your lips at all' (v.i.190–91, 201). (Hinely 1987: 129)

In addition, the wall of parental restraint is also the hymen, 'the wall-within-the-wall' (Goldstein 1973: 194); and Theseus' remark, 'Pyramus draws near the wall' (v.i.168), invokes the *double entendre* about walls and the drawing of phallic swords so popular with the servants in the opening lines of *Romeo and Juliet*. However, the hymeneal wall is made of testicular stones and pubic hair, yielding a corporeal sign of monstrously mixed nature, its parts fragmented and fused, its sex a puzzlement.

Shakespeare's Wall encloses a world of suggestiveness: psychoanalytic-ally, the bar of repression separating the conscious from the unconscious; politically, the barrier between Hegel's 'master' and 'slave' (nobles/work-men); linguistically, the bar dividing the symbolic from the real as well as the signifier from the signified (S/s); sexually, the hymen that separates a maiden like Thisbe from what Flute calls 'a thing of naught'; legally, the Athenian law that keeps desire from its satisfaction; and theatrically, the transparent (or in *Pyramus and Thisbe* the opaque) window of mediation that stands between audience and illusion. No wonder the artisans find Wall a problem. From the beginning, they realise that representing Wall presents difficulties, in part because they cannot get a wall on stage and in part because they are required to display an absence, the cranny, when their passion is for making things present. As always, however, Bottom is quick with solutions:

> Some man or other must present Wall. And let him have some plaster, or some loam, or some roughcast about him, to signify wall; and let him hold his fingers thus, and through that cranny shall Pyramus and Thisby whisper. (iii.i.63–7)

Precisely what is meant by 'let him hold his fingers thus' is open to debate. Should Wall display a two-fingered V-like cranny, and, if so, should his fingers point up or down or sideways? Should he form a sinister < or a less suspicious, right-angled > or even a four-fingered < >: There is not much to choose among these on the basis of Bottom's cryptic 'thus'. However, when *Pyramus and Thisbe* is performed, certain bawdy images and phrasings suggest, as we shall see, that Snout shapes the cranny by spreading his legs and making a two-handed circle with his cupped palms, so that when he announces, 'And this the cranny is, right and sinister' (v.i.162), he illustrates by first cupping his right hand, then joining his left to it.[6]

As a tinker, Snout is surely the right man to fashion a cranny, because according to a familiar proverb tinkers are better at making holes than at patching them: 'A tinker stops one hole and makes two' (T. Clayton 1974: 107) – although the proverb may also refer lewdly to tinkers who multiply the population by making non-professional housecalls when husbands are at work. In either case, Snout's attempts at representing a hole translate this proverb into theatrical and bodily form – and appropriately so because the entire production of *Pyramus and Thisbe* figures and disfigures verbal constructions.

Wall himself is of course a personification – and yet less a personification, Thomas Clayton wittily observes, than 'one of its species, still further altered, which might be called, in this context, a "bathetic phallusy"' (T. Clayton 1974: 107). The aptness of this term, the unexpected aptness even of the word 'altered' in this context, is indicated by another Clayton (F. W. 1979), who cites the relevance of Topsell's *Historie of Foure-Footed Beastes* (1607) to the line 'Thy stones with lime and hair knit up in thee'. Speaking of how farmers geld rams, Topsell says 'Then do they use to knit them, and ... their stones, deprived of nourishment ... by reason of *knitting*, do *dry* and consume off' (Topsell 1981:442). Of which Clayton observes: 'An Elizabethan farmer proposing to knit would not be designing small garments. He might well say he was going to knit a *tup*' (F. W. Clayton 1979: 7, my italics). A 'tup', that is, was a ram; Shakespeare compresses the phrase 'knit tup', or gelded ram, into the verb 'knit up'. Thus if Wall is a bathetic phallusy, it is in part because his knit stones render his phallus fallacious, a disfigurement that has significant implications a bit further on with regard to the identity of Wall's cranny.

As a rhetorical figure of sorts, Wall, like Moon, figures and dis-figures at once. He decorporealises his body into a sign, as indeed (he makes us realise) all actors do, Laurence Olivier no less than Snout; and he corporealises a sign into his body. This is hard enough for an amateur actor like Snout, but the hardest part remains: to represent the cranny, he must take upon himself the perplexing task of Theseus' poet and somehow body forth 'airy nothing'. As Snout manages it, this is both a logical and a paradoxical business. To figure an absence, he relies, consistently enough, on an absence: the hole defined by his hands. However, since the absence he figures is itself an absence – a hole in a wall – we in the audience find ourselves tracing in imagination something of a vicious circle from symbolic airy nothing to real airy nothing, a vicious circle that in Snout's hands risks the vacuous fate Lear's Fool alludes to when he tells the disenfranchised king, 'now thou art an O without a figure' (I.iv.189).

'Vicious circle' is connotationally apt here because the cranny is in part that 'dark and vicious place' where Edgar says the begetting of bodies takes place (*King Lear* v.iii.175). This place of 'naught/nought' is suggested earlier when Quince compliments Bottom as 'a very paramour for a sweet voice', and Flute (who will later play Thisbe and is hence anxious to defend good women) admonishes him: 'You must say "paragon". A paramour is, God bless us, a thing of naught' (IV.ii.9–11).[7] This feminine nought, the hole in need of the male tinker's 'stopping', the structural 'flaw' that kindles desire, is the centre of biological reproduction. The 'wooden O' of the theatre is another reproductive centre – too small, the Prologue to *Henry V* admits, to hold the 'vasty fields of France' but, like a cipher that contains 'in little place a million', capable of engendering in the audience's imagination not merely France's fields but France herself, and England, and the tumbling seas between. As a nought formed by the hands of Snout, this cipher can frame a hole in a wall that represents the source of representation itself – sexual, symbolic and theatrical.

In attributing the origin of reproduction to the 'O' of lack, Shakespeare finds allies among modern critical theorists. Anthony Wilden, explaining Lacan's notion of the origin of meaning, says 'it is this implied circularity and autonomy of language that leads Lacan into postulating a sort of fault in the system, a hole, a fundamental lack into which, one might say, meaning is poured' (Wilden 1968: 217). And in an illuminating article on 'Shakespeare's Nothing' (1980), David Willbern makes the theatrical connection thus:

> Just as 'O' as exclamation represents a primitive word at the threshold of speech and 'O' as mark designates the origins of writing, so the various symbolisms of 'O' as creative no-thing, or circle, mouth, or womb, underlie primitive conceptions of the theatrical stage itself.[8]

The theatre reproduces bodies not biologically but by symbolic doubling, miraculously making the body of Bottom out of the body of Will Kempe, or indeed a thousand bodies at Agincourt out of one on stage, imagination willing. The emblem of this bodiless embodiment in *A Midsummer Night's Dream* is Puck, who as we have seen is always where he is not and constantly not where he is, a very patron spirit of the histrionic, so great an actor that when he plays a part he becomes a circle without an 'O' and disappears.

Given the significance of this 'O', the speech by Pyramus immediately following Wall's announcement of his identity is instructive. Pyramus opens on an orotund note:

> O grim-looked night! O night with hue so black!
> O night, which ever art when day is not!
> O night, O night!
>
> (v.i.169–71)

Then, with an explicitness that lacks for nothing, Pyramus identifies what is common to the hollow 'O', the black night and the stricken speaker: 'Alack, alack, alack'. The 'O' is bereft of substance, the night of daylight and poor Pyramus of Thisbe. In this dim light, things look bleak for the lovers. However, from another perspective, the reiteration of 'O' equates grammar and sex, provided you had studied with Shakespeare *The Shorte Introduction of Grammar* by William Lily (1549) and learned that 'O' signals the 'vocative case', a term Shakespeare translates from Latin into bawdry, so that 'case' functions the way a scabbard does for a phallic sword and the 'vocative' becomes, in the Welsh of Sir Hugh Evans, the 'focative' (*The Merry Wives of Windsor*, iv.i.45). This makes things look more sexually promising for the lovers. And although in the absence of Thisbe, Pyramus returns to his exclamatory 'Os', they are now made to suggest the vulvate cranny in the wall – 'And thou, O wall, O sweet, O lovely wall' – so that the wall is, Sir Hugh would say, focative, at least visually:

> Thou wall, O wall, O sweet and lovely wall,
> Show me thy chink, to blink through with mine eyne!
>
> (v.i.173–4)

But, alas, when Wall displays his chink, the hand-formed circle between his legs, Pyramus is presented with an 'O' that is not only a metaphor for Thisbe's vulva but also, in virtue of its physical contiguity, a more immediate metonym for Snout's anus as well. This disconcerting sugges-tion – no doubt 'interlaced', as Philip Stubbes said the players were wont to do, 'with bawdry, wanton shewes, & vncomely gestures, as is used (every Man knoweth) in these playes and enterludes' (Chambers 1923: 4, 220) – is confirmed later when Snout makes his exit with the words 'Thus have I, Wall, my part discharged' (203) – the 'part' in question being both his histrionic role and his cleft buttocks (compare 'Nick Bottom' = 'split bum' (Rubinstein 1984: 77, 185)). No wonder, then, that the peering Pyramus cries, 'O wicked wall, through whom I see no bliss!' No bliss for Pyramus – and less than none for Flute/Thisbe, when Snout's posterior partition becomes the wind instrument played by him/her ('I kiss the wall's hole, not your lips at all') in Shakespeare's version of the amorous Absalon's kissing of Alison's 'nether yë' in Chaucer's *Miller's Tale*.[9]

This scatological gamesomeness gives a bawdy turn to Theseus' scoffing speech about the poetic imagination and Plato's *furor poeticus*. For if the notion of inspiration suffers a metamorphic come-down in that speech, as metaphoric visions become imbruted in metonymic bodies, it experiences here an embarrassing pratfall, as Plato's divine afflatus is downwardly transformed into Snout's profane flatulence, as a seething in the brain becomes a bedlam in the bowels. Not only inspiration but language as well takes a tumble, since Wall's efforts corporealise the phrase *flatus vocis* ('words are but air'), so often invoked by medieval nominalists to deny substance to universals and later by puritan iconoclasts to inveigh against rhetorical imagery.[10] In *A Comedy of Errors* Shakespeare makes game of the whole business by taking literally the figure Puttenham calls 'the preposterous' (*hysteron proteron*), obliging Dromio of Ephesus to insult Antipholus thus: 'A man may break a word with you, sir and words are but wind – / Ay, and break it in your face, so he breaks it not behind' (*A Comedy of Errors*, III.i.75–6). Shakespeare is not above breaking a word here himself, by splitting signifier from conventional signified and wedging a bawdy meaning in between.

Splitting signs, like splitting atoms, can prove explosive. Hence 'discharge' – used by Bottom (I.ii..84) and Quince (IV.ii..8) as well as by Snout and Theseus during the performance of *Pyramus and Thisbe* – is loaded with meanings for Shakespeare to detonate. Its Elizabethan meanings include to fire (a weapon); the noise of such a firing; to unload (a cargo) or disburden; to acquit or perform; to emit or eject; that which is emitted; to release, get rid of; to exonerate, exculpate, or free from responsibility. In the sense most obviously called forth by Wall, the workmen's performance of *Pyramus and Thisbe* amounts to a windy explosion in the presence of their social betters, an offensive act (created backstage by some sort of raspberry noise) in keeping with the carnivalesque tendency to displace idealistic values downward to 'the lower stratum of the body, the life of the belly and the reproductive organs; . . . to acts of defecation and copulation, conception, pregnancy, and birth' (Bakhtin 1984: 21). But whereas medieval festive rituals often deliberately degrade the higher orthodoxies, nothing is further from the workmen's minds than subversion or disrespect, and no one is more startled and embarrassed than Snout himself. Thus in a better sense of 'discharge', they are exonerated by their good intentions and so, in a better sense yet, they honourably fulfil their social obligation to the duke. Like the lunatic, the lover and the poet, they have made something of nothing – not a superfluity of devils, a Helen of Troy or an imagined world of words but, as Theseus himself says, a 'palpable-gross play' (v.i.362). His phrase captures the material obstructiveness of their production while suggesting as well its coarser aspects as 'vile wall', 'wicked wall'.

At the same time, Quince's men have made of something, nothing, having reduced the tragic tale of the Babylonian lovers to verbal flatulence, to a cranny that becomes, when Snout parts his hands, mere nothing – as Philostrate warned Theseus the whole play would be: 'It is not for you. I have heard it over, / And it is nothing, nothing in the world' (v.i.77–8). When Hippolyta also demurs – 'He says they can do nothing in this kind' – Theseus replies generously, 'The kinder we, to give them thanks for nothing' (88–9). For if the play comes *to* nothing, it also comes *from* nothing, from the lack that motivates desire – in this case the social and psychological space that divides workmen from duke and generates in them the desire to please. After all, the rites of courtship depicted in *Pyramus and Thisbe* are re-enacted in the duke's court; the performance of the play constitutes a love-token in the workmen's wooing of Theseus. The 'O' of their theatrical performance is the cranny in the wall of social difference through which they would speak their piece to authority. Unfortunately, the piece they speak discharges most indecorously.

PARTINGS

Discharging a part, playing a role, sheer performing, it seems, is a risky endeavour. It brings the body into play, and as Wall testifies, the body is not to be trusted. Wall's representational mishaps would make anthropologists nod knowingly, since they have taken much note of the fact that the apertures of the body are sites of danger. Through them pass substances that are neither exclusively inside nor outside the body – tears, spittle, blood, milk, urine, faeces, and, to be sure, airy nothing above and below (Douglas 1966: 121). These transgressions of the margins of the body occasion anxiety because we should like our bodies to remain well defined and identifiably our own, indeed to assume the classical configuration of the Renaissance body – reassuringly complete, contained and individual (Bakhtin 1984: 29; Stallybras 1986: 124). Disfigurements like Moon and Lion, whose parts are outside their wholes, blur the boundaries of the body and give comic form to fears about identity that appear elsewhere in the play. Wall illustrates the problem even more paradoxically, inasmuch as he

represents a whole that is not whole because it 'contains' a hole. This paradox is disembodied, as Shakespeare was well aware, in the word 'whole', best represented as w(hole).[11] In this symbolic form, hole can be incorporated into whole as unobtrusively as horn and thorn can be into lanthorn. In embodied form, however, it is otherwise. After Wall has discharged his part, ceased representing the hole with his hands, and become plain Snout again, his name – like that of Bottom, Peter (Quince) and Flute – continues to remind us of the orifices that call in question our bodily wholeness. If even our bodies are incomplete and pervious to a world that keeps pouring in and out of them, how can we hope to define the far more elusive structures psychologically inside and socially outside us that contour our sense of who we are?

This anxiety about the integrity of the body and self is pervasive in *A Midsummer Night's Dream*. As we have seen, the origin of the young women's trials appears to lie in the parting and consequent sense of loss they suffered in childhood. So close were they, Helena says, that they 'chid the hasty-footed time / For parting us' (III.ii.200–1), and, more famously: 'So we grew together, / Like to a double cherry, seeming parted, / But yet a union in partition' (208–10). But the double cherry had to become not just 'seeming' but really parted for the girls to graduate from childhood and acquire independent identities (at a cost discussed in Chapter 1). Again, in the opening scene of the play Egeus regards Hermia as a part of his own body, to do with as he wishes, especially if she disregards his wishes at that crucial moment for a daughter, when she parts from her father to join with her husband. The bodily fusions and confusions here are almost as strange as they are for Moon or Wall. Theseus says Hermia lacks her father's 'voice', she replies by wishing 'my father looked but with my eyes', and he says, 'Rather your eyes must with his judgment look' (I.i.55–7). Where one body ends and the other begins is not easy to establish. Still another example in that vein: if Helena had her wish, her and Hermia's bodies would merge even more indistinguishably. Painfully parted, she would like first to share Hermia's parts – her voice, her eyes, her looks – and then to become wholly her, 'to be to you translated' (I.i.191), as if she could recover their childhood indivisibility by rejoining her under the same skin.

Partings are no less prevalent or painful in the wood. Titania cannot bear to part with the changeling because it would mean a definitive parting with her dead votaress – 'And for her sake do I rear up her boy, / And for her sake I will not part with him' (II.i.36–7). The changeling, caught in the cleft between the feuding monarchs, is a part also: for Titania, he is a detached synecdoche recalling the Indian queen and maternity; for Oberon, a fetish representing the alienated love of Titania. As for the humans: if they are women, they are so many divisible pieces of property – for the possessive

Egeus in the opening scene, of course, but later too for an over-generous Lysander anxious to part with Hermia and acquire a stake in Helena:

> And here, with all good will, with all my heart,
> In Hermia's love I yield you up my part;
> And yours of Helena to me bequeath,
> Whom I do love, and will do to my death.
>
> (III.ii.164–7)

Finally, even bodily parts can be parted, a fate suffered by Hermia's eye when at their awakening she says, 'Methinks I see these things with parted eye, / When everything seems double' (IV.i.188–9). The pun on 'parted *I*' sums up the frightening divisions and multiplications of identity experienced by the lovers; and her phrase 'when everything seems double' reminds us that the apparently stable Theseus and Hippolyta (at whom Hermia might well direct a quizzical look as she says this) have but recently metamorphosed into their current identities from their doubled roles as Oberon and Titania.

PRESCRIPTS AND PERFORMANCES

The desire and fear to be other than who we are is institutionalised in acting and theatre, and thus it is appropriate that we be introduced, in the second scene, to the cast of *Pyramus and Thisbe* as they decide who shall play whom. Bottom, who despite his 'nick' is indivisibly himself, would nevertheless like to 'make all split' by playing Ercles, and would make himself split even further by assuming the parts of Lion and Thisbe as well as Pyramus. This histrionic 'parting' of Bottom accurately reflects the split that takes place in acting when the player's identity divides in varying proportions between self and role. But Bottom's desire virtually to fragment himself onstage sums up in small the implications of Quince's 'But, masters, here are your parts'. For this assignment of parts is a kind of theatrical *sparagmos* inherent in the dramatic mode. The seemingly unified imaginative vision is parted in the script into a cast of characters, and then this script is itself dismembered in the theatre, its parts distributed among players who too often, and most villainously, Hamlet complains, depart from what is set down for them (*Hamlet*, III.ii.38–45).[12]

Hamlet's advice to the players reflects an anxiety about the subversiveness of theatrical performance that is illustrated most obviously in the discharging of Wall's part in *Pyramus and Thisbe* but also throughout *A Midsummer Night's Dream*. In the opening scene, Hermia refuses to play

her assigned part in the cultural script written as it were by her father and the law, thus raising questions about just how faithful the Amazonian Hippolyta will be to the part she has undertaken as Athenian duchess. In fairyland, Titania's performance as queen and wife departs so radically from the role Oberon would have her play that he must correctively recast her as Bottom's lover. Similarly, the inversion of roles he witnesses in Helena's pursuit of Demetrius inspires him to revise their script ('Ere he do leave this grove, / Thou shalt fly him and he shall seek they love' (II.i.245–6)), only to have the errant Puck fail to perform his part ('Thou hast mistaken quite' (III.ii.88)). Even Theseus proves a bad actor upon discovering the lovers, quite abandoning his role as enforcer of the law in a script he had declared inviolable ('Egeus, I will overbear your will' (IV.i.178)).

Scripts, prescripts, texts, pretexts and laws possess an impressive unity and coherence. The body, on the other hand, does not lend itself to holistic pretensions gladly, as we have seen. Thus to remain intact, scripts do well to keep a safe idealistic distance from corporeal entanglements: 'for there was never yet philosopher / That could endure the toothache patiently' (*Much Ado About Nothing*, v.i.35–6). In *A Midsummer Night's Dream* love is the toothache in the jaw of patriarchal philosophy, so persistent that Theseus can cure it only by excising part of that philosophy itself. But then his own magisterial script – in which reason plays the hero while lovers, madmen and poets must take the fool's part – is subjected to parodic subversion by the performance of *Pyramus and Thisbe*, in which all of his claims for compartmentalised wholes – for the clean separation of 'As' from 'not-As' – are discharged as sheer illusion. Within its own bounds, the symbolic order can impose restraints and limits and exercise a certain mastery. As mentioned earlier, the word 'elephant' will bring the creature lumbering into the imagination of Lacan's audience, and with a slight modification of spelling, 'lanthorn' can accommodate both 'thorn' and 'horn', as 'whole' can contain 'hole'. But on the stage, in performance, Robin Starveling's body, his dog, the thorn-bush and a cuckold's horns cannot be stuffed into the lantern, however symbolic it may be; nor can Snout's body be entirely whole when it is partly holes.

Similarly, the law of Athens can contain the actions of all Athenians within its abstract prohibitive purview, but only until actual Athenians begin to act. Again, those tales and histories that augured an unsmooth course for the true love of Lysander and Hermia seem as prescriptive as the law (I.i.131–2). Indeed, to Hermia, they 'stand as an edict in destiny' (151); and when she proposes that they acquiesce to this script and their roles in it ('Then let us teach our trial patience'), Lysander readily agrees, 'A good persuasion'. Then with an air of sweet reason signalled as usual by a

'therefore', he adds 'Therefore, hear me, Hermia. / I have a widow aunt' (156–7), and flinging aside love's doleful script, they flee to the woods to play an unwitting part in Oberon's and Puck's madly misperformed comedy.

Scripts and theatre are everywhere; to escape from them is like trying to escape from signifiers into signifieds. Every epilogue, Stoppard's Guildenstern might say, is a prologue somewhere else. Even Shakespeare must write a script in order to burlesque the Senecanised scripts of popular rip-roarers like *Cambises* that served as a recipe for the revenge drama of his time ('This was lofty!' (I.ii.35)). In a slide of cultural signifiers, the harsh Athenian law, nullified by the aberrant performances and non-performances of the lovers, has metamorphosed into a benign marriage ceremony, a revised script to govern the performance of love. Surely this is a vast improvement; and yet we may wonder if the wedding ceremony, which awaits its uncertain performance in marriage, will have a better run in the theatre of daily life than the law had in the woods. Certainly marriage did not play well in fairyland; witness the brawls of Oberon and Titania and the flooding of Graeco-England. No less disconcerting is the fact that Demetrius' eyes, and hence his love for Helena, remain flower-bedewed. The imaginary invades the symbolic, conveying love from the wood back to Athens, where it is ratified by marriage in the temple. But if the charm of Oberon wears off, can the script of marriage take its place and keep Demetrius' gaze from wandering once again?

Perhaps performance by its nature can never be true to its script, any more than a script can ever be true to itself, all of its parts in perfect accord.[13] For, after all, the relation of performance to script is supplementary, which means that performance is paradoxically outside and in addition to, but also inside and part of, the textual 'whole' that precedes it. Yet unlike most supplements, theatrical performance is an outside part that, rather like Moon outside his lunar lantern, is larger than the script it is supposed to be part of. All in all, a curiously liminal entity.

INTERLUDE

Liminality brings us back to *Pyramus and Thisbe*, because if performance as such is liminal, the performance of *Pyramus and Thisbe* is especially so, as Quince implies by calling it 'an interlude' (I.ii.5).[14] His term is doubly appropriate, first because the play is performed during a liminal period between the weddings and the beddings of the nobles (Carroll 1985: 159), after the certifications of the symbolic but before the consummations of the body. This is important because, as we have seen, *Pyramus and Thisbe*

features a peculiarly disjunctive junction between signs and bodies. Second, 'interlude' is appropriate because the play acts as a comic partition that joins and disjoins social classes. The cultural wall that normally divides workmen from aristocrats is here provided with a theatrical chink through which the workmen can speak to the duke, who plays Thisbe to their courting Pyramus – or, for that matter, who plays Hermia to their Lysander, insofar as the rhymes and love tokens with which Lysander wooed Hermia (I.i.28-36) take the form here of the rhymes and 'verses of feigning love' spoken in *Pyramus and Thisbe* for the duke's pleasure and, hopefully, his largess (Krieger 1979: 61):

> If our sport had gone forward, we had all been made men. . . . O sweet bully Bottom! Thus hath he lost sixpence a day during his life; he could not have 'scaped sixpence a day. And the Duke had not given him sixpence a day for playing Pyramus, I'll be hanged. (IV.ii.17–23)

Fortunately Bottom returns in time for the artisans' sport to go forward, very much as the sport of Shakespeare's company is going forward at this moment. For it seems very likely that at the manor-house performance of *A Midsummer Night's Dream* the Lord Chamberlain's Men are in a situation analogous to that of Peter Quince's players: they are putting on a play chosen by their 'master' Henry Carey, Lord Chamberlain, at the wedding of his granddaughter Elizabeth Carey to Thomas Berkeley (see A Note on the Text, p. xvi). If so, then they too can expect to receive a sixpence a day for at least a portion of their lives.[15] Shakespeare again associates his company with that of the workmen by having Puck's Epilogue echo Peter Quince's prologue: Puck asks the audience's indulgence if the players 'have offended' and promises if pardoned that as conscientious artisans they will 'mend' their ill work in order to make 'amends'.

If the interlude serves as a comic go-between that unites the disparate social orders, it also serves as a comic get-between that separates them. To this end, it relies on the tendency of carnival to parody the pretensions and practices of high culture (Bakhtin 1984: 1–58).[16] For medieval and early Renaissance carnival, high culture usually meant religious culture, but here it takes a literary and generic form: a dramatic tragedy that becomes in the acting a parodic comedy. In the process of pulling the rug out from under the noble genre of tragedy, *Pyramus and Thisbe* also pokes fun at the social pretensions of its noble audience. It may even poke fun at English nobles like Sir Philip Sidney, to whom the mixture of genres in a play advertised as 'The most lamentable comedy and most cruel death of Pyramus and Thisby' was anathema (I.ii.11–12).[17] For of course an aesthetic interest in

maintaining the purity of generic hierarchies often reflected a social anxiety about maintaining the purity of class distinctions.

This interpenetration of the aesthetic and the social even takes on a spatial or geographical cast, for the introduction of low comic effects into the high tragedy of *Pyramus and Thisbe* corresponds to the introduction of the workmen into an aristocratic setting. Constraints of class are relaxed by the admission of the workmen into the palace but also reasserted by defining their 'place' there as the circumscribed area of theatrical performance. To stretch the limits of that area requires permission: 'Let him approach', Theseus says of Quince's prologue, addressing Philostrate as mediator between highness and lowness (v.i.107). To 'keep their place', then, the workmen must keep their play in its place, discrete from its audience both physically and artistically: a wall should appear between play and audience; the illusion should not be broken.

Yet this prescript fails, like all others. A spate of illusion-breaking announcements from the players inspires not only interruptive comments from the audience but even extemporaneous dialogue between the two (181–6, 235–57, 345–57). As a result, we witness a general and largely genial transgression of the borders between play and audience and between lower and upper orders. The well-articulated body of society is theatrically dismembered, as the body of Quince's prologue is by his failures of punctuation, as the bodies of Moon and Wall are by their disjunctive efforts at representation. In fact the entire performance of *Pyramus and Thisbe* is a study in entropy, the randomising of energy brought about by the breakdown of (in Rudolph Arnheim's happy phrasing) the 'constraining partitions' that constitute order (Arnheim 1971: 27–8). Because Shakespeare concentrates this process in the performing body, it is appropriate that the performance winds down to a state of maximum entropy in Pyramus' death and especially in Thisbe's confused lament over his body:

> These lily lips,
> This cherry nose,
> These yellow cowslip cheeks,
> Are gone, are gone!
> Lovers, make moan.
> His eyes were green as leeks.
> (327–32)

Here are two kinds of entropy: one turbulent, in which colours slide irresponsibly from part to part over the surface of Pyramus' body (even as words are sliding randomly over the surface of Thisbe's speech under the nervous pressure of performance); the other passive, a chaos of equilibrium

as Pyramus, his odd colours now 'gone . . . gone!', pales in the end to death's one drab hue.[18] This is the sort of entropy that seeps across social boundaries and takes a little colour from the cheeks of noble newly-weds in the manor-house audience, as implied by the inclusiveness of Thisbe's 'Lovers, make moan'. Death is 'common', as Hamlet says; its vulgarity touches everyone with a body, even lovers.

Thus it is appropriate that Bottom should leap to his feet at this point, vaulting the wall between illusion and reality, death and life, to declare that with the death of the lovers 'the wall is down that parted their fathers' (347–8). Appropriate because, as his own transgressive speech illustrates, the wall is also down between the childlike players and the paternalistic nobility. Similarly, although the Chamberlain's Men presumably refrain from talking to their audience while performing *A Midsummer Night's Dream*, the wall between them and their social patrons disappears when they follow Oberon's instructions and pass from the stage out through the manor house blessing 'each several chamber' with field dew (v.i.413). No doubt this quasi-egalitarian moment is as brief in England as it is in Athens. The dew-sprinkling fairies will gather again downstairs (while the servants of the manor check the valuables in each several chamber upstairs!) and not long afterwards will depart, like the workmen, for their own proper 'place' in the city, having created a delightful interlude in the lives of those they played before.[19]

So if some walls come down, they go back up fairly quickly. But that is just as well, since in this context the disappearance of a wall would mean the crannied 'O' had lost its figure, freeing emptiness, like Pope's 'great Anarch' Dulness in *The Dunciad*, to take dominion everywhere. Insofar as the wall symbolises culture's script for constraining desire, what is wanted is neither a whole wall nor a whole hole, neither a repressive all-governing law of the sort the play began with nor the kind of unchecked licence we witnessed in the wood. The solution would seem to lie somewhere liminally in between; perhaps, to bring Puck's door back into it, we need a wall with a door in it. And yet, if I follow Shakespeare's metaphoric argument at all correctly, not even this sort of wall will be proof against the anarchic inroads of performance, which will make its own crannies where it will, no matter how many doors and windows the wall's building plan has provided.

Less metaphorically: as if reacting against an over-simplified conception of order represented by Theseus, the workmen's entropic performance risks dissolving all boundaries, social as well as artistic. It does so not simply because Quince's players are bad actors but because all actors are bad actors, because performance is unavoidably transgressive. In order to re-present, it must present, and presentation in the theatre, not to mention in the *theatrum mundi*, inevitably incarnates itself in the stuff of human bodies.

Pyramus and Thisbe can come before the duke only by means of the performing workmen; language, Saussure's *langue*, can enter the world only in the form of *parole*, by means of speakers and writers; and metaphoric visions can make their way to the printed page only in the embodied shapes of metonymy. This would cause little complaint if it were not for the fact that bodies are inherently flawed and disgracefully untrustworthy, as the discharging of Wall's part makes clear. Therefore, as long as we humans occupy this local habitation of skin and bone, our re-presentations will always also be presentations, that is to say performances, and therefore misrepresentations and misperformances. All actors are bad actors, and, alas, we are all actors. Plays, language, Theseus' reason, Plato's ideas, Athenian law: all of culture's scripts will inevitably come to corruption from that one particular fault of which Hamlet speaks, the cranny in every wall.[20]

DOUBLINGS AND DISFIGURINGS

In its transgressive and entropic aspects, then, *Pyramus and Thisbe* is a bawdy hole in the wall of social and theatrical constraint, a hole that enables a return of the repressed in the guise of carnival. That is, if Wall represents, among other things, the bar of repression between the conscious and unconscious, then this bar is crossed, as Freud maintained, by means of jokes, slips of the tongue, dreams, omissions, puns, figures, which is precisely what occurs when Snout, Pyramus and Flute struggle to represent and to make contact through the cranny. Wall manages to prevent the lovers' lips from touching through the cranny, but even in doing so it unwittingly allows the Rabelaisian unconscious to enter and have its say.

This does not mean, however, that Wall is down. Wall is not remiss in his duty; he keeps his place. Even if the unconscious has found a cranny through which it can speak, still it cannot speak openly but only through a veil of figuration. It crosses the bar of repression in disguise, which means the audience can acknowledge its presence, remain oblivious of its presence, or pretend to remain oblivious of its presence. What do they do? On the basis of the text alone, we would assume that they disregard or simply fail to recognise the bawdry, since none of them replies in kind. Of course they could acknowledge it non-verbally, by glance or gesture; but if this were intended, it seems likely the text would supply a verbal clue of some sort. As it is, the *double entendres* function as a kind of authorial aside addressed by Shakespeare to his own audience, quite bypassing, for all we can tell, both Quince's players and their Athenian audience. But what of the Elizabethan audience, who are in the same position as their Athenian

counterparts? Do they recognise the bawdry, recognise it but ignore it, or fail to recognise it at all? Surely it must register with someone besides vile-minded critics![21]

These questions come to practical focus on a remark by Theseus at the end of the performance. He says that if 'he that writ it had play'd Pyramus and hang'd himself, it would have been a fine tragedy', but then adds generously, 'and so it is, truly, and very notably discharg'd' (v.i.352–5). If this 'very notably discharg'd' is accompanied by a wry smile and a glance at Snout, then the discharge of the unconscious has been heard and given at least part of its due.[22] If, on the other hand, Theseus speaks in all innocence, then the unconscious (not to mention Shakespeare) is as assiduous as lovers in finding holes in the walls of repression; it will have its joke, whether officially acknowledged or not, even if it has to speak through the unwitting lips of a hyper-rational duke.

Either openly or by accident, then, the repressed has returned; and whether it can ever be entirely banished again is hard to say. In its socialised form, as carnival, the repressed is usually conceived of as the excess steam released through the safety valve of condoned festivity. It is not totally expunged by this means, but at least its subversive temperature is reduced and the establishment kettle is kept intact (safe from Snout's tinkering!).[23] If that is how the workmen's play functions, as a release of carnival within the palace, what dangerous impulses does it cathartise? Steamy lower-class resentment on the part of the workmen would seem the logical answer. And yet the only evidence of such resentment is in the unhappy inversion of meaning in Quince's prologue, which, however, seems less the voice of an angry unconscious expressing a desire to offend than the voice of the playwright desiring to amuse.

On the other hand, what has been accentuated throughout the play, in what I have called 'Theseus' Dream' but also in the lovers' woodland experience, is the marital anxieties of the nobles.[24] A major anxiety at this late point, as the newly-weds pass the time before consummating their marriages, is the spectre of sterility and impotence. Somewhat surprisingly, that spectre also ghosts about in *Pyramus and Thisbe*, because for all its stress on the transgressiveness of the body in performance, the workmen's play also emphasises the inability of the body to perform, either sexually or histrionically. The two 'acts' fuse in failure: Pyramus and Thisbe cannot consummate their love in Babylon, nor can they consummate it in the theatre. Although Pyramus 'draws' near the wall and issues a plethora of 'Os' that should invoke the 'vocative case', he finds the wall as impenetrable from his side as Thisbe, straining to kiss him, does from hers. And just as well, too, since Snout's announcement that he has discharged his part suggests a metonymic displacement of sexuality from phallus to anus, with

a consequent substitution of flatus for seminal seed. This and the fact that Wall's 'stones' are impotently 'knit up' does not augur well for lovers' couplings, quite apart from mousing lions.

But of course this is all fiction, and not very persuasive fiction at that. At best, perhaps, it is a form of apotropaic art, designed to drive away the danger it features – the danger of true love brought to grief through 'filial disobedience' and 'arbitrary parental rigidity' (Bristol 1985: 178). But that danger has been done away with already by the duke's dismissal of Egeus and the law. Now, as Quince's play ends, phasing back into Shakespeare's, pre-marital 'tragedy' yields to marital comedy and a happy ending defined in terms of wedding night couplings and the prospect of procreation. Thus, having thanked the players, Theseus observes that midnight has tolled, which means that the dial's pointer has risen to twelve, a moment rudely glossed by Mercutio's observation in *Romeo and Juliet* that 'the bawdy hand of the dial is now upon the prick of noon' (ii.iv.110–11). Time itself thus stands in phallic readiness for Theseus' next words: 'Lovers, to bed' (359). Now all walls will be down: those that parted Amazonian queen from Athenian king and those that parted lover from lover in the wood. In their place will be unions, mergers, couplings and doublings.

Which of course cannot be staged.

So the wall is up again – the invisible wall of fiction that blocks the audience's voyeuristic view of imaginary beddings backstage. With the departure of the newly-weds, the play recalls Puck to deliver a talismanic speech ridding the palace of baneful influences; and, as a substitute for human consummations elsewhere, the audience is offered the sight of elves and fairies coupling in dance and the sound of fairy voices harmonising in song. Finally, Oberon blesses the house and especially the bodies presumably about to be begotten within it:

> the blots of Nature's hand
> Shall not in their issue stand;
> Never mole, hare lip, nor scar,
> Nor mark prodigious, such as are
> Despised in nativity,
> Shall upon their children be.

Like Puck's earlier speech, Oberon's blessing subjects real evils to the nullifications of the symbolic, erasing disfiguring bodily 'marks' with verbal signs. Yet the erasure is not as easily accomplished as it seems, since like all negations it must foreground what it negates and therefore to some extent defeat its own intent. Moles, hare-lips, scars and marks prodigious, once imagined, are only slightly easier to unimagine than fairies are to un-see

when they are standing right before you. The curse of every blessing is that it invokes the evils it seeks to ward off. This is true of Oberon's blessing insofar as it seeks to purge *A Midsummer Night's Dream* of its disfigurements – the blots made not by 'Nature's hand' but by the 'hard-handed men' who performed *Pyramus and Thisbe*. For by mentioning disfigured bodies, Oberon inevitably reminds us that all bodies are disfigured: parted, fissured, crannied, cracked, un-whole. And this applies also to the disfigured body of *Pyramus and Thisbe*, fragmented into 'parts' that, as played by the workmen, can never achieve wholeness.

If dramatic wholeness and closure are figured as sexual union, as they are at the end of most comedies, then Oberon's blessing of such unions is additionally compromised by his unfortunate mention of disfigured bodies, which reminds us of the disfigurement suffered by the fundamental bodily figure in *Pyramus and Thisbe*, Snout's encircled hands, when the anamorphous split–crack–fissure–cleft–part–hole, initially a metaphor for Thisbe's vulva, becomes, on second glance, a metonym for Snout's anus. This anamorphic refocusing constitutes a Brechtian *Verfremmdungseffekt* as the relocated 'part' combines punningly with its histrionic meaning of 'role' to foreclose on heterosexual action and enactment. The transvestite nature of the workmen's theatre thwarts the desires of *Pyramus and Thisbe* far more irrevocably than parental walls and mousing lions. And what is true of *Pyramus and Thisbe*, we are forced to recognise, is equally true of the newly-weds in Athens, a fact that should give the audience a disconcerting pause as they watch the married couples sweep offstage to sexual consummations that are perfectly imaginable in the script, where men are men and women women, but that prompt an anamorphic double-take in the theatre, where men are men and women are too. Here again the perils of performance and the subversiveness of the body embarrass the action and short-circuit the audience's impulse towards an automatic endorsement of the happy ending.

At the same time, we are asked to imagine beyond the imperfections and disfigurements of bodies on stage and celebrate their one great biological and cultural virtue; they can couple, double and reproduce. In the Old Testament this endless doubling, beginning with Cain and Abel and recorded in great lists of offspring, provides corporeal confirmation of the oft-repeated divine word, 'Be fruitful and multiply' (Scarry 1985: 191–205). In Shakespeare's comedies it provides figurative confirmation of the theatrical power to reproduce by representation. In the most obvious case, Theseus/Oberon and Hippolyta/Titania are the product of doubling actors. Yet even actors of undoubled parts engage in a form of doubling: 'The best in this kind are but shadows; and the worst are no worse, if imagination amend them' (v.i.210–12; Marshall 1982: 563). Hippolyta

replies, 'It must be your imagination then, and not theirs'. That is true enough for *Pyramus and Thisbe*. However, if *A Midsummer Night's Dream* is to prove not merely better than *Pyramus and Thisbe*, but the very best in this kind – if its shadows are to be given body, and its bodies are to cast shadows – then it must be accomplished by the audience's imagination, and the players' and the playwright's too – a veritable orgy of coupling imaginations, all growing to something of great constancy, a play. In this manner, the theatre will transcend its own transvestite limitations and the inability of the players to perform. Unlike Robin Starveling, who cannot get his body into his lunar lantern, Theseus and Hippolyta and all the lovers can get into bed and beget bevies of undisfigured bodies. This, God bless us, would be a thing of naught, were we of the workmen's cast of mind; but fortunately it will all take place between the chaste sheets of our imagination.

Surely this imaginative transcendence of sexual verisimilitude is precisely what is called for. After all, the apparent alternative is to join with the workmen in their naïve desire for a theatre of pure presence, as indistinguishable as possible from life itself. That of course is not what the workmen give us in their hilarious performance of *Pyramus and Thisbe*. Their efforts to launch our imagination beyond the stage by means of props and costumes and prologues serve merely to overload the imagination and cause it to plummet back down to the stage again. We are obliged to take material account of the presence of walls and bodies and hence of the limitations of theatre – and not entirely in order to overcome those limitations. Wall's 'knit up' stones and his botched effort to represent the vulvate cranny imply that even in the best of cases representation is impotent. Hegel's *Aufhebung* and Freud's sublimation are symbolic liftings up, not phallic erections. On the stage, in the form of Bottom and Flute, they will never enable Pyramus and Thisbe to do the deed of darkness, at least not as the play intended. But then, for that matter, Pyramus and Thisbe – the lost 'real', whoever they were, if ever they were – are impotent also. They will never do the deed of darkness either, their flesh having turned to grass, or into mulberry leaves, long ago. This means that we are left in betwixt and between, on a threshold, in an interlude, half-in and half-out of the play, made to realise that we are always to some extent squinting through crannies, angling for a glimpse of something on the far side that has no existence apart from the wall of representation itself. We cannot penetrate that wall and wholly enter the world of Pyramus and Thisbe. If we could, if the wall of representation were a window and perfectly transparent, then *Pyramus and Thisbe* would be a tragedy, and we lovers could make genuine moan. Then Hippolyta's 'Beshrew my heart, but I pity the man' would represent our emotional involvement in the seeming reality of Pyramus' grief (v.i.286). But the emotional rewards of

this 'tragic' involvement would come at the expense of comic detachment. We would lose an opportunity to say, with the amused Theseus, 'This passion, and the death of a dear friend, would go near to make a man look sad' (284–5), an opportunity made available to us because Pyramus, like Wall, makes the window of representation so grotesquely opaque to all but the super-sympathetic Hippolyta.

Theseus' remark underscores the fact that the symbolic may be impotent really, but it is potent symbolically. It offers us substitute gratifications that can cease to be substitutes and become rewarding in themselves, as the workmen's play is, as Shakespeare's play is too. When a tragedy meant to please the duke by making him weep turns into a farce that pleases him by making him laugh, mediation is no longer mediate, a means to an end, but has become an end in itself. And the same is true when a performance meant only to open the duke's purse ends with the players basking in the glow of theatrical success. For of course the only illusion created by *Pyramus and Thisbe* is the players' belief that they have, as the duke says, 'very notably discharg'd' their fine tragedy.[25] But that is the only illusion necessary. If nothing else, *Pyramus and Thisbe* has instructed us in the pleasures of anti-illusionary theatre, of a theatre that not only figures but also disfigures, that provides us with translations but arrests them in process, that opens a cranny for our imaginative vision but intrudes a wall that stops sight – and makes us delight in seeing nothing but what is immediately before us.

The question now is, how does all this bear on the audience's response to *A Midsummer Night's Dream*? That is what Puck asks in his Epilogue. Will the Elizabethan audience, like the duke in Athens, play an applauding role and leave the players with an illusion of success, or have the players foisted illusions on the audience? Who is pouring flower juice in whose eyes?

· 7 ·

Making Amends: Puck's Epilogue

At the end of *Pyramus and Thisbe*, when Bottom leaps to life again and offers
Theseus an Epilogue or a Bergomask, the duke wisely chooses the
Bergomask. Thus as we lost the ballad of 'Bottom's Dream' but gained
Pyramus and Thisbe, so we now lose an epilogue to *Pyramus and Thisbe* and
gain one to *A Midsummer Night's Dream*. Puck delivers it in conciliatory
tones:

> If we shadows have offended,
> Think but this, and all is mended,
> That you have but slumbered here,
> While these visions did appear.
> And this weak and idle theme,
> No more yielding but a dream,
> Gentles, do not reprehend.
> If you pardon, we will mend.
> And, as I am an honest Puck,
> If we have unearned luck
> Now to scape the serpent's tongue,
> We will make amends ere long;
> Else the Puck a liar call.
> So, good night unto you all.
> Give me your hands, if we be friends,
> And Robin shall restore amends.   [*Exit.*]

At first glance Puck seems as anxious about giving offence as Peter Quince was in his prologue. He is sensitive to the 'gaze'. And so he should be, at the end of a play that seems composed like a set of Chinese optical boxes, so that its plot can be defined by charting the path of various glances: first, the narcissistic gazings of the hermaphroditic Hermia–Helena whose mirror is shattered when the appearance of the young men diverts glances and brings about a Hermia–Lysander and Helena–Demetrius pairing off, subsequently destroyed when Demetrius looks from Helena to Hermia. The presentation itself begins with Hermia and Lysander exposed to the oppressive super-vision of Egeus, Theseus and the law, from which they flee to the wood, only to come under the supervision of Oberon. The fairy king's well-intended refocusing of gazes is temporarily thwarted by Puck's mis-mediations, which cause love-looks to glance from their proper object and ricochet hatefully through the forest, until at last all eyes are closed in sleep. When they open, they find themselves under the beneficent gaze of a Theseus whose own eyes have been opened, and his anxieties allayed, by a dream in which he was Oberon and Hippolyta was Titania and . . . but of course that is all fairy toys and antic fables. Still, whatever his reason, Theseus blinkers the forbidding gaze of the law, and everyone goes off to exchange rings and loving gazes, and then to look bemusedly on the strange staging of *Pyramus and Thisbe*. And so, as Pepys would say, to bed.

But before we theatregoers can retire, Puck comes forth to ask what we, who have o'erseen all, have actually seen. Like Bottom gearing up to play Pyramus, Puck says in effect, 'Let the audience look to their eyes' (i.ii.22), and if we cannot do that for ourselves, he will do it for us. In fact, he will look to our eyes in a couple of senses. First, he will look *into* our eyes. As a representative of the play, he is anxious, as players always are, to be the desire of the other, to be as his audience would have him; so he looks into our mirroring eyes to discover what that might be. What he hopes to see there is not of course a dismissive Sartrian look of the sort implied by Theseus' line 'the best in this kind are but shadows' (v.i.210) but something more auspiciously Lacanian, perhaps the lost loving gaze of the mother that most actors would like to recapture.

But as we saw in Chapter 3, the gaze in which players can be caught and their play defined is itself vulnerable to entrapment, most noticeably when it encounters anamorphic diversions. Thus the audience to whose judgement Puck so humbly defers should beware being taken in, for in looking to our eyes the sly one looks not only inquiringly *into* them but also thera-peutically *to* them, tending to our gaze as he tended to that of Lysander and Demetrius. Some of the flower juice he drops in our eyes is contained in his invitation to 'think but this', that all 'these visions' have come dreamingly from within ourselves and hence cannot be attributed, if we do not like them, to a bad play or a clumsy performance. He seems to have taken his cue from the Prologue to Lyly's *Sapho and Phao* (1584), who, with Elizabeth in attendance, makes amends beforehand: 'We all, and I on knee for all, entreat that your Highness imagine yourself to be in a deep dream, that staying the conclusion, in your rising, your Majesty vouchsafe but to say *And so you waked.*' This is but minimally apologetic, for to be in a 'deep dream' is not necessarily a bad thing, nor is a play that puts one there. Puck speaks more disparagingly of a theme 'weak and idle' and un-'yielding' as a dream, as if he were of Mercutio's mind, who debunked dreams as 'begot of nothing but vain fantasy' (*Romeo and Juliet*, I.iv.98). This view of things may exonerate the players, but at the expense of making their performance dissolve into airy nothing. That, according to William Hazlitt, leaving a rather operatic performance of the play at Covent Garden in 1816, is precisely what it ought to do. For, as he complained in an influential report in *The Examiner*, plays like *A Midsummer Night's Dream* are flagrantly inhospitable to the romantic imagination:

> Poetry and the stage do not agree together. The attempt to reconcile them fails not only of effect, but of decorum. The *ideal* can have no place upon the stage, which is a picture without perspective; everything there is in the foreground. That which is merely an airy shape, a dream, a passing thought, immediately becomes an unmanageable reality. Where all is left to the imagination, every circumstance has an equal chance of being kept in mind, and tells according to the mixed impression of all that has been suggested. But the imagination cannot sufficiently qualify the impression of the senses. Any offence given to the eye is not to be got rid of by explanation. Thus Bottom's head in the play [as imagined while reading] is a fantastic illusion, produced by magic spells: on the stage it is an ass's head, and nothing more; certainly a very strange costume for a gentleman to appear in. Fancy cannot be represented any more than a simile can be painted; and it is as idle to attempt it as to personate Wall or Moonshine. Fairies are not incredible, but fairies six feet high are so. (*The Examiner*, January 1816)

Even more loudly than *Henry V*, then, *A Midsummer Night's Dream* seems to call for a choral prologue which would apologise for 'the flat unraised spirits that hath dared / On this unworthy scaffold to bring forth / So great an object' – or, rather, so small an object – as fairies. Shakespeare does indeed apologise in Puck's Epilogue, asking us to forgive all offences and to imagine that what Hazlitt would prefer to happen has happened: actors, stage, the theatre itself have all vanished, and we who thought we were an audience have awakened to find ourselves, strangely enough, in a theatre, rubbing our eyes and wondering like Keats, 'Was it a vision, or a waking dream?'

Since waking and wondering are precisely what six of the characters in *A Midsummer Night's Dream* spend much of their time doing, we may wonder just whom we should take for a model. Should we wake like Lysander and Demetrius, eyes beflowered and affections gone mad, or like all the lovers later, affections set right but memories confused, or, worst of all, like Bottom, mind and senses bafflingly unhinged? No doubt some of the audience will be as anxious as Demetrius to put fairies and fantasy behind them – 'These things seem small and undistinguishable, / Like far-off mountains turned into clouds' (IV.i.186–7).[1] But surely there will be others, less certain, who will murmur with Hermia 'Methinks I see [this play] with parted eye, / When everything seems double' (188–9), and still others who, like Bottom and Samuel Pepys, will have seen everything and experienced nothing. Who does Puck have in mind for us?

To help answer that question, let me return to the affairs in the wood from which the lovers and Bottom awoke, since these woodland experiences, though looked back on as a dream, took place as if they were a play, very much as if Shakespeare were suggesting to the Hazlitts in his audience that the two are, as Demetrius says, indistinguishable.

FESTIVAL FAIRIES AND MECHANICAL PLAYERS

Act 4, Scene 1 seems to establish the wedding date as 1 May. On the eve or early morning of that festive day, in rites whose origins were lost even by Shakespeare's youth, young men and women went into the forest to gather boughs and branches – of hawthorn, for instance, also called 'may' – to decorate their homes. But as the Puritan Phillip Stubbes vigorously yet also rather attractively complains, more went on in the woods than bough-gathering. Not only do 'all the yung men and maides, old men and wives run gadding over night to the woods, groves, hils, & mountains, where they spend all the night in plesant pastimes', but he has heard it credibly reported, '(and that, *viva voce*), by men of great gravitie and reputation, that of forty, threescore, or a hundred maides going to the wood overnight, there have scarcely the third part of them returned home againe undefiled. These be the frutes which these cursed pastimes bring forth.' And no very large wonder either, because 'there is a great Lord present amongst them, as superintendent and Lord over their pastimes and sportes, namely, Sathan prince of hel' (Stubbes, 'Lords of Misrule', 1972: 4).[2]

On the other hand in the section on May in *The Shepherd's Calendar*

Spenser describes the custom of 'fetchen home May' as presided over not
by Satan but by May himself, who was

> in a royal throne,
> Crowned as king: and his Queene attone
> Was Lady Flora, on whom did attend
> A fayre flocke of Faeries, and a fresh bend
> Of lovely Nymphs

If fairies were a feature of May festivals, as they are here – that is, if the
country folk dressed up and played the role of fairies – then Shakespeare's
audience must have been momentarily confused when Puck and a Fairy
first appear on stage in Act 2. Both identify themselves precisely – the one
as servant to the fairy queen, the other as 'that merry wanderer of the night'
who delights in domestic mischief – but it is not clear if they are real fairies
or festival fairies played by Athenian citizens. For all we know, we may be
in the position of Queen Elizabeth during her progress of 1578 when the
villagers at Norwich 'had seven boys dance before her (as neare as could
be ymagined) like the Phayries' (Brooks 1979: fn. lxxxiv) or during her
progress of 1591 when at Elvetham the entertainment featured a dance of
fairies led by Queen Aureola, who announced herself as the wife of
Auberon, the fairy king (Griffin 1951: 141; Montrose 1983: 50).[3] If so,
then the appearance of Puck and the Fairy will seem like a staged prologue
to the quarrelling exchange between Oberon and Titania, a prologue
telling the audience that Oberon and Titania are *not* fairies but Athenians
playing those roles. Obviously this is not the case. But for a while it appears
possible; and the reason seems to be Shakespeare's desire to create a
metadramatic blur at the border between theatre and reality (or unreality in
this case). The illusion of Athenian play-fairies fades, leaving us with real
fairies who, on second glance, are the Chamberlain's Men's play-fairies.
Add to this the workmen's preparations for rehearsing *Pyramus and Thisbe*
and a double patina of theatricality overlies the appearance of Demetrius
and Helena, and later of Lysander and Hermia. The audience is given a
theatrical perspective from which to view the transformations of identity
that occur when Puck blunders with the flower juice, that is, when as stage-
manager trying to dramatise Oberon's script he miscasts Lysander as
Demetrius.

The second scene, with Bottom and the players, reveals what we might
not have noticed in the first scene, that Athens is itself a theatre in which
Theseus serves as stage manager for a play governed by the law. However,
as in the 'plays' with which *Richard II* and *King Lear* begin, the actors do not
keep to their parts. Like Bolingbroke and Cordelia, Hermia and Lysander

refuse to speak the speeches set down for them, as it were; and so the plot is suspended for four days, and theatricality shifts to the wood, where fairies like Puck play to perfection any part they choose.

To 'act' presupposes 'to be seen', and to adopt a role and enter a play means to triangularise desire on a larger scale. The third party to desire in the theatre, analogous to the law in Athens, is the audience. Without an audience, a play is not a play but a form of theatrical narcissism. Hermia and Lysander refuse to adopt the proper roles required of them by Athenian law, but they do not disavow the law; they simply try to evade it, to hide from its judgmental gaze. The gaze they cannot hide from is that of the audience. They are like Peter Quince's company, who intend to rehearse their play in the wood to escape the gaze of Athens:

> and meet me in the palace wood [Quince says], a mile without the town, by moonlight. There will we rehearse; for if we meet in the city, we shall be dogged with company, and our devices known. (i.ii.92–5)

But the Peter Quince players are dogged with company even in the wood: 'What a play toward?' Puck exclaims, 'I'll be an auditor; / An actor too perhaps, if I see cause' (iii.i.74–5). The lovers are similarly dogged by Oberon: 'But who comes here?' the fairy king asks, 'I am invisible. / And I will overhear their conference' (ii.i.186–7). Oberon quickly decides not merely to overhear as audience but to reshape the plot – he is, after all, 'king of shadows' (iii.ii.347); and so his woodland script replaces the Athenian law and wends its rather episodic way to an ending that both he and his counterpart Theseus can happily applaud.

Whereas the lovers do not know they have been in a play, Bottom does not know he has ever left one. At the woodland rehearsal he frightens his companions by appearing with the ass's head on, declaiming, still deep in Pyramus, ' "If I were fair, Thisby, I were only thine" ', unaware that he has already become a part of Puck's impish production. Later, when he awakens, his first words are 'When my cue comes, call me, and I will answer. My next cue is "Most fair Pyramus" ' (iii.i.98; iv.i.398–9). But his next cue actually comes from his colleagues – 'Let us hear, sweet Bottom' – and he finds he has no speech that will account for a dream that seems indistinguishable from a play: 'Not a word of me' (iv.ii.31–2).

SHADOWS CASTING SHADOWS

In various ways, then, Shakespeare identifies the woodland experience of the lovers with drama, casting it as a comic interlude, though hardly as comic as the one Quince prepares for the duke. This provides the basis for

Puck, in the Epilogue, to invite the audience to share the awakened lovers' confusion about the identity of their theatrical experience. The lovers had little choice in defining what happened to them, either as it happened, owing to Puck's flowerings, or afterwards, owing to Oberon's charm: 'When they next wake, all this derision / Shall seem a dream and fruitless vision' (iii.ii.370–1). Puck is better off; he can fashion images and focus gazes. But even he lacks Oberon's magic with awakened minds and can only suggest, not command, that we call the play 'a dream and fruitless vision'. This suggestion is not as dismissive as it seems, for if we accept it we must then account for the fact that the lovers' experience was by no means fruitless. That is, the illusions fostered by Puck in the forest may have created fictional enmities and dissolved them into general concord, but they have also dissolved real enmities as well. And through the agency of Theseus' royal command, they even dissolve the hard stuff of patriarchal law and overbear the will of Egeus, thus enabling the marriage of true minds in the wood to be ratified in the temple. In this light, Puck's invitation loses its modesty and takes on an ironic cast: 'Play at being rational, if you like, and regard the play as Theseus and the lovers would, as no more significant than a dream. But as with the lovers, all your minds transfigured so together more witnesseth than fancy's images, and grows to something of great constancy, howsoever strange and admirable.'

But what is this something of great constancy? What profit in this dream? Perhaps we get a clue in Puck's opening line, 'If we shadows have offended', which creates in the word 'shadows' something of an anamorphic blur that calls for a cocked head and an oblique glance. Seen straight on, 'shadows' refers to fairies – Puck has himself called Oberon 'king of shadows' (iii.ii.347) – and Puck is suggesting that the little people may have been the origin of mischief in the play, as rural folk say they are in life itself. And to be sure, the fairies *are* the major source of trouble in the play. Why? Because they are the source of desire: because Puck is an Elizabethan substitute for Eros, firing flowers instead of darts, and because Oberon and Titania are erotic will-o'-the-wisps flitting before and flirting after Hippolyta and Theseus. Precisely because they are not there – for their magical presence is sadly lacking – the fairies constitute a kind of primal incompleteness or absence that stirs our desire and sets our imagination in search of them, that is, in search of more romantic visions than the drab world offers. Fools that we mortals are, we can never make do with joint-stools and crab-apples; we must have Puck. Nor can we accept inexplicable natural disasters when marital quarrels in fairyland can explain them, or be content with a brow of Egypt when the cosmetic fancy can paint Helen's beauty over it. And by no means can we put up with a dull midsummer afternoon, real as rain, when *A Midsummer Night's Dream* is playing at The Theatre and bully Bottom is cocking his ear for the tongs and the bones.

Part of the profit of this dream, then, is the knowledge that the fairies flit before all of us, gilding nature with the tricks and fantasies of strong imagination, the way Titania flitted before Theseus in the form of, but always just a little beyond, Perigenia and Aegles, Ariadne and Antiopa. In this sense, these shadows have indeed offended; they always do. Their offence is to reveal to us the nomadic nature of desire as it makes its way in our minds from oasis to oasis in pursuit of the grand mirage of paradise.

Some further profit from this dream lies in a theatrical direction, for on second glance, an anamorphic glance, Puck's word 'shadows' reveals that it was also a term for 'players': 'The best of this kind are but shadows'. Players and fairies are both shadows, are indeed shadows of one another, the players being fairies, the fairies players, in which case they have doubly offended. If the fairies offend because they are the illusory lack that generates desire, the players offend for the same reason. They lack the presence of what they can only re-present, and hence they generate a desire in us for that presence, seducing us Titania-fashion to abandon this boy actor in favour of the Hermia he portrays and to forsake this crude wooden 'O' for the palace of Theseus and an enchanted wood. The desiring gaze of the audience, then, is not much different from the desiring gaze of the lover. For as Puck himself has so vividly demonstrated with his flower juices, lovers like Lysander, inspired by a more than willing suspension of disbelief, do not really *see* their beloved but only an idealised image of her. She, whoever she is – 'Am not I Hermia? Are not you Lysander?' (iii.ii.273) – is no more present in fact than is the character Hermia in the boy who plays her. But we in the audience, eyes beflowered by female costumes and mincing manners, will pursue Hermia or Helena with all the doting desire of a Demetrius or Lysander. That is how our eyes work, or, rather, our gaze, which consists of all the additions desire makes to eyesight in the process of creating vision(s).

The fairy shadows may have offended by seducing the gaze of the audience, but the offence of the player shadows consists not so much in seducing our gaze as in deflecting it, in thwarting our desire for perfect access to a world of imagined presence. This thwarting achieves a kind of perfection in *Pyramus and Thisbe* as it thrusts its physical and representational crudities wall-like between us and any illusions we might have of fictional reality, casting its all too substantial shadow over fairies and Athenians alike and debunking the Romantic critique of the stage as a product of chimerical idealising desire. For Lamb and Hazlitt are seduced by a disembodied non-presence, by the not-thereness of poetic fairies. They are quite right to complain that 'the ideal can have no place upon the stage', because the ideal is incorporeal and the stage, as *Pyramus and Thisbe* makes bawdily clear, is nothing without bodies. Nor will Hazlitt's ideal find comfortable habitation on the global stage of human affairs either, where it can only provoke dissatisfied longings for what is not and a refusal of all that imperfectly is. If the stage cannot reproduce Hazlitt's imaginings perfectly, he will no more put up with it than Theseus will with antic fables and fairy toys. And yet Hazlitt might take caution from Theseus, for in the half-light of *A Midsummer Night's Dream* even he grows shadowy. It would be insulting to call the sceptical duke a 'fairy toy' (even though, as Oberon, that is precisely what he is), but as an antic player bodying forth an antique fiction he can hardly escape being labelled an 'antic fable' and hence forfeiting any claim he might make to being more real than the supersonic globe-girdling Puck.

Shakespeare's play fails on stage for Hazlitt much as Peter Quince's production of *Pyramus and Thisbe* does for the aristocrats, but at least Theseus and Hippolyta have the good grace to admit how needful all plays are of the audience's imagination. Otherwise, as Hamlet would ask, who among actors and playwrights should escape whipping? That is Puck's theme, the offence of playing – the lack, flaw or fault that mars the best of plays and must be mended by an imaginative audience and by the forgiveness that acknowledges a common plight. In this respect the play and its audience serve rather as the deep-gazing eyes of lovers do, each a mirror to the other. Thus the play will discover what it is – a splendid vision or an awful sight – in the audience's response; and the audience will discover what it is as the play reflects back an image of itself caught in the complicitous act of seeing–desiring–dreaming. Two quotes seem relevant here, one by Lucian:

> When every spectator becomes one with what happens on the stage, when everyone recognises in the performance, as in a mirror, the reflection of his own true impulses, then, but not until then, success has been achieved. Such a dumb spectacle is at the same time nothing less than the fulfilment of the Delphic maxim 'Know thyself', and those who return from the theatre have experienced what was truly an experience. (Hammelman 1957: 35)

And one by Antonin Artaud:

> The theatre will never find itself again – i.e., constitute a true means of true illusion – except by furnishing the spectator with the truthful precipitates of dreams, in which his taste for crime, his erotic obsessions, his savagery, his chimeras, his utopian sense of life and matter,

even his cannibalism, pour out, on a level not counterfeit and illusory, but interior. (Artaud 1958: 92)

Both seem descriptive of Shakespeare's achievement in *A Midsummer Night's Dream*, which enables its audience, as Oberon's play enabled the lovers, to experience and at some level of consciousness to come to terms with desire in both its destructive and irrational as well as its creative and imaginative modes. The wall of repression has temporarily come down, permitting the fairies not merely to enter the palace but, even as Puck speaks, to wend their way through the manor-house or out among the audience in The Theatre, bestowing the blessings of fantasy everywhere in accordance with Oberon's instructions: 'Now until the break of day, / Through this house each fairy stray' (v.i.397–8). This uniting of fairyland with theatre and of theatre with off-stage reality seems a distant forecast of Prospero's great speech 'Our revels now are ended', in which the melting away of spirits presages the deliquescence of the Globe theatre and ultimately of that vaster theatre of illusions, the great globe itself (*The Tempest*, IV.i.148 ff.).

Less cosmically, because the term 'shadows' envelops players as well as fairies, it harks back to the blurring of social distinctions during the performance of *Pyramus and Thisbe* and extends that blur into *A Midsummer Night's Dream*. For as the gamboling fairies reassemble downstairs in the Elizabethan manor house and trot offstage for the last time, they, like the audience itself, are awakening from *A Midsummer Night's Dream* and returning to their reality as actors. In their temporary dressing room, all fictional partitions now are down. Bottom rises to the top and freely consorts with the duke, Egeus chats in friendly fashion with Lysander, Hermia and Helena slap one another boyishly on the back, and characters as discrete as Hippolyta and Titania or Theseus and Oberon fuse into a single male actor. This dissolving of fictional partitions into a mingling camaraderie of players, if it does not subversively hint at a levelling of the social and political order in the manor house or in England, it at least suggests that this seemingly firm-fixed structure is also something of a revisable fiction.[4]

DREAMS

A number of walls come down at the end of the play, but the wall of repression that keeps *A Midsummer Night's Dream* outside the pales and forts of its audience's reason still stands, propped up partly by Puck himself. For one illusion humans cannot seem to do without is the illusion of reason, and that is what Puck offers the audience when he invites them to dismiss the play as a dream. The problem with this is that the entire play has demonstrated that reason is itself a dream from which we are always awaking.[5] In Shakespeare's day, Copernicus, Galileo and Kepler were all in the business of exploding centuries of galactic dreams induced by Ptolemy, even while Paracelsus, Paré and Vesalius were awakening medicine from its long Galenic sleep and Bacon was rousing philosophy from the fantasy of scholastic rationality.[6] Most Elizabethans thought it very reason to regard their queen as Gloriana, the Virgin Vestal, inheritor of the glories of Arthur and ancient days. The dream of reason was everywhere; it merely depended on who did the dreaming. Campion was ripped from groin to sternum and his guts spilled in the dust because he insisted on the dream of Catholicism and his tormenters on the dream of Anglicanism. The bodies of old crones were stretched and broken on the rack because in the dream of theological reason they had compacted with Satan. What other 'reason' could one find why the neighbours' cow stopped giving milk or, as Stubbes maintained, why all those young folks frolicked into the woods on the eve of May and came back the next morning with green boughs in hand and young maids in the family way? Satan or Robin Goodfellow, take your choice.

What reason cannot or prefers not to understand, it declares is a dream – airy nothing. What cannot fit inside its whole must be cast out. Unfortunately, every whole contains a 'hole' that paradoxically cannot be contained and therefore, like the cranny in the wall in *Pyramus and Thisbe*, breaks down the distinction between inside and outside. Michael Serres, deploring a division between the hard sciences and the liberal arts – C. P. Snow's 'two cultures' – might be addressing Theseus when he says:

> Knowledge without illusion is an illusion through and through, in which everything is lost, including knowledge. A theorem of it might be sketched like this: *there is no myth more innocent than that of a knowledge innocent of myth.* I can think of no others, so imbrued are myths with knowledge, and knowledge with dreams and illusions.[7]

As we saw earlier, the fairies, descendants of Aristotle's Unmoved Mover, are a kind of imaginative mortar that plugs the hole in causation's wall – but in doing so advertises the presence of that hole. Indeed, pure chimera that he is, Oberon is the hole in the seemingly solid wall of Theseus, the airy nothing into which the man of cool reason dissolves when, in the form of a doubling actor, he moves from palace to wood and dons the fairy king's invisibility. Thus what Theseus would banish beyond reason's pale, he cannot even banish from his own body. No sooner does he terminate the action of the play with his 'Lovers, to bed; 'tis almost fairy time', than in his role as Oberon he returns to perforate the solid whole he has just defined. More important is the fact that Oberon does not entirely remain in fairyland, not as long as he is theatrically incarnated in Theseus. Thus the fairy king will always be visibly invisible in the figure of the duke, a kind of illusive corporeal baggage Theseus unwittingly carries with him when he leaves fairyland and re-enters Athens. His body invaded thus, Theseus 'dis-figures' Serres' metaphoric phrase about how 'imbrued are myths with knowledge, and knowledge with dreams and illusions'. Moreover, he renders visible Puck's sly implication in his Epilogue that, unbeknownst to us, we too carry away from the theatre, inspirited in us somewhere, the virtues of our theatrical sojourn in this fairyland of a play.

Finally, in that Epilogue – a part of the play that is both inside and outside it at once, rather as Oberon and Theseus are inside and outside one another at once – here is Puck, airy nothing in the role of spokesfairy for the play itself, pretending to make it dramatically whole and complete by telling us to think it is, like him, nothing at all.

Yet reason will have its 'wholes' and its 'causes', as fairies are well aware. That is why Oberon creates for the lovers one final illusion, that when they wake 'all this derision / Shall seem a dream and fruitless vision'. No doubt the lovers would have come to that conclusion anyhow, just as Lysander, squinting at Helena through Puck's flower juice, came to realise that 'The will of man is by his reason swayed, / And reason says you are the worthier maid' (ii.ii.115–16). As kings of shadows, Oberon and Shakespeare know that their theatrical productions must always be sacrificed to reason's insistence on an impenetrable wall between dream and reason, myth and fact, play and reality. But that is how a sacrificial object does its work, by being sacrificed. What good is a *pharmakos* if he dies of old age?

A Midsummer Night's Dream cannot be ritually killed like a *pharmakos*, but it can be expelled from consciousness like Oedipus from Thebes. What will be denied are not visions of supernatural forces operating behind or above the scenes of this world. The 'life is a dream' metaphor does not imply that we have witnessed truths that transcend reason but rather truths to which reason will not stoop to see. But if we do bend a bit, looking in a low mirror, we will discover, as Artaud would wish, though not as rawly as Artaud would wish, 'the precipitate of dreams' – a taste for crime, erotic obsessions, savagery, chimeras, even (in Hermia's nightmare) cannibalism – all of which sits as badly with our sense of ourselves as the paragon of reason as Bottom's hairiness about the face does with his sense of himself as a man of wit and wisdom.

Bottom forgets his dream and goes out to bray his lines in *Pyramus and Thisbe*, but Shakespeare may hope from his audience a response more like that of the lovers, not a complete erasure of the play but a sacrificial sublimation. The hierarchical wall between reason and *A Midsummer Night's Dream*, like that between conscious and unconscious, will then be up again, no getting around or over it. Through it, though, is another matter. For like all walls, it will have a cranny in it – through which, if cool reason were to draw near, it might discern, on the far side, strange shadows dancing like elves in fairy circles or like child actors in a wooden 'O', and through which a hobgoblin like Puck, seeing a spy, might squirt the juice of love-in-idleness. Cool reason should look to its eyes. And so should we. But Puck and the play have already seen to that.

Notes

THE STAGE HISTORY AND CRITICAL RECEPTION
(pp. xx–xxvi)

1. Attempting to situate *A Midsummer Night's Dream* within the ideological manoeuvrings of its time is an admirable enterprise, but one
that is no more exempt from misprision than any other, especially
when the critic's own ideological axe comes in for grinding. For
instance, Puck's phrase 'The hungry lion roars', in his apotropaic
speech near the end of the play, has been said to represent the
'ideological threat of working-class resentment' (Schneider 1987:
205). Certainly no one would deny that the *Elizabethan* working class
had good cause for resentment (see Patterson 1989, for example), but
to attribute a similar plight and feeling to the Athenian artisans one
must take a detour around or through Shakespeare's text: 'To arrive
at this class-conscious rendering of the text requires that one read
through the polite surface to the aggressive gestures underneath'
(Schneider 1987: 204). At some time or another all critics succumb
to the attractions of this strategy by citing the text when it says what
they want it to and reading through its surface when it does not. But
when a failure in reading becomes a principle of reading, even in a
good cause, surely something has gone wrong.
2. If, for instance, 'The hungry lion roars' can be taken as a metaphor
for working-class resentment, it can even more obviously be taken

as a literal statement reflecting the abysmal treatment of animals in Elizabethan England. I think of the menagerie of exotic animals kept since the twelfth century in the Tower of London and especially of the lions, whose roaring must have been audible far around, or even of the lion that was to have drawn a chariot at the baptismal feast of Prince Henry in 1594 but whose roaring was thought too frightening for the ladies (see the section on 'Date', pp. xv–xvi above). But much as I should like to think Shakespeare condemned the mistreatment of animals as well as workmen, in this case Puck's roaring lion stands much more plausibly for wild and frightening creatures in general – possibly even for the diabolical lion of whom Peter warns ('Be sober, be vigilant; because your adversary the devil, as a roaring lion, walketh about, seeking whom he may devour' (1 Peter 5:8)) – creatures that must be kept at bay if newly-weds are to go about their business more securely than poor Pyramus and Thisbe in the lion-infested woods outside Babylon.

3. Leonard Tennenhouse also associates Oberon as well as the workmen with carnival (1986: 73) – rather surprisingly, inasmuch as Oberon is himself royal and his intentions are always strictly patriarchal and phallocratic. The only candidate for carnival in fairyland would seem to be Puck; but even he, though a product of the rustic imagination, shows no interest in mocking the higher orders, only in creating mischief wherever possible.

CHAPTER 1 (pp. 1–22)

1. Freud assumed that the incest taboo is peculiarly human, marking a division between us and 'lower' animals. Since his time, however, ethologists, anthropologists and sociobiologists have claimed (1) that incest-avoidance is found in other animals whose survival depends on genetic variation, especially primates, and (2) that the human taboo seeks to suppress not a natural but an unnatural desire on our parts. That is, we have evolved in such a way as to make us 'naturally' non-incestuous (because non-incestuous creatures survive), and we outlaw incest simply because it is eccentric and distasteful (Fox 1980: 1–14). Hence in a roundabout way Freud was right.

2. For Lacan the imaginary is a fusional mode of mind, a sophisticated human version of the imprinting mechanism that establishes identity for animals. It first manifests itself in the illusory union between infant and mother, and then later, during the 'mirror-state', in the alienating identifications of the child with its image. The imaginary is

oppositional and dyadic, whereas the symbolic is mediational and triadic. The ego is formed via the agency of a specular other and is thus estranged from itself in the very process of achieving a seeming unity. Although the imaginary later interacts with the symbolic, its imaging tendency might be taken as an attempt to arrest and crystallise into form the transiency of the symbolic's pursuit of desire, to fuse the fragmented and fleeting in an illusion of wholeness, while the symbolic tends to shatter the mirrors that magnetise the dreaming gaze of the imaginary.

3. In place of Freud's instinct or drive, Lacan attributes human motivation to need, demand and desire. 'Need' is biological, appetitive, non-verbal, and, because it is focused on specific objects, capable of being satisfied. Once language is acquired, need is expressed verbally as 'demand' – an appeal to others not so much for specific objects (say, food) as for gifts that can be taken as proofs of love. 'Desire', on the other hand, 'is neither the appetite for satisfaction, nor the demand for love, but the difference that results from the subtraction of the first from the second, the phenomenon of their splitting [*Spaltung*]' (Lacan, 'The Meaning of the Phallus' (1958), in Mitchell and Rose 1983: 80–1). This apparently means that stated demand is always in excess of need and that this excess ('the difference') somehow splits off and assumes new form as an unfocused yearning for consummation, well expressed in the double senses of 'wanting' and perfectly illustrated in the Canadian movie *Maria Chapdelaine*.

4. Lacan, on the other hand, interprets the child's game as symbolising the disappearance of his own self, not of his mother's goings and comings (although in the imaginary the two would seem bound together), and of his entrance into the symbolic (Lacan 1978: 62).

5. What follows is by no means a rigorous psychoanalytic analysis of *A Midsummer Night's Dream*, merely an intermittent employment of Freudian–Lacanian concepts, modified by reference to Elizabethan culture and practices, as a framework for discussion. I cannot even claim to have read all of Lacan's Delphic signifiers, let alone to have grasped their signifieds. My colleague Michael Clark has patiently identified for me a few perceptible shapes amid the shadows flickering on the Lacanian cave wall, as a result of which he has my gratitude and I have a permanent squint. Less personally, I am also obliged to him, as all students of Lacan must surely be, for his monumental *Jacques Lacan: An Annotated Bibliography* (1988), the annotations in which are marvels of compressed lucidity. Other writers on Lacan who have been particularly helpful (see References): Malcolm Bowie

1979; Juliet Flower MacCannell 1986; Juliet Mitchell and Jacqueline Rose 1983; John P. Muller and William J. Richardson 1982; Kaja Silverman 1983; Ellie Ragland-Sullivan 1986, 1989; Sherry Turkle 1978; and Anthony Wilden 1968.

6. Stephen Greenblatt says that in reading Renaissance texts psychoanalysis 'can redeem its belatedness only when it historicizes its own procedures' (Greenblatt 1986b: 221). One might argue, as Barbara Freedman does (1991: 36), that any rereading of the past – psychoanalytic, feminist, Marxist, new historicist – is necessarily belated. For that matter, psychoanalysis is belated even in post-Freudian–Lacanian times. Since everyone goes mad or neurotic in his or her own way, not according to a pre-existent psychoanalytic recipe, the analyst always comes to the analysand's discourse as the literary critic comes to the text, after the fact – and yet sufficiently conscious of that, one hopes, to 'historicise' or customise the interpretation in light of the individual case. Or, as François Roustang says, from the perspective of the analyst, 'The certainty that one knows is useless; psychoanalysis is possible when the psychoanalyst has forgotten the theory' (Roustang 1982: 70). My own rudimentary customisings, historical and other, appear sometimes in the text, sometimes in notes, and always in a spirit of uncertainty.

7. It may be worth mentioning that a journey into the forest might well be associated in Shakespeare's mind with his mother. Mary Arden grew up at Wilmcote, a few miles north of Stratford 'in the valley of the Alne, divided from the Avon by low wooded hills', part of the Forest of Arden (Fraser 1988: 18). Moreover, since her father, Robert Arden, had been a prosperous man, and more than generous to her in his will, it is likely that as the poet's father fell on hard times in the 1570s, his mother's Arden past loomed more largely in her mind (and perhaps in a few wry comments) as a time of lost affluence.

8. 'Irrecoverable' because in Elizabethan times, where divorce and remarriage were virtually impossible, children did not have step-dames unless their real mother was dead (Stone 1977: 37–41) or unless she had abandoned them, as mothers did with appalling frequency from Hellenistic antiquity to the Renaissance (Boswell 1988). In Shakespeare's time the psychological absence of the mother resulting from (and causing) the child's graduation from the imaginary to the symbolic was considerably exacerbated and confused by the oedipal situation that often prevailed in the Elizabethan family. One reason for this was the practice, so common among the upper classes, of wet-nursing babies, the effect of which was to

deprive infants of a single nurturing figure in their earliest years of life. As Lawrence Stone observes,

> These nurses were often cruel or neglectful, and they often ran out of milk, as a result of which the baby had to be passed from nipple to nipple, from one unloving mother-substitute to another. If the infant stayed with one wet-nurse, then it became deeply attached to her, as a result of which the weaning process at about eighteen months inflicted the trauma of final separation from the loved substitute mother-figure and a return to the alien and frightening world of the natural mother. (Stone 1977: 100)

In cases like these the 'loss of the mother' is not a metaphor for psychic alienation or repression but a plain physical fact; at weaning time the substitute mother was banished and permanently lost to the infant. To make things more confusing, such a procedure reverses the normal oedipal pattern. Instead of the father calling a halt to the fusion of mother and child, the natural mother herself must speak the paternal No and assume the role of stepdame to her own infant. In a worst-case scenario – i.e. distant mother, unloving nurse(s) – the child would suffer a series of abandonments and grow up in a maternal vacuum very likely to produce what psychologists today call 'deprivation syndrome'. Even in the best of cases it could hardly avoid experiencing a fundamental lack of love and deep anxieties about where and to whom it belonged.

9.   Both aspects of the symbolic need acknowledgement, as Juliet MacCannell observes:

> If you see the Symbolic Order as merely coercive . . . not as benign mediator or broker, the linkage Lacan makes between the structure and aim of civilisation and the process of symbolisation is obscured, just as it is exaggeratedly rationalised in a schema that sees its positive 'civilising' qualities alone. (1986: 135)

10.   On the other hand, Pearson argues that Shakespeare was simply following earlier Renaissance accounts of Theseus, which painted the hero in a darker moral light than most critics have done. Recalling the unhappy story in which Theseus unjustly accuses his son and calls for his death contributes to this disapproving portrayal.

11.   Shakespeare's awareness of this is suggested in *Pericles* when the visionary Diana announces, 'My temple stands in Ephesus', speaks of 'my silver bow', and is called by Pericles 'Celestial Dian, goddess

argentine' (v.i.241 ff.), not to mention his situating *The Comedy of Errors* in Ephesus with its temple of Diana. In the most complete version of the myth available to Shakespeare, Seneca's *Phaedra* – translated by John Studley as *Hippolytus* and printed by Thomas Newton in a collection called *Seneca, His Tenne Tragedies* (1581) – Hippolytus is identified as a votary of Diana (Pearson 1974: 277–8).

12. A major Lacanian refinement of Freud is precisely this shift of emphasis from the biological to the symbolic – for instance from the father as a person to the 'name-of-the-father' or from gender as anatomically caused to gender as culturally caused. According to Fredric Jameson, a failure to acknowledge these Lacanian distinctions has inspired many of the attacks on Lacan as phallocentric (1982: fn. 352–3).

13. Aquinas, *Summa Theologica*, I, 92, 1c; cited by Mary Daly in the *Dictionary of the History of Ideas*, vol. IV, ed. Philip P. Wiener (New York: Charles Scribner's Sons, 1973), 525. Aristotle's view of conception accords with his general view that for any object to come into existence a form or universal had to impress itself on the medium or substance, in itself shapeless and inert, albeit desirous of being so impressed. Ignorant of the role of ovaries and testicles in reproduction, he thought that male and female both emitted 'sperma' from their blood. The male seed supplied form and movement; the female menstrual fluid supplied matter and passivity. The Aristotelian 'mother' was less a mother than an incubator of male seed (McClaren 1984: 16; Needham 1959: 37–74; Preus 1977: 65–85). The imprisoned Richard II transfers this notion of sexual conception to mental conceptions when he says:

> My brain I'll prove the female to my soul,
> My soul the father, and these two beget
> A generation of still-breeding thoughts;
> And these same thoughts people this little world,
> In humors like the people of this world,
> For no thought is contented.
>   (Richard II 5.5.6-11)

14. My feminising of Lacan's masculine pronouns here falsely implies that both genders engage with the symbolic alike, whereas in Seminar XX Lacan says that woman enters the symbolic quite differently from man, on the one hand denigrated as a 'not-all' – the negative that shapes man's positive – and on the other hand mystified as the Other who promises to be the end of all quests.

15. The Athenian law here, the very epitome of the symbolic as societal superego, illustrates how interinvolved the symbolic and imaginary are. It exhibits, albeit in non-visual form, the principal tendency that motivates the ego in the imaginary register, a unifying drive for wholeness. As the ego seeks to compose truth-laden gestalts out of the flux of subjective experience, so the law seeks to impose definitive order on human affairs, reducing the sundry to the simple. It exhibits another tendency of the imaginary also, the aggressiveness that results when its idealisations are threatened (Lacan 1977: 22; Muller and Richardson 1982: 49). The Athenian law incorporates that aggressiveness as the penalty of death for those who challenge its authority. In fact, so grotesquely rigid and prohibitive is the law here that it belies the restless nature of the symbolic itself. It is as if the imaginary has invaded the symbolic and converted its diachronic chain of signifiers into a synchronic legal icon. The question is how to free desire from this tyranny. The answer is not by transforming the law, which seems unalterable, but by disengaging its authority from its power, which lies with Theseus.

16. 'In the 1640s both Connecticut and Massachusetts turned [Calvin's] precept into legislation, although so far as is known only a handful of children were ever executed for this crime' (Stone 1977: 175). As Stone records, the Reformation and Counter-Reformation gave new righteousness and vigour to parental discipline, especially among Puritans, because of a redoubled preoccupation with Original Sin, the seductiveness of the Devil, and the sweeping authority of the Bible with its harsh instructions about raising children (174–8). See also Cook (1991: 98–9). But disregarding a parent's wishes in marriage was no cause for killing a child in England, even though, as Ann Jennalie Cook notes, 'not a single work [on the subject of marriage] advocates the primacy of personal affection in the face of legitimate parental objections. The veto some allow when children cannot accept their elders' selection has not yet become a right of absolute individual choice' (Cook 1991: 75). In short, Shakespeare's death-dealing patriarchy here is a caricature of a society that, although severely patriarchal, was by no means this bad.

17. Not quite all cultures: see Riane Eisler's *The Chalice and the Blade* (1987) for evidence of a pre-patriarchal 'partnership' society in neolithic Europe and Crete.

18. A similar monstrousness was attributed to Elizabethan women who wore masculine clothing, those who,

from the top to the toe, are so disguised, that though they be in
sexe Women, yet in attire they appeare to be men, and are like
Androgini, who counterfayting the shape of either kind, are in
deede neither, so while they are in condition women, and would
seeme in apparell men, they are neither men nor women, but
plaine Monsters. (Averell, *Mervailous Combat*, 1588 (Shepherd
1981: 67))

19. Plutarch's tale appears in Bullough 1957: 386–7. Louis Adrian
    Montrose cites several Elizabethan accounts of Amazons, both
    ancient and contemporary (though always just beyond the horizon),
    and summarises: 'Amazonian mythology seems symbolically to
    embody and to control a collective anxiety about the power of the
    female not only to dominate and reject the male but to create and
    destroy him' (1983: 36).
20. See also Lévi-Strauss 1963: 58–62. Lévi-Strauss' theory is based on
    Marcel Mauss' *The Gift*, which argues that the earliest form of
    exchange was not economic barter but gift-giving, a practice that has
    been endorsed in modified form more recently by Jean Baudrillard
    (1975). Lacan echoes Lévi-Strauss' claims about women and
    symbolism (1978: 150–1).
21. Among the property-owning classes in Elizabethan England mar-
    riage was usually more economically oriented and more successfully
    controlled by parents than it is in Shakespeare, where love ushers
    young couples to the altar either with or without the company of
    fathers (Stone 1977: 86–7). This accords with middle-class practice
    in Warwickshire, if not with that of the nobility: in Stratford, for
    instance, 'couples in the middling ranks often seem to have taken the
    initiative themselves, entering into matches to which parents sub-
    sequently acceded without much fuss' (Neely 1989: 215).
22. This sense of loss follows from the notion that we become human
    when we enter the symbolic; for if the symbolic implies a lack – the
    not-thereness of an immediate world which the symbolic can only
    represent – then our humanity or selfhood is founded on lack and
    loss, and hence we are driven by a desire for recovery.
23. Lacan regards the longing of Aristophanes' hermaphrodites to
    recover a lost wholeness as a reflection of human desire in general
    (1978: 196–7, 204–5); Ragland-Sullivan discusses *The Symposium* in
    terms of Lacanian desire (1989: 725–55); and David Marshall notes
    the relevance of the myth to Hermia and Helena (1982: 558–62). In
    the Renaissance a somewhat similar view of desire focused on the
    incompleteness and sense of lack brought about by the creation of

Eve out of the body of Adam. 'For if Lady Eve had been formed otherwise than from the body of man', Paracelsus says, 'desire would never have been born from both of them. But because they are of one flesh and one blood, it follows that they cannot let go of each other' (Paracelsus 1979: 33). The satisfactions of oneness, however, are called in question by the fact that Adam was not content when he 'contained' Eve and that Aristophanes' hermaphrodites, even in their original globular state, were still desirous of more, and hence proposed to assault Olympus and the gods.

24. When the drugged Demetrius awakens and sees Helena, he addresses her in terms that leave little to choose between her and Aphrodite: 'O Helen, goddess, nymph, perfect, divine! / To what, my love, shall I compare thine eyne? / Crystal is muddy' etc. (III.ii.137 ff.).

25. Lacan, invoking Aristophanes' story about the origin of desire, says the subject suffers its first loss, of androgynous wholeness, when it undergoes sexual differentiation in the womb (Lacan 1978: 204–5). This physiological process occurs in the 'real', prior to signification, but will be confirmed later by symbolic distinctions. Indeed, culture is always already there, a play with a role set aside for us even before we make our entrance. Hence the joke about two infants lying side by side in the maternity ward. The first says, 'I'm a boy; what are you?' The other replies, 'I don't know; how can you tell?' Lifting up the bedcover, the first points downward, and after a dramatic pause says, 'See, blue booties.'

26. From Egeus' standpoint it is pure witchcraft, which was thought capable of generating a false love. Thus in 1542 Parliament passed a statute making it a felony (the offender subject to pillorying and a year in jail) 'to provoke any persone to unlawfull love' (Kittredge 1929: 115); and Thomas Newton sounds very much like Egeus when he asks in his *Tryall of a Man's Owne Selfe* (London: unpublished, 1602) 'Whether by any secret sleight, or cunning, as drinkes, drugges, medicines, charmed potions, amatorius philters, figures, characters, or any such like paltering instruments, devises, or practises, thou has gone about to procure others to doate for love of thee' (p. 116).

CHAPTER 2 (pp. 23–47)

1. Terry Eagleton (1986: 19) appropriately quotes Jonathan Culler (1975: 120) to make this intertextual point about love:

To say 'I love you', as Jonathan Culler points out, is always at some
level a quotation; in its very moment of absolute, original value,
the self stumbles across nothing but other people's lines, finds
itself handed a meticulously detailed script to which it must
slavishly conform. It discovers, that is, that it is always already
'written', scored through in its noblest thoughts and most spontaneous affections by the whole tediously repetitive history of
human sexual behaviour, subjected to impersonal codes and
conventions at exactly the moment it feels most euphorically free
of them.

2. Helena's desire to exchange identities with Hermia instances a
   selfishness that is pervasive in the play. Exchanging identities ought
   to be a metaphor for identification, empathy, sympathy, all of which
   depend on imagination, the active agent behind Aristotle's concept of
   mimesis, and hence of most learning, and the inactive agent behind
   most instances of what in its simplest form we call lack of consideration and in its most heinous form prejudice. Yet failures of
   empathic imagination abound in the opening scene. Egeus is too
   wilfully absorbed in his own paternal despotism to take account of
   Hermia's feelings, even to take account of her life. Theseus has been
   too blithely 'overfull of self-affairs', as he says (i.i.113), to investigate
   Demetrius' jilting of Helena. Demetrius is too preoccupied with
   desire for Hermia to be troubled by her unhappy plight; and Helena
   is too full of self-pity to sympathise with anyone. Her desire to
   exchange identities with Hermia is purely and selectively selfish;
   she wants to be the Hermia who is loved by Demetrius, but she
   never utters a kind word to the Hermia who is faced with death,
   sequestration or an undesired marriage. At this early stage, only
   Hermia and Lysander, whose sympathy for Helena causes them to
   confess their intent to flee Athens (i.i.202–3, 224–5) and perhaps
   Hippolyta, who may be troubled by Hermia's misfortunes (i.i.122),
   demonstrate a capacity to imagine what another feels.

3. This thesis, that love must simply see, its gaze unrefracted by the
   prism of the mind, is inexhaustibly scrutinised, discussed, catalogued, illustrated and analogised by Louis Zukovsky in *Bottom: On
   Shakespeare* (1987).

4. René Girard takes Hermia's line here as the keynote to his
   interpretation of the play. Focusing on mimetic desire, he argues that
   the 'hell' experienced by the lovers in the forest is engendered not by
   the 'parental and supernatural bugaboos that are supposed to be its
   cause' but by the self-defeating nature of mimetic rivalry: 'The

midsummer night is a hell of the lovers' own choosing, a hell into which they all avidly plunge, insofar as they all choose to choose love by another's eyes' (Girard 1979: 194). In Girard's neo-Hegelian theory, that is, desire is not kindled by the object itself but by another's desire: the reason I want that peach, dissertation topic or Magic Johnson T-shirt is because I see you want it, and the more you want it the more I want it (Kojève 1969: 6). But this auction theory of desire, however relevant elsewhere in Shakespeare, has little bearing on the lovers, who do not 'all choose to choose love by another's eyes'. There is no evidence that Demetrius or Lysander loves Hermia because the other loved her first; nor does Hermia love Lysander because someone else does / because no one else does. Helena is indeed jealous of Hermia, but she doesn't love Demetrius because Hermia does / because Hermia does not (though by the criterion of mimetic desire, she should, because Helena does). For that matter, the fact that Demetrius is distasteful to Hermia ought to devalue him in Helena's eyes, but it does not.

Girard is more accurate when he says that Helena desires to be 'metamorphosed into Hermia, because Hermia enjoys the love of Demetrius' (1979: 191). But desiring to *be* the other is quite different from desiring what the other desires. Helena wants to be Hermia, not in order to desire Demetrius, whom she already desires, but in order to be desired *by* him; and Demetrius wants to be Lysander in order to be loved by Hermia.

In a sense, however, this finding reasons for love flies in the face of the play's insistence on its irrationality. For whatever sense it fails to make, love is a force that operates as impersonally as electro-magnetism. Whether inspired culturally by bookish traditions or naturally by flower juices, once its victims are plugged into it they are in its power.

5. Columbus employed this method on his third voyage. But it was not all this easy or accurate, actually. Even when old beliefs about Polaris being a fixed star suspended directly over the pole were disproved, its degree of variation from the pole was often confused. Still, cal- culating its height with even the most primitive instrument was an improvement on the technique described by an Icelandic priest newly (and miraculously) returned from a visit to the Holy Land in the year 1150. By his account, there was nothing to it: 'if a man lies flat on the ground [in Jordan], raises his knee, places his fist upon it, and then raises his thumb from his fist, he sees the Pole Star just so high and no higher' (E. G. R. Taylor 1971: 129).

6. Of course the empirical 'seeing is believing' school of thought has

always given rise to a counter-realisation that believing is seeing, that is, that preconceptions subtly control our vision. Helena illustrates this position when she complains that 'Things base and vile, holding no quantity, / Love can transpose to form and dignity' (i.i.232–3), a complaint echoed by Theseus in his indictment of the transforming imaginations of lovers, madmen and poets (v.i.2–22).

7. Even apart from the degrading sexual aspects of this, equating woman with truth overtly celebrates her while covertly denying her a role in the truth-seeking process. Man is the active seeker, woman the passive object of knowledge. Similarly, at the other end of the line, figuring woman as the inspirer of truths, as in the case of the muses, aggrandises her at the cost of making man the exclusive creator of art.

8. In his *Eroici furori* Bruno treats Actaeon as the hunter of the universal light that will reveal God:

> Hence the wonderful image of Actaeon and his dogs, hunting after the 'vestiges', which recurs again and again . . . until, by progressive insights, the dogs, thoughts of divine things, devour Actaeon and he becomes wild, like a stag dwelling in the woods, and obtains the power of contemplating the nude Diana, the beautiful disposition of the body of nature. He sees All as One. (Yates 1964: 278)

9. The association of the witch's seductive eye and sexual congress is repeated in a kind of inverse form in the Elizabethan belief that the act of procreation was powerfully dependent on a form of reflective seeing. Discussing the stress on erotic pleasure in medical treatises of the time, Stephen Greenblatt paraphrases the physician Jacques Duval (1612):

> Sexual pleasure may be thought to link us to the beasts, writes Duval, but in fact in its specifically human form it is one of the marks of God's special favor. The Sovereign Creator was not content that his best-beloved creatures mate as the other animals do, with the male mounting on the female's back or, in the case of elephants, camels, and other heavy beasts, with the male and female turning their backs to one another. For human coition God ordained a different practice: men and women look into each others' faces – 'the beautiful lines and features' of the human face – so that they may be aroused to a more fervent desire to generate images of themselves, to make those beloved faces live again in their offspring. And as they look upon one another and make love,

drawn into the genital 'labyrinth of desire' that God creates specially for them and obey the 'tacit commandments' engraved as a benediction in their very bodies, men and women avenge themselves upon their enemy, death. For to leave behind one's own image – 'drawn to the life in one's child' ('vif et naiuement representé en son successeur') – is not to die. (Greenblatt 1986a: 43–4)

Here the reflected images of husband and wife mingle in an act of visual congress that conveys the fused image to the loins and thence to the child. Instead of the child perceiving itself, as in the mirror-state, the parents see the child in themselves, or forcibly see themselves *into* the child, conquering death the while.

10. The point about Shakespeare's hawking imagery and the restraint of female sexuality is obvious. To tame the shrew in *The Taming of the Shrew* Petrucchio follows the approved procedures carefully; and the metaphor echoes in the hearts of many a husband, in Othello's most ominously: 'If I do prove her haggard, / Though that her jesses were my dear heartstrings, / I'd whistle her off' (III.iii.266–8).

11. The painter André Marchand said,

> In a forest, I have felt many times over that it was not I who looked at the forest. Some days I felt that the trees were looking at me . . . I think that the painter must be penetrated by the universe and not want to penetrate it. (Cited by Merleau-Ponty 1964: 167)

This is of course a gentler view of the 'look' than Sartre's. Merleau-Ponty also notes that painters like to paint themselves in the act of painting because they are keenly aware that while they see things they are being seen *by* things (1964: 169). Again, Lacan tells a story about himself as a young man in an alien environment, aboard a boat with some professional fishermen. A sardine can floats by and Lacan, reflecting afterwards, decides that in a sense the can was looking at him, marking him as an outsider (1978: 95–6).

12. The quote from Cusa appears in an insightful discussion of Renaissance perspectivism in Barbara Freedman's extraordinarily fine book on postmodernism, psychoanalysis and Shakespearian comedy, *Staging the Gaze* (Freedman 1991: 19).

13. On a lighter note, the perils of 'perceivedness' are amusingly illustrated in a cartoon by Gary Larson showing a lone executive seated at his desk in a barren office, his expression thoughtful but impassive. Visible through the large window at his back are tall

buildings with vaguely eye-like windows that may be aimed in his direction. The caption says: 'Anatidaephobia: The fear that somewhere, somehow, a duck is watching you.'

I should add, however, that perceivedness is sometimes far preferable to invisibility. People on the societal margin, like the manic-depressive patient just quoted, may be scrutinised by the police or other authorities, but their existence with respect to ordinary citizens is usually marked by averted looks, blank looks and other signs of the social invisibility illustrated in Ralph Ellison's novel *The Invisible Man*.

14. Obviously replying to Sartre, Maurice Merleau-Ponty presents a less paranoid view: 'Immersed in the visible by his body, itself visible, the see-er does not appropriate what he sees; he merely approaches it by looking, he opens himself to the world' (1964: 162). Merleau-Ponty gets no closer to appropriation than the following:

> Visible and mobile, my body is a thing among things; it is caught in the fabric of the world, and its cohesion is that of a thing. But because it moves itself and sees, it holds things in a circle around itself. Things are an annex or prolongation of itself. (1964: 163)

15. This notion of identity as locational, rather than romantically lodged in a unique indwelling self, is often found in other cultures. Among the Balinese, for instance, as Clifford Geertz puts it,

> It is not ... their existence as persons – their immediacy and individuality, or their special, never-to-be-repeated impact upon the stream of historical events – which [is] played up, symbolically emphasized: it is their social placement, their particular location within a persisting, indeed an eternal metaphysical order. (Geertz 1973: 390)

A similar view, a stress on social allegiances and positioning, is evident in the elaborately serialised personal names of the Nzema of West Africa (Grottanelli 1988: 7–13). I should add that Geertz's distinction has a generic parallel in Shakespeare, where 'locational identity' is more likely to be found in the comedies and romances than in the tragedies and histories, and, in addition, is more likely to be found in supporting characters like Pistol and Horatio, who occupy a typical site in fictional societies and plays, than in major characters like Falstaff and Hamlet, whose various and elusive individuality is always in excess of defined social roles and fixed locations.

16. In imagining a snake as an extension of Lysander's gaze, Shakespeare may have been influenced by stories of the basilisk or cockatrice. In ancient Greece the basilisk was a serpent whose look was said to kill. After the fourteenth century it became confused with the cockatrice (see the discussion by T. H. White 1984: 168–9). The basilisk got its name from the Greek *basileus* ('king') 'because he does not creep on the earth like other serpents', Topsell declares, 'but goes half upright, for which reason all other serpents avoid his sight' (1981: 43). It may be that the basilisk was originally a cobra, perhaps a spitting cobra that could give the impression of shooting poison from its eyes.

    It is difficult to tell just what frightens Hermia about Lysander. If you take the snake as a phallic symbol, it would represent her feeling that, despite his protests, Lysander was eyeing her lasciviously earlier, when they lay down to sleep (ii.ii.35–65). This would emphasise her fear of Lysander's getting too close to her. On the other hand, his eyeing her suffering from a distance during the dream would represent her fear of his getting too far away from her, her fear of abandonment. And of course he *is* abandoning her for Helena even as she is dreaming. For perceptive analyses, see Faber's traditional psychoanalytic interpretation (1972) and, more flexibly, Garber (1974: 72–4) and especially Holland 1960.

17. 'The subject of the picture', as Elizabeth Wright describes it (1984: 118),

    > is apparently a face, framed in what is clearly a woman's hair, styled in what was then a consciously fashionable manner. It turns out, however, that the eyes are nipples, the nose a navel, and the mouth the pubic hair of a woman. If the cultural frame (the woman's hair) is ignored, the naked torso is plainly seen, hidden in full view. The picture is a metaphor for any gaze, signifying desire and an invasion of the other's desire ('The Rape').

18. As Couliano reports (1987: 29), Ficino believed this theory was 'confirmed by Aristotle himself, who relates that menstruating women who look at themselves in the mirror leave little drops of blood on its surface. This can only mean that it is the thin blood brought to the eyes along with the pneuma (*Amore*, VII, 4)'.

19. Welsford's stress on patterned movement among the lovers reflects an interest in design that runs throughout the play, as Mark Rose has charted (1972: 17–20), tending to subordinate the individuality of the lovers in particular to structural relationships.

20. It is worth mentioning that the constancy of Hermia and Helena

complicates the recently popular view that in seeking 'to legitimise the distorted vision of a patriarchal order' the play functions rather like Oberon, whose 'manipulation of vision, however tricky, ultimately affirms a patriarchal ideology that equates men with right perspective and women with an irrational nature that defies orderly sight' (Freedman 1991: 184). It seems arguable that Oberon's treatment of Titania, while it may legitimise the patriarchal order in fairyland, repellently equates patriarchy with tyranny in the theatre. Nor does this argument seem to apply to Oberon's treatment, via Puck, of the lovers, the result of which is that the defining male gaze is made to appear errant and ridiculous beside an admirable (albeit baffling) female fidelity.

21. I should add that Lysander's flower-induced gaze at Helena may only render explicit a secret gaze that he was directing at her even in Athens, despite his love for Hermia. Which is only to say that love is never so absolute as to render the lover entirely blind to other attractions.

CHAPTER 3 (pp. 48–71)

1. Jurgis Baltrusaitis says one must stand 'very close, looking down on it from the right' to see the skull properly (1977: 91). Having seen the painting only in relatively small reproductions, I am obliged to take his word for it. Everyone I know has got cross-eyed trying to see a normal skull, and one suffered paper cuts on the nose for the sake of perspectival science. For the less daring, Baltrusaitis has a photograph showing how the skull appears in proper focus: it lies on its right cheekbone, eye-sockets to the left, jaw to the right (1977: 103), looking in fact very much like the viewer.

2. Shakespeare may or may not have seen Holbein's painting, but as Ned Lukacher points out, it is very likely that he saw the anamorphic painting of Edward VI by a Holbein follower, one William Scrots, whose very name invites anamorphic glances. Citing Baltrusaitis (1977: 16, 18–19, 109), Lukacher writes, 'Scrots' portrait hung in Whitehall Palace during the 1590s when Shakespeare's company, the Lord Chamberlain's Men, played there; this portrait was to be viewed through a viewing hole drilled through a screen off to the side of the painting' (1989: 873).

   That Shakespeare is playing with perspective in *A Midsummer Night's Dream* would be in keeping with his interest in anamorphism in *Richard II*, which was written around the same time (Pye 1988: 581–8; Lukacher 1989: 863–78). See also Barbara Freedman's brilliant chapter studying 'the crossroads where learned ignorance, trick perspectives, and Shakespearean comedy meet' (1991: 7–42; 10), and, for a more strictly psychoanalytic consideration of anamorphism, Lacan 1978: 79–104.

3. The four parts are so amenable to doubling that they seem designed for that purpose. The only difficulty is the need for a couple of quick costume changes when one pair exits just before the other enters – at iv.i.101 and at v.i.365. But changing time for the latter occasion is supplied by Puck's speech about dread spirits and frolicsome ones (v.i.366–86), and for the former occasion it can be managed if the stage direction 'Wind horn' were taken as authorising several windings and perhaps a few musical discords and sweet thunderings from Theseus' hounds before the duke and his train put in an appearance. If the parts were doubled in Shakespeare's time, the practice was subsequently abandoned (at least there is no mention of it for two centuries), only to be recovered in recent years.

    As Graham Bradshaw observes, 'doubling [the roles of Theseus and Oberon] makes excellent dramatic, psychological and symbolic sense, because they are the respective representatives of reason and of those life mysteries which reason cannot encompass or control'. Doubling 'underlines the irony that these seemingly opposed realms are properly interdependent and need to be integrated, brought into harmony with each other' (Bradshaw 1987: 69). However, see Roger Warren (1983: 60, 64) for objections, as well as for excellent analyses of the productions not only by Brook and Phillips but by Peter Hall and Elijah Moshinsky as well.

4. Krieger also believes that the discord between Oberon and Titania, which reflects the conflict between Theseus and Hippolyta, implies that the wars between the Athenians and the Amazonians have disrupted all nature. But this is to translate the Athens–fairyland metaphor into literal identity, leading Krieger to add that it 'indicates Shakespeare's understanding of the strategies used by the ruling class to justify its power and its retention of centralized authority through hypothetical analogy with the forces of nature' (1979: 56). Grounding one's authority on 'nature' is a strategy no doubt employed by all ruling classes (not to mention parents, trade union leaders and English professors), and certainly Shakespeare understood as much. However, Theseus' anxieties seem less those of a ruler desperate to legitimate his political authority, which no one has challenged, than those of an about-to-be husband concerned about his sexual dominance. Of course sexual dominance can be an important element in domestic politics, and the politician who cannot

rule in his own bedroom may not be able to rule elsewhere, as Antony discovered during the sea battle near Actium (*Antony and Cleopatra*, Act 3 Scene 10).

5. Among the villainously imperceptive critics who have been taken in by this surface view of Theseus I am afraid I must number myself: 'In affairs of love Theseus has a normative role in the play; his marriage to Hippolyta, the preparations for which structurally bracket the trials of the young lovers, operates as the social ideal against which other relationships are measured' (1965: 124).

6. That is, Hippolyta keeps her counsel and remains an enigma to the interpreter of the script. But of course directors and actors must decide how she is to be played – somewhere along the spectrum from loving and obedient (the traditional presentation) to fiercely resistant (as in a 1967 Greenwich Village production by John Hancock in which she was 'brought back in captivity, robed in leopard skins, was caged and guarded' (Lewis 1969: 251)).

7. An identification of Theseus and Hippolyta with Oberon and Titania is of course not dependent on doubling the parts, though much is lost, I think, if that is not done. But the identification is made when Titania reproves Oberon about 'the bouncing Amazon, / Your buskined mistress and your warrior love', and he accuses her of loving Theseus and leading him from woman to woman (ii.i.70–80). For Theseus to marry Oberon's beloved, with Oberon's approval, is tantamount to his being Oberon. And if Theseus is Oberon, then he is Titania's husband, and she a fairy version of Hippolyta.

8. 'That the Indian boy is an Eros figure', MacCary argues, 'cannot be doubted, and by my definition that means he represents an archaic self-image. Thus the male facing marriage nostalgically returns to an earlier, easier pattern of desire' (1985: 147). On this view, that is, the Indian boy represents the classical *eromenos* or boy-beloved of the older male *erastēs*, and Oberon–Theseus is regressing to a more narcissistic and manageable kind of desire, easier than negotiating with a fairy queen. It is not clear whether MacCary means what he seems to say (what Jan Kott said earlier (1964: 214)), that Oberon reverts to pederasty. If so, we would expect the boy to appear on stage and exhibit some of his seductive charm. However, it is hard to see how this, or any solution involving a love for the boy, helps the Theseus who, in MacCary's otherwise persuasive argument, is experiencing this therapeutic dream. There is no Ganymede in Theseus' palace; and if the Duke must resort to a simpler mode of love it would more likely be the series of nomadic heterosexual encounters cited by Oberon rather than something homoerotic. It

seems to me that the boy merely plays a symbolic role in the contest for power. See also Shirley Nelson Garner, who argues for an Indian boy in whom both Titania and Oberon are erotically interested (1981: 49–50).

9. If Oberon and Titania treat the changeling child as a signifier they do no more than other parents do with their children, converting them into objects of symbolic exchange even before they are born. Allen Dunn makes as much of the Indian boy's absence from the stage as I do of the absence of mothers. He regards the Bottom–Titania episode as the Indian boy's dream, a dream designed to defend himself against an oedipal expulsion from Titania's maternal bower by having Bottom expelled instead, while his 'ultimate defense is his [own] absence' (1988: 22). Eliciting a dream from a character who never appears on stage is no mean feat, and may risk being called 'The Critic's Dream', as may my own argument for regarding regal quarrels in fairyland as 'Theseus' (and Hippolyta's) nightmare'. Be that as it may, Dunn's essay is an insightful exploration of oedipal crises in the play. Despite the script, incidentally, directors began putting the Indian boy on stage as early as a New York production in 1853 (Sprague and Trewin 1970: Chapter 3).

10. In a brilliant article on the play, Louis Adrian Montrose shrewdly regards Titania's speech about motherhood as a counterpoint to Theseus' earlier speech about fatherhood (i.i.46–52), in which Theseus overcompensates for the '*natural* fact that men do indeed come from women [and] for the *cultural* facts that consanguineal and affinal ties *between* men are established through mothers, wives, and daughters' (1983: 42).

11. The delightful scene described by Titania reveals what Helena's account of her and Hermia's childhood also reveals, the presence of difference within an idealised recollection of oneness. In Titania's case feminine friendship does not paper over hierarchic distinctions. What she chooses to remember is an occasion when the Indian mother playfully went about the beach 'to fetch me trifles'. No question who is fairy queen and who is votaress here.

12. 'Companionate marriage' is what Theseus proposes for him and Hippolyta when he speaks of their 'everlasting bond of fellowship' (i.i.85), a common Protestant term for marriage. However, Protestants were not hospitable to fairies, companionably married or not. Puritans in particular regarded them as an invention of the Catholic Middle Ages, 'devised by Popish priests to cover up their own knaveries' (Thomas 1971: 610). But this was untrue, as Thomas points out, because fairies antedated the Church and because the

medieval Church had been hostile to such beliefs, not anxious to compete with indigenous deities and spirits. The existence of fairies was much debated, and although an effort was sometimes made to distinguish good fairies from bad ones, most theologians, Protestant or Catholic, thought them all devilish. For a survey of the various opinions, see Briggs (1959: 163–83).

13. Lacan's notion of the phallus (Lacan 1977: 281–91) is difficult to set forth clearly. First, it is 'neither a fantasy, nor an object, nor an organ (whether penis or clitoris), but a signifier – indeed the signifier of all signifiers' (Muller and Richardson 1982: 335). What this master signifier signifies is something like 'being the object of desire', possessing the power to compel recognition, desire, love, respect. For the child, male or female, the original phallus is the mother, whom the child both wants and wants to be wanted by. At the oedipal crisis the child must repress the desire for the mother and for the mother's desire by transferring the phallus to the name-of-the-father, thus enabling his or her admission to the symbolic. From this time on, the phallus is associated with the power and privilege of patriarchy, not because it should be, but simply because in patriarchal cultures it is.

Lacan's apparent transcendence of biology in making the phallus a signifier rather than the penis is compromised by his very choice of the phallus to serve as this signifier and by his associating the 'rise' (*Aufhebung*) and 'fall' (repression) of desire as it becomes symbolised with tumescence and detumescence (Lacan 1977: 288). At one point he says the question is whether one physically 'has' the phallus (hence men) or symbolically 'is' the phallus, with or without having it (either women or men).

14. 'The changeling', as David Marshall notes in an unusually perceptive essay,

> comes to represent all of the characters in the play who are traded or fought over as property. It also shows us that the other characters are changelings in the sense that the play's plot revolves around their exchanges: their substitutions and their interchangeability. (1982: 568)

15. Although Kott's claim has been much contested (by J. R. Brown 1971; McFarland 1972; Bevington 1978; Marcus 1981; Brooks 1979: cxv; Empson 1986: 224 among others), it has inspired directors like Peter Brook to all but stage the ravishment by Titania of a monstrously priapic Bottom. Brook's production prompted from Kott later a 'mea culpa!' (1987: 52), evidently more self-congratulatory

than apologetic, since in the same essay he likens Titania to a lascivious matron in *The Golden Ass* who 'has a specific urge for animal sex' (1987: 35). For a learned response to Kott's stress on the priapic connotations of the ass, see Deborah Baker Wyrick on the permutations of the 'ass motif' (1982). As she concludes, 'Thus, even as a sexual cipher the ass is unstable; under his shaggy skin lurks a remarkable ability to shift symbolic significance. The "licentious ass", the "foolish ass", and the "admirable ass" inhabit one skin' (1982: 438). (See Tobin (1984) as well for the general influence of Apuleius' novel on the play.) As a final flourish of learning in this connection, let me note that Theseus shapes his dream in accord with the principle of Artemidoros Daldianus (second century AD), who in his *Oneirokritika* revealed the significance of dreaming of an ass:

> Asses, if they carry a burden, obey their driver, are strong and walk quietly, bode good for marriage and partnership, for they indicate that the wife or partner will not be wasteful but obedient and compatible. (N. Lewis 1976: 70)

Thus an unexpected virtue of watching *A Midsummer Night's Dream*, our own theatrical dream about an ass in fairyland, is that we can return home to a 'wife or partner' not only frugal but – trust Artemidoros – amiably subservient.

16. This all depends, however, on a Titania whom Swander regards as full of 'wildly lust-driven desires' (1990: 96) – desires made evident through stylistic devices so subtly meaningful as to boggle the imagination. For instance, of her lines – 'Out of this wood, do not desire to go. / Thou shalt remain here, whether thou wilt or no' (III.i.126–7) – he says, 'Her sudden violent lust is all available in the arrangement of the "t-d-g" consonants, the basically monosyllabic diction, the opening trochee, the firm metrical regularity thereafter, and the caesura defined by the identical hard consonant ("d") on both sides' (1990: 97). Even so, Swander's otherwise careful and interesting argument makes the best case yet for a ravishment of Bottom that does not require a wild disregard of the text.

17. In keeping with his argument that Titania's bower is in an offstage fairyland, Homer Swander takes this stage direction, with its 'and the king behind them', to imply that Oberon may have followed the errant couple to the bower, spied upon them *in flagrante delicto*, and now, as they return for a few post-coital pleasantries, trails behind in dejected jealousy (1990: 105). If, on the other hand, Titania's bower is the onstage 'bank where the wild thyme blows', then the mismatched pair

is entering the bower in this scene (Act 4 Scene 1), and a ravishment must be managed in the awkward presence of both Oberon and the audience.

18. J. Dennis Huston shrewdly observes that Titania's tyrannic bent is part of a more pervasive pattern of tyranny in the play, beginning with Egeus and the law but also including the despotism of love itself (Huston 1981: 105–7).

19. Robbe-Grillet claims that the modern novel

> has the great advantage of calling attention to its own artificiality, of pointing to its mask with its finger, instead of hiding behind the appearance of something natural, an essence, an ideological trap. It is artifice itself which appears on the scene in the novel. (1977: 5)

True enough, but only if we include Cervantes and Sterne among modern novelists. In the graphic arts, Roger Poole cites an interesting example of anamorphism – Naum Gabo's sculpture 'Spherical Theme' (1964):

> [It] appears from directly in front of it to be a construction in one circular piece of metal. Only when one moves round it does it appear that there are two curved circles of metal bent and placed back to back. From a position at a ninety degree angle to one's first position, one can in fact look right through the two halves of what appeared at first to be a solid object. At forty-five degrees to one's original position, the ambiguity is perfectly established, as the rhythmic quality of the whole forbids a final decision as to whether or not the construction is in one piece. (Poole 1972: 113)

Within the realistic sphere, the most obvious example is pornography, which places the viewer in the position of a voyeur, seeing without being seen. But insofar as the picture has been staged to catch the gaze of the viewer, it has 'seen' him before he sees it.

20. Theseus would have been better off simply to assert the authorising agencies of nature and God, like the well-known preacher William Whately, author of *A Bride-Bush; or, a direction for married persons* (1619), who admonishes women:

> If ever thou purpose to be a good wife, and to live comfortably, set down this with thyself: mine husband is my superior, my better; he hath authority and rule over me; nature hath given it to him . . . God hath given it to him. (Quoted by Stone 1977: 55–6)

For a good analysis of Theseus' speech, see David Marshall (1982: 551–2).

21. Egeus *is* absent from the last act in Quarto 1. In the Folio, however, he appears and is given the lines assigned in Q1 to Philostrate. As critics have recently noted (Hodgdon 1986; McGuire 1989), whether Egeus is present or absent here can have a crucial effect. His absence implies his refusal to acknowledge Hermia's wedding and his alienation from Athenian society, whereas his presence speaking Philostrate's lines implies his full acceptance of the marriage. His absence makes far better sense: in part because the radical reversal of attitude required by the Folio seems so implausible – for instance, an Egeus shedding 'merry tears' while watching a rehearsal of *Pyramus and Thisbe* taxes credulity (v.i.69) – and in part because it parallels the earlier absence of the mother and, following logically upon the dismissal of the law, sweeps the stage clear of the harsher aspects of patriarchy.

22. Not, of course, that Theseus is wiping patriarchy off the cultural slate, only its most repressive features as represented by the tyranny of the law. After all, Athens and Elizabethan England *were* patriarchal, and although Shakespeare could movingly represent injustices brought about by and within the system, it is questionable whether he could entertain the idea of the kind of just social order that has only become politically imaginable in the late twentieth century.

23. Ann Jennalie Cook, on the other hand, finds sufficient reason for Theseus' change of mind about the law in the awakened Demetrius' acknowledgement of his former betrothal to Helena, in Theseus' realisation that he, who knew of the betrothal, should have done something about it earlier, and in Theseus' acquiescence to the *fait accompli* of an unchaperoned night in the wood together (Cook 1991: 203–4).

CHAPTER 4 (pp. 72–95)

1. As a matter of fact, in one of his sixteenth-century manifestations, Puck *was* averse to dust, more so at any rate than the lax housewives and maids whom he befriended by doing their work for them. This good-natured Puck appeared in a more devilish version, usually put about by Puritans like William Warner (*Albion's England*, 1602), as a hobgoblin who pulled maids out of their beds at night, put a spell on them, and made them do the work for which he later took credit (Briggs 1959: 72–3).

2. For a perceptive reading of the play as a rite of passage, see Florence Falk (1980); also Marjorie Garber (1980, 1981); and, for a view of the play as part of a generic Shakespearian stress on rites of passage in the festive comedies, Edward Berry (1984).

3. Not that the changeling boy has not been brought on stage in certain productions, only that there is no textual justification for doing so. He first appeared in a New York production in 1853 (Sprague and Trewin 1970: Chapter 3). In Elija Moshinsky's BBC television production of 1981, for instance, the boy was obtrusively present (Warren 1983: 69).

4. Not only does the moon shine graciously on Athens and the woods but words about the moon glimmer far more frequently in *A Midsummer Night's Dream* than in any other Shakespearian play: 'moon' thirty-one times, 'moonlight' six, 'moonshine' eight, 'moonbeams' one. For an excellent discussion of moonshine as a dissolvent of cultural order, an intensifier of love's illusions and ultimately a beneficent therapeutic, see Harold E. Toliver (1971: 82–93).

5. In fact, Actaeon's experience, as Ovid narrates it, might well have conspired with that of Apuleius to fashion bully Bottom's (Barkan 1980):

> . . . [Diana] makes no further threats, but by and by doth spread
> A payre of lively olde Harts hornes upon his sprinckled head.
> She sharpes his eares, she makes his necke both slender, long and
>   lanke.
> She turnes his fingers into feete, his armes to spindle shanke.
> She wrappes him in a hairie hyde beset with speckled spottes,
> And planteth in him fearefulnesse.
>
> (*Metamorphoses*, Book iii, 229–34)

Actaeon's pathetic fearefulnesse is justified when his own hounds pursue and destroy him. Bottom's friends, on the other hand, do not pursue their suddenly transformed leader but flee from him. Yet although this would produce at least a trace of Actaeon's fear in lesser men ('Why do they run away? This is knavery of them to make me afeard' (iii.i.107–8)), Bottom responds heroically:

> I see their knavery. This is to make an ass of me, to fright me, if
> they could. But I will not stir from this place, do what they can. I
> will walk up and down here, and I will sing, that they shall hear I
> am not afraid. (iii.i.115–19)

Later of course, in the presence of the fairy queen and her retinue, his apprehensions are translated into comic insouciance and a passion for a bottle of hay. And later yet the chorusing of Theseus' hounds, which echoes that of Actaeon's hounds in Ovid, precedes his awakening.

6. I should add parenthetically that the bent bow is not the only interpretation possible. Golding's Ovid (Rouse, 1966) repeatedly refers to the crescent moon as 'horned', an image not calculated to strike joy in an about-to-be married man's heart, particularly one who is marrying an Amazon of unknown propensities.

7. As Sidney Homan says, 'Far from being antithetical to Athens, the forest at times seems to be more a projection of the mortals' collective unconsciousness' (1969: 75).

8. Beside the romanticising of schizophrenia by Deleuze and Guattari, it is worth placing, as Sherry Turkle does (1978: 155), the words of an unidentified French psychiatrist:

> I know that it passes for humanism, but I find it dehumanizing. I know how psychotics are, I worked, lived among them. They are sad, isolated, resigned, overwhelmed by boredom . . . for one Artaud, how many patients stay in the hospital for all of their lives and never get up out of a chair?

And for that matter, who would exchange places with Artaud, whose whole life was an articulate primal scream?

9. Perhaps the more relevant saying being literalised here is the one uttered in Shakespeare's time, sometimes about Maying, sometimes about Valentine's Day, that a maid would marry the first bachelor she met (A. R. Wright 1938, vol. 2: 137). As regards the potency of flower juices on the eyes:

> Percy (*Reliques* iii, b.2) quotes a receipt by the celebrated astrologer, Dr. Dee, for 'an unguent to anoynt under the eyelids, and upon the eyelids eveninge and morninge, but especially when you call', that is, upon the fairies. It consisted of a decoction of various flower. (Dyer 1883: 216).

10. The role of Orphic harmonies in Shakespeare's early work and their relation to poetic language is learnedly discussed by Keir Elam (1984: 140–8); see also Elizabeth Sewell (1960), who argues that *A Midsummer Night's Dream* exhibits the character of mythological thought and testifies to the Orphic power of poetry in the natural world.

Oberon's speech may also hint at an allegorised parody of astrological influence passing from the heavens through flowers into the liver of the impassioned Lysander, as though Cupid's arrow were brought in to serve as a mythological connection between the stars and the potent flower, a connection that was omitted in the alchemy of the day:

> Celestial flower is the name given to a meteorite or a shooting-star by the alchemists, and the flower was, for them, symbolic of the work of the sun. The significance would be adapted according to the color of the flower. So, for example, orange or yellow-colored flowers represent a reinforcement of the basic sun-symbolism; red flowers [presumably including one 'now purple with love's wound'] emphasize the relationship with animal life, blood, and passion.

This is from J. E. Cirlot's *Dictionary of Symbols* (1962: 110); he cites his source as Gino Testi, *Dizionaria di Alchimia e di Chimica antiquaria* (Rome, 1950). The identification of red flowers with 'animal life, blood, and passion' in humans may be less fantastic than it seems (provided it seems enormously fantastic), if we note that in Paracelsian alchemy the colours (or the configuration) of a herb's flowers can reveal its affinity with a certain organ (or star or disease) (Pagel 1982: 148–9). Paracelsus also held that although the stars had no power over the wise physician or philosopher, or in this case an 'imperial vot'ress' – '[the stars] must follow him, not he them' – they could control 'the man who is still animal', as Lysander and Demetrius would appear to be.

11. The revelation of the 'lie' in Lysander's name is like the revelation of the secret names archaic peoples refuse to reveal to outsiders – the key to their true identities. Instead of a different name, however, Lysander's 'secret' name is merely suppressed within his public one, a visible but unseen syllable, a verbal analogue to Holbein's anamorphic skull. In a sense, what happens to Lysander's name happens to all of the lovers: partially hidden aspects of their characters become visible in the wood – visible to others and to themselves as well, however confusedly – and become hidden again when they awaken, though presumably not *as* hidden as before.

12. The ancestor of all these is Lykaon, whose story is told by Ovid in the *Metamorphoses* (Rouse, 1966, I: 233–85). Briefly, insulted by Lykaon, Zeus not only turned him into a wolf but, because Lykaon typified human sin and arrogance, determined to destroy all mankind for good measure and so flooded the earth.

13. In France in Shakespeare's time a veritable epidemic of fear spread about men being turned into wolves. In 1580 Jean Bodin was inspired to write a treatise on lycanthropy in which he attributed the transformations to Satan, presumably also with the permission of God, although the authors of the *Malleus Maleficarum* and the Church generally held that only the appearance of a transformation occurred (Kramer and Sprenger 1970: 122–24). The spiritual upheavals of the Reformation and Counter-Reformation, as Michael Cheilik observes, might well have led to 'such mass counter-Christian psychoses as witchcraft and lycanthropy' (Cheilik 1988: 276).

14. 'A sanctuary for animals' only in the most ironic sense. Deer might be protected from poachers – usually the poor who actually needed the meat – but what they were saved for was the kind of royal 'hunt' in which Elizabeth, an indefatigable rider, followed as the deer were hauled down by packs of hounds chasing them in relays or waited with her ladies and fired her crossbow into herds driven or lured past their 'stand' (Strutt 1968: 9). Then they could all ride back to London and enjoy bear-baiting, another passion of hers.

15. In his chapter on 'The forest, the wild, and the sacred' (*New Perspectives on the Shakespearean World*, 1985: 11–39) Marienstras brilliantly connects these matters to constitutional debates about the king's prerogatives and powers.

16. Of course there is another animal at large in the wood, one not terribly wild yet capable of roars so lion-like that they would make the duke cry, 'Let him roar again, let him roar again'. But when the royal party enters the wood Bottom lies asleep, perhaps snorting a little as donkeys will, but not roaring. Besides, by this time Bottom is no longer adorned with his ass's head, Puck having removed it about the time the duke entered the forest (iv.i.82). This coincidence might have appealed to the aristocratic hunters at the theatre, those who knew for instance that once a hart had been killed it was the envied prerogative of the prince to slit its throat and cut off its head. Moreover, the 'doucets' or testicles of the animal were cut off and presented to the prince on a handkerchief (Marienstras 1985: 33). What happens to Bottom is not metaphorically so distant. He suffers both of these cuttings off, as it were, losing both ass's head and ass's virility, when he is restored to his normal state. A proper punishment for a beast beloved by a queen and, if not bedded by her, at least slept with by her, coming dangerously near to putting horns on the head of Oberon/ Theseus also and justifying the duke's metaphorical revenge.

Actually, however, instead of cropping Bottom's head and other incidentals, Theseus might have taken a more appropriate revenge by trimming his bottom. More appropriate, that is, in reference to the myth about Theseus aiding Pirithous in his attempt to steal Persephone from Hades. When the two warriors demanded the maid, Hades politely asked them to be seated, and they did so, only to discover that the chairs they sat on were the Chairs of Forgetfulness, which, for reasons no one can remember, at once became part of their bodies. Stuck in this unseemly manner, the heroes remained in Tartarus for four years, until Hercules came to their rescue. Unfortunately even Hercules could not detach Pirithous, and though he did wrench Theseus from his chair some of his flesh tore away in the process, which is why, according to legend, the buttocks of Theseus' descendants were notoriously thin-skinned. In light of this mythical incident, so inexplicably neglected by critics, it would seem entirely fitting for Theseus to exact reparations where Bottom has too much and he himself too little. (An additional virtue of this interpretation is the enhanced meaning it would impart to Bottom's remark about calling his dream ' "Bottom's Dream", because it hath no bottom'.)

17.   Another interpretation of Puck's sweeping would refer it to carnival and spring rituals that mark the end of one cycle and the beginning of another, or even as a 'sign of death and of a wedding which is a renewal' (Kott 1987: 59).

18.   For instance, responding to Kott's dark view of the play, Thomas McFarland refers to it as 'very possibly the happiest work of literature ever conceived' (1972: 90). Yet the harmonious ending has a few slight discordances. For instance, the silence of Hermia and Helena during the performance of *Pyramus and Thisbe* can be troubling, especially since it recalls the silence of Hippolyta during the trial of Hermia in the opening scene (Huston 1981: 161). Have the young women been 'silenced' by marriage the way the conquered Amazon may have been, or the way Titania's assertions of independence were silenced by Oberon? It seems unlikely in light of the fact that Titania awoke happily and lovingly enough from her dream, as did Hermia and Helena when they found themselves paired off with the right young men. Hippolyta speaks freely in the final scenes, albeit not often, which would seem to belie the notion that the other brides have been struck dumb by the repressive force of marriage – the marriage that is precisely what they wanted from the beginning. Perhaps they are simply laughing too hard to speak.

Or, to underscore another possible point of friction, perhaps their silence points to a different issue, the suppression not of women but of the lower class. That is, the ladies may remain silent Cordelia-like, because they are unwilling to join the unpleasant aristocratic critique of Quince's company. But *is* the critique unpleasant? Even discounting for late twentieth-century sensitivities, one cannot imagine it reflecting very favourably on the nobles at any time. Still, as Anne Barton observes (1974: 219–20), Theseus' gracious preferment of the artisans' play to begin with suggests that he and the other nobles make fun of the players in a spirit of Horatian amusement rather than Juvenalian spite, and, moreover, in the knowledge that some of their comments cannot be heard and those that can cannot penetrate the armour of naïve vanity in which the players are encased (surely Bottom proves as impervious to the nobles' mockery as he was to Titania's enticements) – in all, a welcome difference from the audience that prompted Holofernes to protest 'This is not generous, not gentle, not humble' at a comparable moment in *Love's Labor's Lost* (v.ii.633). In Chapter 6, however, I will discuss some other points of friction.

19. Of course we do not leave the real world entirely behind during the theatrical performance, any more than a neophyte leaves his or her past entirely behind during the liminal phase of an initiation ritual. But that is what liminality consists of. To the Coleridgian extent that we exercise 'poetic faith', we exchange 'reality' for imagined life in Athens and the woods, but to the Johnsonian extent that we exercise our unpoetic common sense, we remain solidly on our chairs in the theatre in Shoreditch. Our liminality is like that of the mirror-state, inasmuch as our identity is in suspension somewhere between the image with which we identify and our body which it reflects. The question raised by Puck's Epilogue, however, is whether we have had a productively liminal experience here or an idly marginal one, whether, that is, the play has somehow transformed us or merely entertained us for a time.

CHAPTER 5 (pp. 96–116)

1. Someone has surely pointed out how well Derrida's notion of the supplement is exemplified by the creation of Eve (1976: 141–64; 1979), who is an excess added to a sufficiency (an Adam even more than sufficient if he can afford the loss of a rib) but who also, because her presence implies a prior insufficiency, is the replacement of a lack (the 'want' that generated Adam's desire).
2. I add 'embrace' here as a demurrer to Freud's and Lacan's bleak view

of the child's entrance into the symbolic as an act of submission, a surrender of the immediacy of the pleasure principle for the deferrals of the reality principle. Both put too much stress, it seems to me, on what is lost, too little on what is gained; and neither takes adequate account of the pleasure and naturalness with which children actually acquire language (recorded most vividly in that ecstatic moment when Helen Keller realised that everything had a name).

3.   This appears in Chapter VII of the *Phenomenology* (Kojève 1969: 140–1). Hegel's metaphor is misleadingly violent: by 'murder' he merely means that symbolising underscores the mortality of real dogs by lending them the immortality they lack – that is, if dogs lived for ever their bodies would preclude a need for names; we could just point. But to attribute symbolism to the fact that we animals are mortal is rather extreme. Our mere mobility would suffice; dogs are not always visible and close enough to point to. There are disappearances and absences less permanent than death that make symbols useful.

4.   My unduly metaphorical account merely notes the fact that no particular pansy is the referent of the common noun 'pansy' or of any of the other more colourful terms for that class of flower. Hegel's particular dog Fido, say, is not murdered by the concept of 'dog'; he or she is simply lost in the generic pack of all dogs, past and future, who run together in the concept. Individual pansies are similarly lost in being labelled 'pansy', but they are additionally obscured by the anthropomorphising involved in their special namings.

5.   Marriage would best suit Lacan's concept of metaphor, inasmuch as he, unlike Jacobson, disregards resemblance as a basis for metaphor; for him it consists simply in the substitution of one word for another, and since this process is endless, meaning is always deferred. By the same token, since no concatenation of signifiers ever captures the totality of its referent, all discourse is metonymic or synecdochic, moving from part to part in search of the whole. For both theorists, the metonymic mode, based on a '*word to word* connexion', is most obviously syntagmatic; but a successive metaphoric substitution of word for word also takes on a syntagmatic character (1977: 156–7). In this respect, Christian Metz argues (1982: 183–206) that Jacobson unjustifiably conflates metonym and syntagma, when in fact metonymy, like metaphor, is a semantic category (based on the signified or referent), whereas the syntagmatic is a syntactic category (based on position).

6.   I mean the full proper name, not one's given name, of whose commonness Montaigne dismissively says, 'Is it *Peter* or *William*? And

what is that but a word for al mouths? or three or foure dashes of a pen' (Montaigne 1965: I, 316).

7. See also Derrida's critique of Lévi-Strauss in *Of Grammatology* (1976: 161–78). According to Derrida, Lévi-Strauss was deluded by the notion that their 'real' names revealed something more fundamental about the individual Nambikwara. These names were no more 'proper' or self-identifying than the names the European outsiders had given them; each was merely part of a different code. Anne Barton gives this dispute over the status of proper names an historical and literary context in *The Names of Comedy* (1990), identifying Lévi-Strauss' notions with Plato's Cratylus and Derrida's with Hermogenes.

8. It is not entirely clear just how metaphoric this notion of embodiment is or just where it takes place. Aristotle held that the action of the imagination, or *phantasia*, is a physical one, and that its images, *phantasmata*, are corporeal, not mental.

> Aristotle holds, that is, that there can be no knowing, no 'nousing', of universals, without particular physical events in the body. This is the main point made by Pomponazzi in 1516, in insisting that intellect cannot for Aristotle exist 'without' images, and hence cannot exist 'without body'. (Randall 1960: 95)

Even Bacon, wishing to disparage words, gives them a certain imagistic body: 'Words are but the images of matter: and except they have life of reason and invention, to fall in love with them is all one as to fall in love with a picture' (Bacon 1960: 30). And Lacan says,

> Speech is in fact a gift of language, and language is not immaterial. It is a subtle body, but body it is. Words are trapped in all the corporeal images that captivate the subject; they may make the hysteric 'pregnant', be identified with the object of *penis-neid*, represent the flood of urine of urethral ambition, or the retained faeces of avaricious *jouissance*. (Lacan 1977: 87)

9. Although the substitution of effect for cause is metonymic, this particular 'cause' is selected from metaphoric paradigms: instead of testy fairies the folk might have substituted any number of causes – malefic witches and devils, late eclipses in the sun and moon, sinful humans, retributive gods. As a result, the mechanism of causation and explanation is sceptically foregrounded, and the speech erases its speaker.

Titania's 'therefore's remind me of some remarks made by William Empson in 'argufying' for a poetry that employs not merely images but muscular images, the sort that can do their share of work in the cause of argument, a cause Empson was almost always engaged in himself:

> Argufying in poetry is not only mental; it also feels muscular. Saying 'therefore' is like giving the reader a bang on the nose; and though it may be said that 'intellectualized' poetry feels stale and unreal, a bang on the nose does not feel stale and unreal; it is just as fresh the twentieth time as it was the first; that is, if you are granted enough leisure for recovery. The word 'therefore' is no more stale than the word 'dawn', and has just as much imagery about it. (1987: 170)

Titania's 'therefore's give the audience several bangs on the nose – enough, at any rate, to make everyone sit up and take note of the fact that her argufying is as specious as her existence is dubious.

10.   As Louis Montrose has noted, the concluding three lines of Titania's speech invite comparison to Theseus' lines at i.ii.46–51 about Egeus as father–author of Hermia (Montrose 1983: 42). Both speeches deconstruct the concept of a natural origin. Patriarchy seeks to validate its property rights by reference to the genetic act, but in fact of course they derive from phallocratic Athenian culture. Had Hermia really been stamped by nature with her father's seal of authority she would not be rebelling, any more than a gosling rebels against the imprinting instinct that seals it to its mother. Hermia's rebellion stamps her as 'unnatural' in her father's eyes, but it is patriarchy itself, as Theseus' speech unwittingly reveals, that is unnatural.

11.   Thus Shakespeare playfully compresses into Puck, in the form of his absent presence, the conflicting beliefs of Elizabethans about his existence. Shakespeare probably agreed with the sceptical Reginald Scot (1584) in assigning Robin Goodfellow to the realm of family fictions, but he grew up among many who must have believed in those fictions. He may even have known that in 1595, perhaps while he was writing his play, a London 'cunning woman' named Judith Phillips 'was whipped through the City . . . after being convicted of extracting large sums of money from gullible clients prepared to pay for the privilege of meeting the Queen of the Fairies' (Thomas 1971: 613). (For a perceptive discussion of the influence of Scot's *Discoverie of Witchcraft* on *A Midsummer Night's Dream*, especially with respect to

the credulities of the imagination, see Barbara A. Mowat (1989: 344–6)). That Puck's role as psychological *pharmakos* was well enough understood by more sophisticated Elizabethans is evident from a passage in a book called the *Apothegms of King James* (1658) cited by Brand (1849: 512):

> Sir Fulk Greenvil had much and private accesse to Queen Elizabeth, which he used honourably, and did many men good. Yet he would say merrily of himself that he was like Robin Goodfellow, for when the maides spilt the milk-pannes, or kep any racket, they would lay it upon Robin; so what tales the ladies about the queen told her, or other bad offices that they did, they would put it upon him.

12. David Marshall points out (1982: 564) that A. W. von Schlegel spoke in his lectures of 'the droll wonder of the transmutation of Bottom' as being 'merely the translation of a metaphor in its literal sense' (Furness 1963: 323). Marshall himself (1982) is typically insightful about disfigurations in the play, as is Barbara Freedman in her chapter on 'Dis/Figuring Power' (1991).

13. Of course Kafka's story is grounded in metaphoric doubleness, and hence it allows us to see through the insect to, not the body, but the thoughts and feelings of the human Gregor. However, if the narrator were not present to tell us what happened, and if Gregor were not allowed to reflect on the curiosity of his transformation, we would simply be reading about the adventures of a remarkably large insect trapped in a human environment, instead of a human trapped in an insect body. In fact this is how Gregor's sister comes increasingly to view him: 'I won't pronounce the name of my brother in front of this monster, and so all I say is: we have to try to get rid of it' (1972: 51).

I should add that the odd conjunctions of malaphor merely take to comic extreme a tendency already present in metaphor, as Paul Ricoeur emphasises in saying that in metaphor

> 'remoteness' is preserved within 'proximity'. To see *the like* is to see the same in spite of, and through, the different. This tension between sameness and difference characterizes the logical structure of likeness. Imagination, accordingly, is this *ability* to produce new kinds by assimilation and to produce them not *above* the differences, as in the concept, but in spite of and through the differences. (Ricoeur 170)

14. The relation of complete metamorphosis to metaphor is analogous to that of a generic concept to metaphor in Paul Ricoeur's formulations. That is, Ricoeur regards a concept like 'dog' as an erasure of individual differences in favour of generic identity: this black poodle and that white Samoyed turn abstractly and identically grey as 'dog'. In the metaphoric process, however, 'the movement toward the genus is arrested by the resistance of the difference, as it were, intercepted by the figure of rhetoric' (Ricoeur 147). Thus in the creation of metaphor the imagination produces new notions 'not *above* the differences, as in the concept, but in spite of and through the differences' (146). Metaphor is somewhat malaphoric then, poised between and embracing individual difference and generic identity.

15. Puck tells Oberon that he has simply placed 'an ass's nole' on Bottom's head (iii.ii.17), but Bottom's pleasure in being scratched by Cobweb and Mustardseed (iv.i.22–3) would authorise a marvailes hairiness about the shoulders and back as well as about the face.

16. It is true too, as Rosemond Tuve pointed out, that in many Renaissance metaphors the signifier and signified are not as discrete as the rhetorical definitions imply. When a neoplatonist refers to God as 'light', it is sometimes hard to tell if this is a metaphor or a proposition. 'Various ways of conceiving of reality as formal coincide in thinking that the rose *is* Transient Loveliness as really as it is a flower of a certain shape or color' (Tuve 224n). Her attempt to distinguish Renaissance uses of metaphor from those of romantics and moderns suggests what is too often forgotten in theorisings about 'the' nature or function of metaphor, that metaphor, like language, can function in a great many ways, ranging from rhetorical ornamentation to cognitive insight.

17. As William C. Carroll observes in his excellent analysis of the play from the standpoint of metamorphosis, '[Bottom's] transformation is far from total. Here, as elsewhere in the play, Shakespeare reminds us of the double nature of metamorphosis, for Bottom is and is not an ass, his identity never clearer than when it has been lost in another shape' (1985: 149–50).

18. Keying on a later passage in I Corinthians (12: 14–15), Annabel Patterson gives Bottom's speech a political turn (1989: 68–9). His synaesthetic confusions imply that the usually suppressed aspects of the body (as a metaphor for the suppressed members of society) are to be seen as respected parts of a unified body (a utopian community).

19. Aristotle tends to collapse metonymy and its subdivision synecdoche into metaphor, so that, for instance, his first two kinds of metaphor are actually synecdoches (*Poetics*, 1986: 1457b). In 1599 John Hoskins

wrote disdainfully of metonymy and synecdoche, both being in his view prosaic and 'easy' (Hoskins 1935). Even Jacobson, although making metonymy one of the poles of discourse, regards it as more likely to be found in realistic novels than in poems, as though poetic metaphor descended to prose under the corruptive influence of metonymy (Jacobson 1960: 375).

CHAPTER 6 (pp. 117–145)

1. The walls surrounding the city, representing the constraints and protections of civilised life, are analogous to the wall inside the city that divides the two families, standing for the constraints and protections of parental authority. Thus the city gate that opens to the wild world of nature outside is analogous to the cranny and is an appropriate point of egress for the lovers, whose wild nature seeks escape from all such walls. These parallels render the lovers' experience a kind of synecdoche for the human plight, caught as we always are between walls of restraint and crannies of desire.

2. Actually, as a sign, Ninus' tomb is as misleading as Thisbe's mantle, since it seems to memorialise a dead father of Babylon, when in fact, or rather legend, Ninus founded Ninevah and was done in by his wife Semiramis before she raised the walls of Babylon, where it is unlikely that her husband would be buried.

3. The divergent opinions of Hippolyta and Theseus at this point forecast the brief dispute between Hamlet and Gertrude in Gertrude's closet (*Hamlet* III.iv.120–62). At issue in each case is the reality of the supernatural. Gertrude accuses Hamlet's heat-oppressed brain of having generated the Ghost he claims to have seen: 'This bodiless creation ecstasy / Is very cunning in' (144–5). Were Theseus there, he would no doubt agree with Gertrude, noting that the ecstatic Hamlet is like the wild-eyed poet whose 'imagination bodies forth / The forms of things unknown' and 'gives to airy nothing / A local habitation and a name', and that both are like a quartet of bemused lovers who once tried to foist 'antic fables' and 'fairy toys' upon him. To Gertrude's charge of ecstasy, however, Hamlet replies by citing the coherence of the 'matter':

> Ecstasy!
> My pulse, as yours, doth temperately keep time,
> And makes as healthful music. It is not madness
> That I have utter'd. Bring me to the test,

> And I the matter will reword, which madness
> Would gambol from.

And surely if Hippolyta were there, she would join in his defence. Their argument is not based on a correspondence theory of truth, since there is no way to compare the rewording of the matter to the fairy and ghostly matter itself, immaterial as it is. As Hamlet puts it, the test of the tale is in the telling itself. Just what it is about Hamlet's rewording of the matter that would confirm his sanity and the presence of the Ghost is unclear – presumably an internal consistency and plausibility so compelling as to belie madness – but it is clear that the burden of knowledge has shifted, as it has in western epistemology in general, from the known object to the knowing subject, or rather from a self-effacing 'objective' knower to one who knows that he knows and whose knowledge will be confirmed not by an object of knowledge but by its expression in language. Somewhat similarly, the lovers' stories of the night persuade Hippolyta because they correspond not to the night but to one another.

4. For a thorough exploration of imagination and lack of imagination in *Pyramus and Thisbe* and *A Midsummer Night's Dream*, see Robert W. Dent's classic article (1964).

5. As David Marshall says, 'But the theater must end by teaching us how to see – not only how to see through – the invisible wall that creates its architecture' (1982: 565). Marshall himself has learned this theatrical lesson well; he consistently not only sees through but also sees *A Midsummer Night's Dream* with great clarity.

6. In a witty and insightful article, Thomas Clayton argues that Snout does not represent the cranny with his fingers or hands but simply with his spread legs. In his view, Bottom's 'let him hold his fingers thus' is meant to show how Snout should represent himself as Wall – by joining index finger to thumb and allowing the remaining three fingers to form an upright 'W' (T. Clayton 1974: 111). This is certainly possible, though rather superfluous in view of Snout's announcement 'That I, one Snout by name, present a wall' (not that superfluity matters in this production). A more serious criticism of doing it this way, instead of by some kind of circle, is that it causes Pyramus' ostentatious repetition of 'O' in his following speech to become pointless and forecloses on other meanings that no indecent interpreter of Shakespeare would want to lose.

7. It is not clear whether Flute means 'paramour' to be male or female. The appropriateness of applying it to Bottom, the future paramour of Titania, is obvious. On the other hand, in three of the four other

appearances of the word in Shakespeare the reference is to women. For that matter, even if Flute refers to Bottom, the pun on 'nought' in his phrase may be female, the 'thing' male, and both 'naught[y]'.

8. The previous quote from Wilden is also taken from Willbern's article (1980: 250). My comments on *Pyramus and Thisbe* and Wall are a belated supplement to Willbern's persuasive argument, illustrated from throughout the canon, that Shakespeare thinks of his art as a kind of creation *ex nihilo*, in which, however, the theological sense of the term suffers a fall into the bawdily/bodily context of sexual generation. In respect of the present discussion, see especially his remarks about the birth and baptism implicit in Theseus' speech on poetic creation (1980: 249) and about the phallic, vaginal and symbolic implications of the Prologue's opening speech in *Henry V* (1980: 255–6).

9. To be sure, Snout's later declaration, 'Thus have I, Wall, my part discharged so', suggests also a seminal emission of the sort Pistol is famous for in *2 Henry IV*, as when Falstaff asks Pistol to 'discharge' the hostess' bill and Pistol replies, 'I will discharge upon her, Sir John, with two bullets', only to have Falstaff say, 'She is pistol-proof, sir; you shall hardly offend her' (ii.iv.120 ff.). In Wall's case, however, stones that have been 'knit up' are incapable of discharging, so that the stress falls not on the potent penis but on the parted bottom. See note 19 below.

10. In medieval philosophy, the term *flatus vocis* usually referred to universals, but Reformation iconoclasts also took aim at words as images. For instance, in his excellent survey of verbal scepticism, Keir Elam says that the Puritan theologian William Perkins 'assails the lexical idol' in part because 'of its merely vocal constitution (all speech is reduced to *flatus vocis*): "All words made and uttered by men, are in their owne nature but sounds framed by the tongue, of the breath that commeth from the lungs"' (Elam 1984: 168).

11. That Shakespeare was conscious of the 'hole' in the word 'whole' when he constructed Wall is evident from Hermia's earlier denial that Lysander could have left her voluntarily:

> I'll believe as soon
> This whole earth may be bored; and that the moon
> May through the centre creep
>
> (iii.ii.52–4)

which is not a bad commentary on the play, the earth taking on itself the role of Wall here, a whole with a hole in it through which love's moon madnesses may pass.

12. The playing of a role is itself a version of the partitioning of self that characterises the mirror-state. That is, the child experiences its body as an external object before experiencing it as its own, and an actor must experience his body similarly, as a malleable object in the mirror of the character he will play. Unfortunately Peter Quince's actors never succeed in closing the part, or in breaching the partition, between themselves and their roles.

13. The relation of performance to script in *A Midsummer Night's Dream* is analogous to that between what John Crowe Ransom called 'texture' and 'structure' in arguing, appropriately enough in the present context, for a poetry that modified romantic idealism and logical coherence by forcing them to encounter the intractability of 'the world's body'. Ransom's theory appears in various places, but perhaps most clearly in 'Criticism as Pure Speculation' in *The Intent of the Critic*, ed. Donald A. Stauffer (Princeton: Princeton University Press, 1941). His notion of a subversive, even 'irrelevant' texture – for that matter, the general new critical stress on irony and Murray Krieger's on literature's self-denying illusions – anticipates the kind of postmodern interest in anti-totalising impulses to be found, for instance, in Bakhtin's carnival and dialogism and Jean-François Lyotard's 'little stories'. See Krieger's 'The Literary, the Textual, the Social' and the essays it introduces in *The Aims of Representation* (1987).

14. Richard Southern says, 'no one has yet been able to put forward an explanation of why the word "interlude" came to be used to name these plays in England' (126). He notes that interludes may have been comic scenes or episodes within longer more serious dramas, or they may have been short plays performed between courses at banquets. But that they were definitely ludic and somehow in-between is the inescapable impression given by the word itself.

15. It might be argued that Shakespeare is hypocritical in mocking the ambitious ineptitudes of the workmen when his own company is engaged in the same sort of thing. But mockery is contagious stuff, and simply by introducing theatrical ineptitude in *Pyramus and Thisbe* Shakespeare puts *A Midsummer Night's Dream* at risk. You could argue that there is more hypocrisy in carefully excluding from the play anything that might be used against it, especially in a play so vulnerable to the Samuel Pepyses in the audience anyhow. On the other hand, you could take the 'lightning rod' view and regard *Pyramus and Thisbe* as a device to deflect criticism away from *A Midsummer Night's Dream* and even to enhance it by contrast.

16. Not that the workmen poke fun at anyone deliberately: no theatrical troupe could be more considerate of the sensibilities of its audience than they. Nor could any monarch be more conscious than Theseus of the courtesy owed those who in 'simpleness and duty' offer their service (v.i.83). In the speech that follows – 'The kindlier we, to give them thanks for nothing' (v.i.89–106) – Theseus might be describing the behaviour of Elizabeth when greeted while on progresses. In 1578 at Norwich, for instance, a schoolmaster faltered at his task of greeting her with a Latin speech. 'Be not afraid', she said graciously and, when he had done, declared, 'It is the best that ever I heard' (Brooks 1979: lxvii). It takes a good sense of balance to stay on the gracious side of condescension, but Elizabeth and Theseus manage it about as well as could be expected; and if they slip a little, still well-intended condescension is preferable to the sort of indifference James I sometimes exhibited (Griffin 1951: 150). See in this connection note 18, Chapter 4 above.

17. At the same time, Quince's interlude pokes fun at the less noble and fastidious – weavers, tinkers, bellows-menders and the like – who crowded into the popular theatres to see plays like *The Lamentable Tragedy, Mixed Full of Pleasant Mirth, Containing the Life of Cambises, King of Persia* (Robinson 1964: 193–4).

18. The actual appearance of Thisbe's dead love is not easily established. On the one hand, it would be perfectly Bottom-like to rearrange nature in the manner described, the ambitious player painting at least an inch thick to acquire what he takes to be the proper colouring for Pyramus. On the other hand, however, it would be perfectly Flute-like to rearrange Thisbe's lines thus in the nervous heat of performance. On still another hand (there is no limit to metonymy), it would be perfectly Quince-like to write Thisbe's lines in the first place just as they are spoken.

19. The Chamberlain's Men create an interlude inasmuch as any play or literary work constitutes an imaginative pause or gap, indeed one might say an 'O', in workaday life. On the other hand, the play also constitutes an exciting presence that 'sticks out' of the drabness of ordinary life. Putting the two together, we have an experience that oscillates optically in and out like the psychologists' ambiguous box.

20. I do Hamlet's speech a disservice here, but Shakespeare repeatedly puns on 'fault' as flaw or crack and hence, as Rubinstein notes (1984: 98), as 'the arse and its flatus'. More decorously, in respect of scripts and performances, one might argue that the Ghost's script for revenge, entrusted to a prince who 'can say nothing' (II.ii.569), let alone do anything, shrinks to an unperformed 'O': the Ghost, no less

than Hamlet and the chameleon, has been made to 'eat the air, promise-crammed' (III.ii.92–3). See Herbert A. Ellis on the use of 'fault' in *Love's Labour's Lost* (1973: 128–30) and William H. Matchett (1979: 187) on Gloucester's 'Do you smell a fault?' at the opening of *King Lear*. However perfect Hamlet's anonymous paragon may seem, his 'particular fault' betrays our 'knowledge' of him, as though implying the unavoidable flaw in the structure of representation – the flaw that Jacques Derrida refers to as the lack of a centre, a kind of floating hole in the wall, as it were (Derrida 1978). Hence our recognitions are misrecognitions, our readings misreadings (as Paul de Man maintains). J. Hillis Miller expands on de Man's notion of misreading by saying, 'To live is to read, or to commit again and again the failure to read which is the human lot' (J. H. Miller 1987: 59). As a dramatist, Shakespeare substitutes 'perform' for read and comes out in pretty much the same place, the place where we all find ourselves, in a bit of a hole.

21. I take comfort from the fact that Thomas Clayton, F. W. Clayton, Wolfgang Franke, Frankie Rubinstein and Jan Lawson Hinely testify to the presence of bawdy meanings which in my innocence I should otherwise never have suspected.

22. I should add that Theseus' phrase 'very notably discharg'd' may have other implications. '*Not*able', for instance, may refer to 'nut' ('testicle'), which, as a consequence of 'knitting', Wall has figuratively 'not' got. Moreover, 'notable' also connotes 'note', hence the penis (a 'prick' was a musical note), which would be the logical organ of discharge here, were it not for the knitting and the stress on 'O'-shaped holes. These testicular and phallic meanings make it clear that we have here a displaced discharge, from penis to anus, from reproductive vitality to scatalogical and theatrical vacuity. See Rubinstein 1984: 171–2.

23. For a review of variations on this essentially reconciliatory view of carnival, featuring the views of Arnold Van Gennep, Emile Durkheim, C. L. Barber, Roger Callois and Victor Turner, see Michael D. Bristol (1985: esp. 26–39), who concludes with a valuable caveat:

> However, all these terms must now be read as historical categories. Carnival in the early modern period is not simply festivity in general, though all festivity is very likely to have a 'conservative' social function. In considering a particular historical instance of festivity, however, it is necessary to ask who is conserving what and at whose expense. The forms of festive life

are always available for appropriation to particular social and political purposes. In early modern Europe such appropriation is by no means exclusively confined to the dominant culture. (1985: 39)

24. In an insightful discussion of the carnival aspects of *Pyramus and Thisbe*, Michael D. Bristol observes that the workmen's play 'seems to warn equally against the dangers of filial disobedience and of arbitrary parental rigidity' (1985: 177–8) – issues obviously of little concern to the workmen but central to the main plot characters who constitute the workmen's audience. The social, economic and political implications of the performance of *Pyramus and Thisbe* pass, like its sexual *double entendres*, over the heads of its immediate audience, and certainly over the heads of its players. And even if we equate the workmen with children and the aristocrats with parents, the terms 'filial disobedience' and 'parental rigidity' do not translate very readily into something like social subversion and political oppression, given the respectfulness of the workmen and the (on the whole) graciousness of Theseus and Hippolyta. But see Krieger (1987), Leinwand (1986), and Patterson (1989) for a more stringent view.

25. That the duke should contribute to this illusion of success is in keeping with his earlier speech about picking an understanding welcome from the botched greetings made him in the past (v.i.89–105). As mentioned earlier, some of the captious comments of the audience should be, I think, spoken as asides, not meant to be heard by the players, and those that are heard simply do not register. Hence I assume that the players conclude their performance and throw themselves into their Bergomask in a triumphant mood (a hit, a hit, a palpable gross hit!). And I see no reason at all why Bottom should be denied his sixpence a day for life, though some have cruelly said he will be. In fact, in my *Never on Sunday* version of it, the entire company will be called to the palace on the morrow, a little bleary-eyed perhaps after a celebratory evening, and not only amply rewarded by the duke but also warmly and meaningfully complimented on the occasion of their permanent retirement from the theatre.

CHAPTER 7 (pp. 146–158)

1. This is of course the Demetrius whose flower-induced fantasies about Helena remain intact. His love is an illusion that carries over

into reality and hence suggests both the power and fragility of the
imaginary.

2. Going a-Maying and theatre-going seem to have much in common
   for Stubbes, who says of the latter: 'but marke the flocking and
   running to Theaters and curtens, daylie and hourely, night and daye,
   tyme and tyde to see Playes and Enterludes, where such wanton
   gestures, such bawdie speaches: such laughing and fleering: such
   kissing and bussing: such clipping and culling: Suche winkinge and
   glancinge of wanton eyes, and the like is used, as is wonderfull to
   behold. Than these goodly pageants being done, every mate sorts to
   his mate, every one bringes another homeward of their way verye
   freendly, and in their secret conclaues (couertly) they play *the
   Sodomites*, or worse' (Chambers 1923, vol. IV: 223).

3. Griffin and Montrose cite John Nichols, *Progresses and Public
   Processions of Queen Elizabeth*, 3 vols. (1823; repr. New York, 1966),
   118–19.

4. This sanguine prospect is clouded, however, by the fact that the
   community of players into which the fictions dissolve is devoid of
   women. In this regard it accurately reflects androcratic constraints
   within which even the most subversive Elizabethan playwright is
   penned. I should add that exposing the 'constructedness' of a play or
   a society is hardly the revelation it is often taken to be. The question
   is not whether something is constructed (everything is) but how well
   or badly.

5. In classical and medieval philosophy, imagination occupied a position
   midway between the world out there (the ground of all knowledge)
   and reason. It was the means, Aristotle said, by which we could
   experience things in their absence, for images could be called up in
   the theatre of memory long after the sensory stimulus itself had
   faded. Yet things themselves (being) were all important, and the
   business of the mind, according to scholastics, was to seek conformity
   to them (*adaequatio intellectus ad rem*). With the Kantian revolution,
   being ceased to be the divine cause or first principle. Instead,
   imagination, no longer regarded as a mimetic mediary between the
   senses and reason, became the source of sensation and understanding. This Kantian revolution is prefigured in *A Midsummer Night's
   Dream* and summarised by Lysander's remark that 'The will of man
   is by his reason swayed, / And reason says you [Helena] are the
   worthier maid' (II.ii.115–16). Far from recording the truths of nature,
   reason serves merely to rationalise irrational imaginings grounded in
   desire.

6. Of course ever since the Romantics, reason has had a bad press.

Nietzsche, Max Weber, Freud, Heidegger, Adorno, Foucault, Derrida – not to mention artists like Artaud, Beckett and Bataille and events like the Holocaust, Hiroshima and planetary pollution – have put paid to the Enlightenment assumption that the proper exercise of reason would dispel superstition and prejudice and, in the spirit of Condorcet's famous 'Sketch for a Historical Picture of the Progress of the Human Mind', unfold a progressive utopia of science, justice, equality and peace. Instead, reason has been shown to be an agent of domination and exclusion. Rational dialogue has meant that white western straight males have talked with white western straight males and been deaf to the speech of women, homosexuals, children, other races, other cultures, and of course those who cannot speak at all and have only recently begun to receive a hearing – other species and the environment.

7. Michael Serres, *La traduction* (Paris: Minuet, 1974), 265; in Vincent Descombes' *Modern French Philosophy*, tr. L. Scott Fox and J.M. Harding (Cambridge: Cambridge University Press, 1980), 91–2.

References

Agrippa, Henry Cornelius (1974), *The Philosophy of Natural Magic* (Seacaucus, NJ: University Books).

Ansorge, Peter (1970), 'Director in Interview: Peter Brook', *Plays and Players*, 18: 18–19.

Aristotle (1986), *De Anima*, tr. Hugh Lawson-Tancred (London: Penguin Books).

Arnheim, Rudolph (1969), *Visual Thinking* (Berkeley and Los Angeles: University of California Press).

Arnheim, Rudolph (1971), *Entropy and Art: An Essay on Disorder and Order* (Berkeley and Los Angeles: University of California Press).

Artaud, Antonin (1958), *The Theater and its Double*, tr. Mary Caroline Richards (New York: Grove Press Inc.).

Bacon, Francis (1859), *The Works of Francis Bacon*, ed. James Spedding, Robert Leslie Ellis and Douglas Denon Heath, vol. 2 (London: Longman and Co.).

Bacon, Francis (1960), *The Advancement of Learning and New Atlantis* (London: Oxford University Press).

Bakhtin, Mikhail (1984), *Rabelais and His World*, tr. Hélène Iswolsky (Bloomington: University of Indiana Press).

Baltrusaitis, Jurgis (1977), *Anamorphic Art*, tr. W. J. Strachan (New York: Harry N. Abrams, Inc.; originally *Anamorphoses ou magie artificielle des effets merveilleux* (Paris: Olivier Perrin Editeur, 1969).

Barber, C. L. (1959), *Shakespeare's Festive Comedy* (Princeton: Princeton University Press).

Barber, C. L. (1980), 'The Family in Shakespeare's Development: Tragedy and Sacredness', in *Representing Shakespeare*, ed. Murray M. Schwartz and Coppélia Kahn (Baltimore: Johns Hopkins University Press): 188–202.

Barkan, Leonard (1980), 'Diana and Actaeon: The Myth as Synthesis', *English Literary Renaissance*, 10: 317–59.

Barkan, Leonard (1986), *The Gods Made Flesh: Metamorphosis and the Pursuit of Paganism* (New Haven and London: Yale University Press): 251–71.

Barton, Anne (1974), '*A Midsummer Night's Dream*', in *The Riverside Shakespeare*, ed. G. Blakemore Evans (Boston: Houghton Mifflin Company): 217–21.

Barton, Anne (1990), *The Names of Comedy* (Toronto, Buffalo: University of Toronto Press).

Baudrillard, Jean (1975), *The Mirror of Production*, tr. Mark Poster (St Louis: Telos Press).

Bernheimer, Richard (1952), *Wild Man of the Middle Ages: A Study in Art, Sentiment and Demonology* (Cambridge, Mass.: Harvard University Press).

Berry, Edward (1984), *Shakespeare's Comic Rites* (Cambridge: Cambridge University Press).

Bettelheim, Bruno (1975), *The Uses of Enchantment: The Meaning and Importance of Fairy Tales* (New York: Random House).

Bevington, David (1978), ' "But We Are Spirits of Another Sort": The Dark Side of Love and Magic in *A Midsummer Night's Dream*', in *Medieval and Renaissance Studies: Proceedings of the Southeastern Institute of Medieval and Renaissance Studies* (summer 1975), ed. Siegfried Wenzel (Chapel Hill, NC: University of North Carolina Press): 80–92.

Bevington, David (ed.) (1980), *A Midsummer Night's Dream*, in *The Complete Works of Shakespeare*, 3rd edition (Glenview, Ill.: Scott, Foresman).

Blanchot, Maurice (1981), *The Gaze of Orpheus* (Rhinebeck, NY: Station Hill Press).

Bloch, R. Howard (1989), 'Medieval Misogyny', in *Misogyny, Misandry, and Misanthropy*, ed. R. Howard Bloch and Frances Ferguson (Berkeley and Los Angeles: University of California Press).

Boswell, John (1988), *The Kindness of Strangers: The Abandonment of Children in Western Europe from Late Antiquity to the Renaissance* (New York: Pantheon Books).

Bowie, Malcolm (1979), 'Jacques Lacan', in *Structuralism and Since: From Lévi-Strauss to Derrida*, ed. John Sturrock (Oxford: Oxford University Press): 116–53.

Bradshaw, Graham (1987), *Shakespeare's Scepticism* (Hemel Hempstead: Harvester Wheatsheaf): 39–47, 66–72.

Brand, John (1849), *Observations on the Popular Antiquities of Great Britain*, vol. 2 (London: Henry G. Bohn).

Briggs, Katherine M. (1959), *The Anatomy of Puck* (London: Routledge & Kegan Paul).

Briggs, Katherine M. (1967), *The Fairies in Tradition and Literature* (Chicago: University of Chicago Press).

Briggs, Katherine M. (1976), *The Dictionary of Fairies* (London: Allen Lane).

Bristol, Michael D. (1985), *Carnival and Theater* (New York and London: Methuen).

Brooks, Harold F. (1979), 'Introduction' to the New Arden *A Midsummer Night's Dream* (London: Methuen).

Brown, James Neill (1980), 'A Calendar, A Calendar! Look in the Almanac!' *Notes and Queries*, 225 (n.s. 27): 162–5.

Brown, John Russell (1971), 'Free Shakespeare', *Shakespeare Survey*, 24, ed. Kenneth Muir (Cambridge: Cambridge University Press): 127–35.

Brown, Norman O. (1959), *Life against Death* (New York: Vintage Books).

Bryant, J. A., Jr. (1964), 'The Importance of *A Midsummer Night's Dream*', *Ball State Teachers College Forum*, 5: 3–9.

Bullough, Geoffrey (ed.) (1957), *Narrative and Dramatic Sources of Shakespeare*, vol. I: Early Comedies, Poems, *Romeo and Juliet* (London: Routledge & Kegan Paul; New York: Columbia University Press).

Calderwood, James L. (1965), '*A Midsummer Night's Dream*: The Illusion of Drama', *Modern Language Quarterly*, 26: 506–22.

Calderwood, James L. (1971), *Shakespearean Metadrama* (Minneapolis: University of Minnesota Press): 120–48.

Calderwood, James L. (1987), *Shakespeare and the Denial of Death* (Amherst: University of Massachusetts Press): 64–7.

Carroll, D. Allen and Gary Jay Williams (1986), *A Midsummer Night's Dream: An Annotated Bibliography* (New York and London: Garland Publishing Inc.).

Carroll, William C. (1985), *The Metamorphoses of Shakespearean Comedy* (Princeton: Princeton University Press): 141–77.

Carson, Anne (1986), *Eros the Bittersweet* (Princeton: Princeton University Press).

Carter, John Marshall (1988), 'Fairies', in *Mythical and Fabulous Creatures*, ed. Malcolm South (New York: Peter Bedrick Books): 325–48.

Chambers, E. K. (1923), *The Elizabethan Stage*, 4 vols. (Oxford: Clarendon Press).

Champion, Larry S. (1970), *The Evolution of Shakespeare's Comedy* (Cambridge: Harvard University Press).

Cheilik, Micháel (1988), 'The Werewolf' in *Mythical and Fabulous Creatures*, ed. Malcolm South (New York: Peter Bedrick Books): 265–89.

Chesterton, G. K. (1904), '*A Midsummer Night's Dream*', in his *The Common Man* (London: Sheed and Ward): 10–21.

Cirlot, J. E. (1962), *Dictionary of Symbols*, tr. Jack Sage (London: Routledge & Kegan Paul).

Clark, Michael (1988), *Jacques Lacan: An Annotated Bibliography*, 2 vols. (New York and London: Garland Publishing, Inc.).

Clayton, F. W. (1979), *The Hole in the Wall: A New Look at Shakespeare's Latin Base for* 'A Midsummer Night's Dream'; the Tenth Jackson Knight Memorial Lecture, delivered at the University of Exeter 13 June 1977 (Exeter: The University).

Clayton, Thomas (1974), ' "Fie What a Question's That If Thou Wert Near a Lewd Interpreter": The Wall Scene in *A Midsummer Night's Dream*', *Shakespeare Studies*, 7: 101–13.

Cohen, Ralph (1982), 'The Statements Literary Texts Do Not Make', *New Literary History*, 13: 379–91.

Collins, David G. (1982), 'Beyond Reason in *A Midsummer Night's Dream*: Stratford, 1981', *Iowa State Journal of Research*, 57 (2): 131–42.

Cook, Ann Jennalie (1991), *Making a Match: Courtship in Shakespeare and His Society* (Princeton: Princeton University Press).

Cope, Jackson I. (1973), *The Theater and the Dream: From Metaphor to Form in Renaissance Drama* (Baltimore and London: Johns Hopkins University Press): 219–25.

Couliano, Ioan P. (1987), *Eros and Magic in the Renaissance*, tr. Margaret Cook (Chicago and London: University of Chicago Press).

Culler, Jonathan (1975), *Structuralist Poetics: Structuralism, Linguistics, and the Study of Literature* (Ithaca, NY: Cornell University Press).

Culler, Jonathan (1982), *On Deconstruction: Theory and Criticism after Structuralism* (Ithaca, NY: Cornell University Press).

Curley, Michael J. (tr.) (1979), *Physiologus* (Austin and London: University of Texas Press).

Curtius, Ernst Robert (1953), *European Literature in the Latin Middle Ages*, tr. Willard R. Trask (New York: Pantheon Books).

Cusa, Nicholas of (1960), *The Vision of God*, tr. Emma Gurney Salter (originally published 1928; repr. New York: Frederick Ungar).

Cutts, John P. (1968), *The Shattered Glass: A Dramatic Pattern in Shakespeare's Early Plays* (Detroit: Wayne State University Press).

De Becker, R. (1968), *The Understanding of Dreams and the Machinations of the Night* (London: Allen and Unwin).

Deleuze, Gilles and Félix Guattari (1983), *Anti-Oedipus: Capitalism and*

Schizophrenia, tr. Robert Hurley, Mark Seem and Helen R. Lane (Minneapolis: University of Minnesota Press); originally *L'Anti-Oedipe* (Paris: Les Editions de Minuit, 1972).

Demetz, Peter (1958), 'The Elm and the Vine: Notes toward the History of a Marriage Topos', *PMLA*, 73: 521–32.

Dent, Robert W. (1964), 'Imagination in *A Midsummer Night's Dream*', *Shakespeare Quarterly*, 15: 115–29.

Derrida, Jacques (1976), *Of Grammatology*, tr. Gayatri Chakravorty Spivak (Baltimore and London: The Johns Hopkins University Press).

Derrida, Jacques (1978), 'Structure, Sign, and Play in the Discourse of the Human Sciences', in *Writing and Difference*, tr. Alan Bass (Chicago: University of Chicago Press): 278–93.

Derrida, Jacques (1979), 'The Supplement of Copula: Philosophy *before* Linguistics', in *Textual Strategies*, ed. Josué V. Harrari (Ithaca, NY: Cornell University Press): 82-120.

Doane, Mary Ann (1989), 'Veiling over Desire: Close-Ups of the Woman', in *Feminism and Psychoanalysis*, ed. Richard Feldstein and Judith Roof (Ithaca, NY and London: Cornell University Press): 105–41.

Dollimore, Jonathan (1990), 'Shakespeare, Cultural Materialism, Feminism and Marxist Humanism', *New Literary History*, 21 (3): 471–93.

Donaldson, E. Talbot (1985), 'The Embarrassments of Art: *The Tale of Sir Thopas*, 'Pyramus and Thisbe', and *A Midsummer Night's Dream*', in his *The Swan at the Well: Shakespeare Reading Chaucer* (New Haven and London: Yale University Press): 7–29.

Doran, Madeline (1960), '*A Midsummer Night's Dream*: A Metamorphosis', Rice Institute Pamphlet, 46: 113–35.

Douglas, Mary (1966), *Purity and Danger* (London: Routledge & Kegan Paul).

Draper, John (1938), 'The Date of *A Midsummer Night's Dream*', *Modern Language Notes*, 53: 266–8.

Draper, John (1972), 'The Queen Makes a Match and Shakespeare a Comedy', *Yearbook of English Studies*, 2: 61–7.

duBois, Page (1982), *Centaurs and Amazons: Women and the Pre-History of the Great Chain of Being* (Ann Arbor: University of Michigan Press).

Duerr, Hans Peter (1985), *Dreamtime: Concerning the Boundary between Wilderness and Civilization*, tr. Felicitas Goodman (Oxford: Basil Blackwell Ltd).

Duncan-Jones, Katherine (1981), 'Pyramus and Thisbe: Shakespeare's Debt to Moffett Cancelled', *Review of English Studies*, 32: 296–301.

Dunn, Allen (1988), 'The Indian Boy's Dream Wherein Every Mother's Son Rehearses His Part: Shakespeare's *A Midsummer Night's Dream*',

Shakespeare Studies XX, ed. Leeds Barroll (New York: Burt Franklin & Co.): 15–32.

Dyer, Rev. T. F. Thistleton (1883), *Folk-Lore of Shakespeare* (London: Griffith & Farran).

Eagleton, Terry (1986), *William Shakespeare* (Oxford: Basil Blackwell).

Edgerton, Samuel Y., Jr. (1975), *The Renaissance Rediscovery of Linear Perspective* (New York: Basic Books).

Edwards, Philip (1968), *Shakespeare and the Confines of Art* (London: Methuen).

Eisler, Riane (1987), *The Chalice and the Blade* (San Francisco: Harper & Row).

Elam, Keir (1984), *Shakespeare's Universe of Discourse* (Cambridge: Cambridge University Press).

Ellis, Herbert A. (1973), *Shakespeare's Lusty Punning in 'Love's Labour's Lost'* (The Hague: Mouton).

Empson, William (1986), *Essays on Shakespeare*, ed. David B. Pirie (Cambridge: Cambridge University Press).

Empson, William (1987), *Argufying: Essays on Literature and Culture*, ed. John Haffenden (Iowa City: University of Iowa Press).

Espy, Willard R. (1983), *The Garden of Eloquence: A Rhetorical Bestiary* (New York: E. P. Dutton).

Evans, Malcolm (1986), *Signifying Nothing* (Hemel Hempstead: Harvester Wheatsheaf): 221–5.

Faber, M. D. (1972), 'Hermia's Dream: Royal Road to *A Midsummer Night's Dream*', *Literature and Psychology*, 22: 179–90.

Falk, Florence (1980), 'Dream and Ritual Process in *A Midsummer Night's Dream*', *Comparative Drama*, 14 (3): 263–79.

Farrell, Kirby (1976), *Shakespeare's Creation* (Amherst: University of Massachusetts Press).

Farrell, Kirby (1989), *Play, Death, and Apocalypse in Shakespeare* (Chapel Hill, NC and London: University of North Carolina Press).

Fender, Stephen (1968), *Shakespeare: A Midsummer Night's Dream* (London: Edward Arnold).

Fontanier, Pierre (1968), *Les Figures du discours* (Paris: Flammarion).

Fox, Robin (1980), *The Red Lamp of Incest* (New York: E.P. Dutton).

Franke, Wolfgang (1979), 'The Logic of Double-Entendre in *A Midsummer Night's Dream*', *Philological Quarterly*, 58 (3): 282–97.

Fraser, Russell (1988), *Young Shakespeare* (New York: Columbia University Press).

Freedman, Barbara (1991), *Staging the Gaze: Postmodernism, Psychoanalysis, and Shakespearean Comedy* (Ithaca, NY and London: Cornell University Press).

Freud, Sigmund (1950), *Totem and Taboo*, tr. James Strachey (London: Routledge & Kegan Paul).

Freud, Sigmund (1961), *Beyond the Pleasure Principle*, tr. James Strachey (New York and London: W. W. Norton).

Furness, Horace Howard (1963), *A New Variorum Edition of Shakespeare: A Midsummer Night's Dream* (New York: Dover Publications, Inc.; originally J. B. Lippincott, 1895).

Garber, Marjorie B. (1974), *Dream in Shakespeare* (New Haven and London: Yale University Press): 59–87.

Garber, Marjorie B. (1980), ' "Wild Laughter in the Throat of Death": Darker Purposes in Shakespearean Comedy', in *Shakespearean Comedy*, ed. Maurice Charney (New York: New York Literary Forum): 121–6.

Garber, Marjorie B. (1981), *Coming of Age in Shakespeare* (London: Methuen).

Garner, Shirley Nelson (1981), '*A Midsummer Night's Dream*: "Jack shall have Jill; / Nought shall go ill" ', *Women's Studies* 9: 46–63.

Garrett, Stewart (1981), 'Shakespearean Dreamplay', *English Literary Renaissance*, 11 (1): 44–69.

Geertz, Clifford (1973), *The Interpretation of Cultures* (New York: Basic Books).

Girard, René (1977), *Violence and the Sacred*, tr. Patrick Gregory (Baltimore and London: Johns Hopkins University Press).

Girard, René (1979), 'Myth and Ritual in Shakespeare: *A Midsummer Night's Dream*', in *Textual Strategies*, ed. Josué V. Harari (Ithaca, NY: Cornell University Press).

Glass, James M. (1989), *Private Terror/Public Life: Psychosis and the Politics of Community* (Ithaca, NY and London: Cornell University Press).

Goddard, Harold (1951), *The Meaning of Shakespeare*, vol. 1 (Chicago and London: University of Chicago Press): 74–80.

Goldstein, Melvin (1973), 'Identity Crises in a Midsummer Nightmare: Comedy as Terror in Disguise', *Psychoanalytic Review*, 60: 169–204.

Greenblatt, Stephen (1986a), 'Friction and Fiction,' in *Reconstructing Individualism*, ed. Thomas C. Heller, Morton Sosna and David E. Wellbery, with Arnold I. Davidson, Ann Swidler and Ian Watt (Stanford: Stanford University Press): 30–52.

Greenblatt, Stephen (1986b), 'Psychoanalysis and Renaissance Culture', in *Literary Theory/Renaissance Texts*, ed. Patricia Parker and David Quint (Baltimore: Johns Hopkins University Press): 210–24.

Griffin, Alice V. (1951), *Pageantry on the Shakespearean Stage* (New Haven: College and University Press).

Grottanelli, Vinigi L. (1988), *The Python Killer: Stories of Nzema Life* (Chicago and London: University of Chicago Press).

Gui, Weston (1952–3), 'Bottom's Dream', *American Imago*, 9: 251–305.

Hall, James (1974), *Dictionary of Subjects and Symbols in Art* (New York: Harper & Row).

Hammelman, H. A. (1957), *Hugo von Hofmannsthal* (New Haven: Yale University Press).

Hanson, N. R. (1961), *Patterns of Discovery: An Inquiry into the Conceptual Foundations of Science* (Cambridge: Cambridge University Press).

Hartman, Vicky Shahly (1983), '*A Midsummer Night's Dream*: A Gentle Concord to the Oedipal Problem', *American Imago*, 40 (4): 355–69.

Hassel, R. Chris, Jr. (1970), 'Shakespeare's Comic Epilogues: Invitations to Festive Communions', *Shakespeare Jahrbuch*: 160–9.

Haydn, Hiram (1950), *The Counter-Renaissance* (New York: Charles Scribner's Sons).

Henderson, Katherine Usher and Barbara F. McManus (1985), *Half Humankind* (Urbana and Chicago: University of Illinois Press).

Henze, Richard (1974), 'A Midsummer Night's Dream: Analogous Image', *Shakespeare Studies*, 7: 115–23.

Herbert, T. Walter (1964), 'Invitations to Cosmic Laughter in *A Midsummer Night's Dream*', in *Shakespearean Essays*, ed. Alwin Thaler and Norman Sanders (Knoxville: University of Tennessee Press): 29–39.

Herbert, T. Walter (1977), *Oberon's Mazed World* (Baton Rouge and London: Louisiana State University Press).

Hinely, Jan Lawson (1987), 'Expounding the Dream: Shaping Fantasies in *A Midsummer Night's Dream*', in *Psychoanalytic Approaches to Literature and Film*, ed. Maurice Charney and Joseph Reppen (Rutherford, Madison, Teaneck: Fairleigh Dickinson University Press): 120–38.

Hodgdon, Barbara (1986), 'Gaining a Father: The Role of Egeus in the Quarto and Folio', *Review of English Studies*, n.s. 37: 534–42.

Hoffer, Peter C. and N. E. H. Hull (1981), *Murdering Mothers: Infanticide in England and New England 1558–1803* (New York: New York University Press).

Hofstadter, Douglas and David Moser (1989), 'To Err is Human; To Study Error Making is Cognitive Science', *Michigan Quarterly Review*, XXVIII (2): 185–215.

Holland, Norman (1960), 'Freud on Shakespeare', *PMLA*, 75: 163–79.

Holland, Norman (1980), 'Hermia's Dream', in *Representing Shakespeare*, ed. Murray M. Schwartz and Coppélia Kahn (Baltimore: Johns Hopkins University Press): 1–20.

Homan, Sidney R. (1969), 'The Single World of *A Midsummer Night's Dream*', *Bucknell Review*, XVII (1): 72–84.

Homan, Sidney R. (1981), *When the Theater Turns to Itself* (Lewisburg, London and Toronto: Bucknell University Press).

Hoskins, John (1935), *Directions for Speech and Style*, ed. Hoyt H. Hudson (Princeton: Princeton University Press).

Hunter, William B. (1983), *Milton's 'Comus': Family Piece* (Troy, NY: Whitson): 95–101.

Huston, J. Dennis (1981), *Shakespeare's Comedies of Play* (New York: Columbia University Press): 94–121.

Iser, Wolfgang (1961), 'Das Spiel im Spiel: Formen dramatischer Illusion bei Shakespeare' (The Play within the Play: Forms of Dramatic Illusion in Shakespeare), *Archiv für das Studium der neuren Sprachen und Literatur*, 198 (4): 209–26.

Jacobson, Gerald F. (1962), 'A Note on Shakespeare's *A Midsummer Night's Dream*', *American Imago* 19 (1): 21–6.

Jacobson, Roman (1956), 'Two Aspects of Language and Two Kinds of Aphasic Disturbances', in his and Morris Halle's *Fundamentals of Language*, Janua Linguarum, Series Minor, I (The Hague: Mouton): 69–96.

Jacobson, Roman (1960), 'Closing Statement: Linguistics and Poetics', in *Style in Language*, ed. Thomas A. Sebeok (Cambridge: MIT Press): 350–77.

James, E. O. (1951), *Seasonal Feasts and Festivals* (London: Thames and Hudson).

Jameson, Fredric (1982), 'Imaginary and Symbolic in Lacan: Marxism, Psychoanalytic Criticism, and the Problem of the Subject', in *Literature and Psychoanalysis: The Question of Reading: Otherwise*, ed. Shoshana Felman (Baltimore and London: Johns Hopkins University Press): 338–95.

Kafka, Franz (1972), *The Metamorphosis*, tr. Stanley Congold (New York: Bantam Books).

Kermode, Frank (1961), 'The Mature Comedies', in *Early Shakespeare*, Statford-upon-Avon Studies, vol. 3, ed. John Russell Brown and Bernard Harris (London: Edward Arnold): 211–17.

Kittredge, George Lyman (1929), *Witchcraft in Old and New England* (Cambridge, Mass.: Harvard University Press).

Knight, G. Wilson (1932), *The Shakespearian Tempest* (London: Oxford University Press): 141–69.

Kojève, Alexandre (1969), *Introduction to the Reading of Hegel*, tr. James H. Nichols, Jr (Ithaca, NY and London: Cornell University Press).

Kott, Jan (1964), *Shakespeare Our Contemporary*, tr. Boleslaw Taborski (Garden City, NY: Doubleday).

Kott, Jan (1987), *The Bottom Translation*, tr. Daniela Miedzyrzecka and Lillian Vallee (Evanston, Ill.: Northwestern University Press).

Kramer, Henry and Jacobus Sprenger (1970), *Malleus Maleficarum* (Lyons,

Junta, 1484), tr. Rev. Montague Summers (New York: Benjamin Blom, Inc.; originally 1928).

Krieger, Elliot (1979), *A Marxist Study of Shakespeare's Comedies* (London: The Macmillan Press).

Krieger, Murray (1987), 'The Literary, the Textual, the Social', in *The Aims of Representation: Subject, Text, History*, ed. Murray Krieger (New York: Columbia University Press): 1–22.

Kristeller, P. O. (1943), *The Philosophy of Marsilio Ficino*, tr. Virginia Conant (New York: Columbia University Press).

Lacan, Jacques (1977), *Ecrits: A Selection*, tr. Alan Sheridan (New York and London: W. W. Norton).

Lacan, Jacques (1978), *The Four Fundamental Concepts of Psycho-Analysis*, ed. Jacques-Alain Miller, tr. Alan Sheridan (New York and London: W. W. Norton).

Lacan, Jacques (1988), *The Seminar of Jacques Lacan*, Book I, Freud's Papers on Technique 1953–1954, ed. Jacques-Alain Miller, tr. John Forrester (New York and London: W. W. Norton).

Lamb, M. E. (1979), '*A Midsummer Night's Dream* and the Minotaur', *Texas Studies in Literature and Language*, 21: 478–91.

Landes, David S. (1983), *Evolution in Time* (Cambridge, Mass. and London: Harvard University Press).

Laqueur, Thomas (1986), 'Orgasm, Generation, and the Politics of Reproductive Biology', *Representations*, 14: 4–16.

Leggett, Alexander (1974), *Shakespeare's Comedy of Love* (London: Methuen): 89–116.

Leinwand, Theodore (1986), ' "I believe we must leave the killing out": Deference and Accommodation in *A Midsummer Night's Dream*', *Renaissance Papers*: 17–21.

Lévi-Strauss, Claude (1963), *Structural Anthropology*, tr. Claire Jacobson and Brooke Grundfest Schoepf (New York: Basic Books).

Lévi-Strauss, Claude (1969), *The Elementary Structures of Kinship*, tr. J. H. Bell, J. R. von Sturmer and R. Needham, ed., rev. ed. (Boston: Beacon Hill); originally *Les structures élémentaires de la parenté* (Paris, 1949).

Lévi-Strauss, Claude (1973), *Tristes Tropiques*, tr. John and Doreen Weightman (London: Cape).

Lewis, Allen (1969), '*A Midsummer Night's Dream* – Fairy Fantasy or Erotic Nightmare', *Educational Theatre Journal*, 21: 251–8.

Lewis, C. S. (1954), *English Literature in the Sixteenth Century* (Oxford: Oxford University Press).

Lewis, Naphtali (1976), *The Interpretation of Dreams and Portents* (Toronto and Sarasota: Samuel Stevens, Hakkert & Company).

Lukacher, Ned (1989), 'Anamorphic Stuff: Shakespeare, Catharsis,

Lacan', *South Atlantic Quarterly*, 88 (4): 863–98.

Lyons, Charles R. (1971), '*A Midsummer Night's Dream*: The Paradox of Love's Triumph', in his *Shakespeare and the Ambiguity of Love's Triumph* (The Hague: Mouton): 21–43.

MacCannell, Juliet Flower (1986), *Figuring Lacan* (Lincoln: University of Nebraska Press).

MacCary, W. Thomas (1985), *Friends and Lovers: The Phenomenology of Desire in Shakespearean Comedy* (New York: Columbia University Press).

McClaren, Angus (1984), *Reproductive Rituals: The Perception of Fertility in England from the Sixteenth to the Nineteenth Century* (London and New York: Methuen).

McGuire, Philip C. (1988), 'Intentions, Options, and Greatness: An Example from *A Midsummer Night's Dream*', in *Shakespeare and the Triple Play*, ed. Sidney Homan (Lewisburg: Bucknell University Press): 177–86.

McGuire, Philip C. (1989), 'Egeus and the Implications of Silence', in *Shakespeare and the Sense of Performance*, ed. Marvin and Ruth Thompson (Newark: University of Delaware Press): 103–15.

Maclean, Ian (1980), *The Renaissance Notion of Women* (New York: Cambridge University Press).

Malcolmson, R. W. (1973), *Popular Recreations in English Society* (Cambridge: Cambridge University Press).

Manwood, John (1598), *A Brefe Collection of the Lawes of the Forests* (London, 1592), private edition. *A Treatise and Discourse of the Lawes of the Forest* (London, 1598), first public edition.

Marcus, Mordecai (1981), '*A Midsummer Night's Dream*: The Dialectic of Eros-Thanatos', *American Imago*, 38 (3): 269–78.

Marienstras, Richard (1985), *New Perspectives on the Shakespearean World*, tr. Janet Lloyd (Cambridge: Cambridge University Press and Editions de la Maison des Sciences de L'Homme; originally *Le Proche et Le Lointain* (Paris: Les Editions de Minuit, 1981).

Marshall, David (1982), 'Exchanging Visions: Reading *A Midsummer Night's Dream*', *English Literary History*, 49: 543–75.

Martindale, Charles and Michelle (1990), *Shakespeare and the Uses of Antiquity* (London and New York: Oxford University Press); see Chapter 2, 'Shakespeare's Ovid'.

Matchett, William H. (1979), 'Some Dramatic Techniques in *King Lear*', in *Shakespeare: The Theatrical Dimension*, ed. Philip C. McGuire and David A. Samuelson (New York: AMS Press, Inc.): 185–207.

Mauss, Marcel (1954), *The Gift: Forms and Functions of Exchange in Archaic Societies*, tr. Ian Cunnison (London: Cohen & West Ltd).

May, Steven W. (1984), '*A Midsummer Night's Dream* and the Carey–

Berkeley Wedding', *Renaissance Papers 1983*, ed. A. Leigh Deneef and M. Thomas Hester (Durham, NC: The Southeastern Renaissance Conference): 43–52.

McFarland, Thomas (1972), *Shakespeare's Pastoral Comedy* (Chapel Hill, NC: University of North Carolina Press): 78–97.

Mebane, John S. (1982), 'Structure, Source, and Meaning in *A Midsummer Night's Dream*', *Texas Studies in Language and Literature*, 24 (3): 255–70.

Mehl, Dieter (1974), 'Forms and Functions of the Play within a Play', *Renaissance Drama*, 7: 41–62.

Merchant, W. Moelwyn (1961), '*A Midsummer Night's Dream*, A Visual Re-creation', *Early Shakespeare*, Shakespeare Institute Studies, ed. John Russell Brown and Bernard Harris (London: Edward Arnold): 165–86.

Merleau-Ponty, Maurice (1964), *The Primacy of Perception*, ed. James M. Edie (Evanston, Ill.: Northwestern University Press).

Metz, Christian (1982), *The Imaginary Signifier*, tr. Celia Britton, Annwyl Williams, Ben Brewster and Alfred Guzzetti (Bloomington: Indiana University Press).

Miller, J. Hillis (1987), *The Ethics of Reading* (New York: Columbia University Press).

Miller, Ronald F. (1975), '*A Midsummer Night's Dream*: The Fairies, Bottom, and the Mystery of Things', *Shakespeare Quarterly*, 26: 254–68.

Mitchell, Juliet and Jacqueline Rose (eds) (1983), *Feminine Sexuality: Jacques Lacan and the école freudienne* (New York: W. W. Norton).

Mitchell, W. J. T. (1986), *Iconology: Image, Text, Ideology* (Chicago and London: University of Chicago Press).

Montaigne, Michel de (1965), *Essays*, 3 vols, tr. John Florio, 1580 (London, Melbourne, Toronto: Dent, Everyman's Library).

Montrose, Louis Adrian (1983), ' "Shaping Fantasies": Figurations of Gender and Power in Elizabethan Culture', in *Representing the Renaissance*, ed. Stephen Greenblatt (Berkeley and Los Angeles: University of California Press): 31–64.

Morris, Harry (1985), '*A Midsummer Night's Dream*: So Quick Bright Things Come to Confusion', in his *Last Things in Shakespeare* (Tallahassee: Florida State University Press): 232–54.

Mowat, Barbara A. (1989), ' "A local habitation and a name": Shakespeare's Text as Construct', *Style*, 23 (3): 335–51.

Muir, Kenneth (1954), 'Pyramus and Thisbe: A Study in Shakespeare's Method', *Shakespeare Quarterly*, 5: 141–53.

Muller, John P. and William J. Richardson (1982), *Lacan and Language* (New York: International Universities Press).

Needham, Joseph (1959), *A History of Embryology*, 2nd edition (Cambridge: Cambridge University Press): 37–74.

Neely, Carol Thomas (1989), 'Constructing Female Sexuality in the Renaissance: Stratford, London, Windsor, Vienna', in *Feminism and Psychoanalysis*, ed. Richard Feldstein and Judith Roof (Ithaca, NY and London: Cornell University Press): 209–29.

Nelson, Robert J. (1958), *Play Within a Play: The Dramatist's Conception of His Art: Shakespeare to Anouilh* (New Haven: Yale University Press).

Nemerov, Howard (1956), 'The Marriage of Theseus and Hippolyta', *Kenyon Review*, 18: 633–41.

Nevo, Ruth (1980), *Comic Transformations in Shakespeare* (London: Methuen): 96–114.

Olson, Paul A. (1957), '*A Midsummer Night's Dream* and the Meaning of the Court Marriage', *English Literary History*, 24: 95–119.

Ong, Walter J. (1967), 'The Lady and the Issue', in his *In the Human Grain* (New York: The Macmillan Company): 188–202; originally in *The Month* (1951) and *Cross-Currents* (1952).

Opie, Iona and Moira Tatem (eds) (1989), *A Dictionary of Superstitions* (Oxford and New York: Oxford University Press).

Orgel, Stephen (1989), 'Nobody's Perfect: Or Why Did the English Stage Take Boys for Women?' *South Atlantic Quarterly*, 88 (1): 7–29.

Ormerod, David (1978), '*A Midsummer Night's Dream*: The Monster in the Labyrinth', *Shakespeare Studies*, 11: 39–52.

Pagel, Walter (1982), *Paracelsus: An Introduction to Philosophical Medicine in the Era of the Renaissance*, 2nd revised edition (Basel: Karger).

Palombo, Stanley R. (1983), 'The Genius of the Dream', *American Journal of Psycho-analysis*, 43 (4): 301–13.

Panofsky, Irwin (1962), 'Blind Cupid' in his *Studies in Iconology* (New York and Evanston, Ill.: Harper & Row): 95–127; originally Oxford University Press, 1939).

Paolucci, Anne (1977), 'The Lost Days in *A Midsummer Night's Dream*', *Shakespeare Quarterly*, 28: 317–26.

Paracelsus (1979), *Paracelsus: Selected Writings*, ed. Jolande Jacobi, tr. Norbert Guterman (Princeton: Princeton University Press).

Paré, Ambroise (1982), *On Monsters and Marvels*, tr. Janis L. Pallister (Chicago: University of Chicago Press).

Parker, Patricia (1986), 'Deferral, Dilation, Différance: Shakespeare, Cervantes, Jonson', in *Literary Theory/Renaissance Texts*, ed. Patricia Parker and David Quint (Baltimore and London: Johns Hopkins University Press): 182–209.

Pascal, Blaise (1962), *Pascal's Pensées*, tr. Martin Turnell (New York: Harper & Brothers).

Patterson, Annabel (1989), 'Bottom's Up: Festive Theory' in her *Shakespeare and the Popular Voice* (Cambridge, Mass. and Oxford: Basil

Blackwell Inc.): 52–70.

Pearson, D'Orsay W. (1974), '"Unkinde" Theseus: A Study in Renaissance Mythology', *English Literary Renaissance*, 4: 276–98.

Pechter, Edward (1990), 'Teaching Differences', *Shakespeare Quarterly*, 41 (2): 160–73.

Pepys, Samuel (1970), *The Diary of Samuel Pepys: 1662*, vol. III, ed. Robert Lanham and William Matthews (Berkeley and Los Angeles: University of California Press).

Plato (1961), *Plato: The Collected Dialogues*, ed. Edith Hamilton and Huntington Cairns (Princeton: Princeton University Press).

Poole, Roger (1972), *Towards Deep Subjectivity* (London: Allen Lane).

Preus, Anthony (1977), 'Galen's Criticism of Aristotle's Conception Theory', *Journal of the History of Biology*, 10: 65–85.

Purdon, Noel (1974), *The Words of Mercury: Shakespeare and English Mythography of the Renaissance*, Salzburg Studies in English Literature, 39 (Salzburg: Institut für Englische Sprache und Literatur, Universität Saltzburg).

Pye, Christopher (1988), 'The Betrayal of the Gaze: Theatricality and Power in Shakespeare's *Richard II*', *ELH*, 55: 575–98.

Ragland-Sullivan, Ellie (1986), *Jacques Lacan and the Philosophy of Psychoanalysis* (Urbana and Chicago: University of Illinois Press).

Ragland-Sullivan, Ellie (1989), 'Plato's *Symposium* and the Lacanian Theory of Transference: Or, What is Love?', *South Atlantic Quarterly*, 88 (4): 725–55.

Randall, John Herman, Jr. (1960), *Aristotle* (New York and London: Columbia University Press).

Reik, Theodor (1957), *Of Love and Lust* (New York: Farrar, Straus, Giroux).

Rhoads, Diana Akers (1985), *Shakespeare's Defense of Poetry: A Midsummer Night's Dream and The Tempest* (Lanham, MD, New York, London: University Press of America).

Richman, David (1990), *Laughter, Pain, and Wonder: Shakespeare's Comedies and the Audience in the Theater* (Newark: University of Delaware Press): 97–102, 127–30.

Richmond, Hugh (1971), *Shakespeare's Sexual Comedy: A Mirror for Lovers* (Indianapolis, New York: Bobbs-Merrill), 102–22.

Ricoeur, Paul (1978), 'The Metaphorical process as cognition, imagination, and feeling,' in *On Metaphor*, ed. Sheldon Sacks (Chicago and London: University of Chicago Press): 141–58.

Roberts, Jeanne Addison (1980), 'Animals as Agents of Revelation: The Horizontalizing of the Great Chain of Being in Shakespeare's Comedies', in *Shakespearean Comedy*, ed. Maurice Charney (New York:

New York Literary Forum): 79–96.

Robinson, J. W. (1964), 'Palpable Hot Ice: Dramatic Burlesque in *A Midsummer Night's Dream*', *Studies in Philology*, 61: 192–204.

Rose, Mark (1972), *Shakespearean Design* (Cambridge, Mass.: Harvard University Press).

Roustang, François (1982), *Dire Mastery*, tr. Ned Lukacher (Baltimore: Johns Hopkins University Press).

Rowland, Beryl (1974), *Animals with Human Faces: A Guide to Animal Symbolism* (Knoxville: University of Tennessee Press).

Rubinstein, Frankie (1984), *A Dictionary of Shakespeare's Sexual Puns and Their Significance* (London and Basingstoke: The Macmillan Press).

Rudd, Niall (1979), 'Pyramus and Thisbe in Shakespeare and Ovid: *A Midsummer Night's Dream* and *Metamorphoses* 4.1–166', in *Creative Imitation and Latin Literature*, ed. David West and Tony Woodman (Cambridge and New York: Cambridge University Press): 173–93.

Sadler, John (1636), *The Sicke Womans Private Looking-Glasse* (London: Stephens & Meredith).

Sālgādo, Gamini (1975), *Eyewitnesses of Shakespeare: First Hand Accounts of Performances 1590–1890* (New York: Harper & Row).

Sartre, Jean-Paul (1956), *Being and Nothingness*, tr. Hazel E. Barnes (New York: Philosophical Library).

Savage, James E. (1961), 'Notes on *A Midsummer Night's Dream*', *University of Mississippi Studies in English*, 2: 65–78.

Scarry, Elaine (1985), *The Body in Pain: The Making and Unmaking of the World* (New York and Oxford: Oxford University Press).

Schanzer, Ernest (1955), 'The Moon and the Fairies in *A Midsummer Night's Dream*', *University of Toronto Quarterly*, 24: 234–46.

Schneider, Michael (1987), 'Bottom's Dream, the Lion's Roar, and Hostility of Class Difference in *A Midsummer Night's Dream*', in *From the Bard to Broadway*, ed. Karelisa V. Hartigan (Lanham, MD, New York, and London: United Presses of America): 191–212.

Schwartz, Robert Barnett (1990), 'When Everything Seems Double: *A Midsummer Night's Dream*', in his *Shakespeare's Parted Eye: Perception, Knowledge and Meaning in the Sonnets and Plays* (New York: Peter Lang): 49–80.

Scragg, Leah (1982), *The Metamorphosis of 'Gallathea': A Study in Creative Adaptation* (Washington, DC: University Press of America).

Sewell, Elizabeth (1960), *The Orphic Voice: Poetry and Natural History* (New Haven: Yale University Press): 53–168.

Shepherd, Simon (1981), *Amazons and Warrior Women: Varieties of Feminism in Seventeenth-Century Drama* (Brighton: Harvester Press).

Siegel, Paul N. (1953), '*A Midsummer Night's Dream* and the Wedding

Guests', *Shakespeare Quarterly*, 4: 139–44.

Silverman, Kaja (1983), *The Subject of Semiotics* (New York: Oxford University Press).

Simon, Bennett (1978), *Mind and Madness in Ancient Greece* (Ithaca, NY and London: Cornell University Press).

Smith, Joseph H. and William Kerrigan (eds) (1983), *Interpreting Lacan*, vol. 6 (New Haven and London: Yale University Press).

Snodgrass, W. D. (1975), *In Radical Pursuit* (New York: Harper & Row): 144–80.

Southern, Richard (1961), *The Seven Ages of the Theatre* (New York: Hill and Wang).

Sprague, Arthur Colby and J. C. Trewin (1970), *Shakespeare's Plays Today: Some Customs and Conventions of the Stage* (Columbia, SC: University of South Carolina Press).

Stallybras, Peter (1986), 'Patriarchal Territories: The Body Enclosed', in *Rewriting the Renaissance*, ed. Margaret W. Ferguson, Maureen Quilligan and Nancy Vickers (Chicago and London: University of Chicago Press): 123–42.

Stewart, Susan (1984), *On Longing* (Baltimore and London: The Johns Hopkins University Press).

Stone, Lawrence (1965), *The Crisis of the Aristocracy 1558–1641* (Oxford: Oxford University Press).

Stone, Lawrence (1977), *The Family, Sex and Marriage in England 1500–1800* (New York: Harper & Row).

Strutt, Joseph (1968), *The Sports and Pastimes of the People of England* (1801), a new edition much enlarged and corrected by J. Charles Cox, LLD, FSA (London: Methuen, 1903; Detroit: Reissued by Singing Tree Press, Book Tower).

Stubbes, Phillip (1972), *The Anatomie of Abuses* (Amsterdam: Theatrvm Orbis Terrarvm Ltd); originally London, 1583.

Swander, Homer (1990), 'Editors vs. A Text: The Scripted Geography of *A Midsummer Night's Dream*', *Studies in Philology*, 87 (1): 83–108.

Taylor, Anthony Brian (1990), 'Golding's Ovid, Shakespeare's "Small Latin", and the Real Object of Mockery in "Pyramus and Thisbe"', *Shakespeare Survey*, vol. 42, ed. Stanley Wells (Cambridge: Cambridge University Press): 53–64.

Taylor, E. G. R. (1971), *The Haven-Finding Art* (New York: American Elsevier Publishing Company, Inc.).

Taylor, George C. (1945), 'Shakespeare's Use of the Idea of the Beast in Man', *Studies in Philology*, 42: 530–43.

Taylor, Mark C. (1980), *Journeys to Selfhood: Hegel and Kierkegaard* (Berkeley, Los Angeles, London: University of California Press).

Tennenhouse, Leonard (1986), *Power on Display: The Politics of Shakespeare's Genres* (New York and London: Methuen): 43–4, 73–6.

Thiébaux, Marcelle (1969), 'The Mouth of the Boar as a Symbol in Medieval Literature', *Romance Philology*, 22 (3): 281–99.

Thiébaux, Marcelle (1974), *The Stag of Love* (Ithaca, NY: Cornell University Press).

Thomas, Keith (1971), *Religion and the Decline of Magic* (New York: Charles Scribner's Sons).

Thompson, Ann (1978), *Shakespeare's Chaucer: A Study in Literary Origins* (Liverpool: Liverpool University Press; New York: Barnes & Noble).

Thompson, Ann and John O. Thompson (1987), *Shakespeare: Meaning & Metaphor* (Iowa City: Unversity of Iowa Press).

Tobin, J. J. M. (1984), *Shakespeare's Favorite Novel: A Study of The Golden Asse as Prime Source* (Lanham, MD, New York, London: University Press of America): 32–40.

Toliver, Harold E. (1971), *Pastoral Forms and Attitudes* (Berkeley and Los Angeles: University of California Press): 82–93.

Topsell, Edward (1981), *Topsell's Histories of Beasts*, ed. Malcolm South (Chicago: Nelson-Hall).

Trewin, J. C. (1971), *Peter Brook: A Biography* (London: Macdonald).

Turbervile, George (1908), *The Noble Art of Venerie or Hunting*, 1576 (Oxford: Clarendon Press).

Turkle, Sherry (1978), *Psychoanalytic Politics* (New York: Basic Books).

Turner, Victor (1967), *Forest of Symbols* (Ithaca, NY: Cornell University Press).

Tuve, Rosamund (1947), *Elizabethan and Metaphysical Imagery* (Chicago: University of Chicago Press).

Van Gennep, A. (1960), *Rites of Passage*, tr. M. B. Vizedom and G. L. Caffee (Chicago: University of Chicago Press); originally *Les rites de passage* (Paris: Emile Nourry, 1909).

Vergote, Antoine (1983), 'From Freud's "Other Scene" to Lacan's "Other"', in *Interpreting Lacan*, ed. Joseph H. Smith and William Kerrigan (New Haven and London: Yale University Press): 193–221, esp. 201–2.

Vlasopolos, Anca (1978), 'The Ritual of Midsummer: A Pattern for *A Midsummer Night's Dream*', *Renaissance Quarterly*, XXXI (1): 21–9.

Vyvyan, John (1961), *Shakespeare and Platonic Beauty* (London: Chatto & Windus).

Warren, Roger (1983), *A Midsummer Night's Dream: Text and Performance* (London: The Macmillan Press).

Welsford, Enid (1962), 'The Masque Transmuted', in her *The Court Masque: A Study in the Relationship between Poetry and the Revels* (1927;

repr. by Russell & Russell, Inc.): 324–49.

Westlund, Joseph Emanuel (1967), 'Thematic Structure in Shakespeare's Middle Comedies', Ph.D. dissertation, University of California, Berkeley, 1966. *DA*, 28: 206A.

White, T. H. (1984), *The Book of Beasts: Being a Translation from a Latin Bestiary of the Twelfth Century* (New York: Dover Publications); originally G. P. Putnam's Sons, 1954.

Willbern, David (1980), 'Shakespeare's Nothing', in *Representing Shakespeare*, ed. Murray M. Schwartz and Coppélia Kahn (Baltimore and London: The Johns Hopkins University Press): 244–63.

Wilden, Anthony (1968), *The Language of the Self* (Baltimore and London: Johns Hopkins University Press).

Wind, Edgar (1968), *Pagan Mysteries in the Renaissance* (New York: W. W. Norton).

Winnicott, D. W. (1971), *Playing and Reality* (London: Tavistock).

Wright, A. R. (1938, 1940), *British Calendar Customs: England*, vols. 2 and 3, ed. T. E. Lones (London: William Glaisher Ltd).

Wright, Celeste Turner (1940), 'The Amazons in Elizabethan Literature', *Studies in Philology*, 37 (3): 433–56.

Wright, Elizabeth (1984), *Psychoanalytic Criticism: Theory in Practice* (London and New York: Methuen).

Wyrick, Deborah Baker (1982), 'The Ass Motif in *The Comedy of Errors* and *A Midsummer Night's Dream*', *Shakespeare Quarterly*, 33: 432–8.

Yates, Frances A. (1964), *Giordano Brune and the Hermetic Tradition* (Chicago and London: University of Chicago Press).

Yates, Frances A. (1975), *Astraea: The Imperial Theme in the Sixteenth Century* (London and Boston: Routledge & Kegan Paul).

Young, David P. (1966), *Something of Great Constancy* (New Haven and London: Yale University Press).

Zilsel, Edgar (1941), 'The Origins of William Gilbert's Scientific Method', *Journal of the History of Ideas*, II (1).

Zimbardo, R. A. (1972), 'Regeneration and Reconciliation in *A Midsummer Night's Dream*', *Shakespeare Studies*, 6: 35–50.

Zitner, Sheldon P. (1960), 'The Worlds of *A Midsummer Night's Dream*', *South Atlantic Quarterly*, 59: 396–403.

Zukovsky, Louis (1987), *Bottom: On Shakespeare* (Berkeley and Los Angeles: University of California Press); originally 1963.

Index

Actaeon, 29, 78, 92, 170, 182–3
Agrippa, H. C., 30,100
allegory, 90–2
All's Well That Ends Well, 62, 78
Amazons, 5, 9–10, 16, 32, 53–4,
    57–8, 78
anamorphism, 49–54, 66–71, 75,
    110, 143, 152, 174–5, 180,
    184
Ansorge, P., 60
Antiochus, 13
Antony and Cleopatra, 176
Antiopa, 5
Aphrodite, 18, 57, 167
Apuleius, xviii, 29, 62, 85–6, 179,
    182
Aquinas, 7, 164
Arden, M., 162
Aristophanes, 17, 48, 166
Aristotle, 7, 109, 189, 192,
    200
Arnheim, R., 33, 49, 138,
Artaud, A., 154-5, 157, 183

Bacon, F., 29, 189
Bakhtin, M., xxv, 131–2, 137, 196
Baltrusaitis, J., 174
Barber, C. L., xix, xxiv, xxv, 6,
    74, 198
Barkan, L., 71, 75, 182
Barton, A., 105, 187, 189
Barton, J., xxii
basilisk, 173
Baudrillard, J., 166
Bentham, J., 34
Berkeley, G., 34
Bernheimer, R., 85–6
Berry, E., xxv, 64, 74–5, 182
Bettelheim, B., 86
Betterton, T., xxi
Bevington, D., xiii, xv, 178
Blake, W., 97
Blanchot, M., 101
Bloch, R. H., 8
Bodin, J., 185
Boswell, J., 162
Bowie, M., 161

Bradshaw, G., 175
Brand, J., 191
Brecht, B., 143
Briggs, K., 75, 104, 178, 181
Bristol, M. D., xxv, xxvi, 142,
     198–9
Brook, P., xxii, 50, 59, 60, 62,
     175, 178
Brooks, H. F., xvi, xvii, 75, 150,
     178, 197
Brown, J. N., xvii,
Brown, J. R., 60, 178
Bruno, G., 29, 170
Bryant, J. A., xxiii
Bullough, G., 53, 82, 166

Calderwood, J. L., 176
Calvin, 8, 165
carnival, xxv, 141, 198–9
Carroll, W. C., xxiv, 62, 75, 136,
     192
Carroll, D. A., 204
Carson, A., 204
Carter, J. M., 204
Chambers, E. K., 130, 200
Champion, L. S., xvii,
Chaucer, G., xvii, xviii, xix, 52,
     105, 131,
Cheilik, M., 185
Chesterton, G. K., xxii
Cirlot, J. E., 184
Clark, M., xiii, 161
Clayton, F. W., xxvi, 128, 198
Clayton, T., xxv, 128, 194, 198
Cohen, R., 205
Coleridge, S. T., 39, 187
Collins, D. G., 205
Comedy of Errors, 62, 105, 131, 164
Cook, A. J., 165, 181
Cope, J. I., 205
Couliano, I. P., 36, 40, 173
Culler, J., 167–8

Curley, M. J., 205
Curtius, E. R., 98
Cusa, N., 34, 171
Cutts, J. P., 55

Daldianus, A., 179
Daly, M., 164
Daniel, S., 28
Daniels, R., xxii
De Becker, R., 88
Deleuze, G., 80, 183
De Man, P., 198
Demetz, P., 62
Dent, R. W., xxiv, 194
Derrida, J., 187, 188, 198
desire, 3–4, 10–14, 70, 118,
     151–3, 161, 166–7, 168–9
Diana, 5, 53–4, 61, 78, 92, 163–4
Doane, M. A., 29
Dollimore, J., 206
Donaldson, E. T., xvii, xix,
Doran, M., 206
doubling, 51–4, 175, 176
Douglas, M., 74, 132,
Draper, J., xvi–xvii,
Dreyer, C., 49
duBois, P., 9
Duerr, H. P., 85
Duncan–Jones, K., xix
Dunn, A., 103, 115, 177
Dyer, Rev. T. F. T., 183

Eagleton, T., xxv, 167–8
Edgerton, S. Y., 40
Ellison, R., 172
Elizabeth, Queen, 6, 148, 150,
     185, 197
Evans, M., xxiv
Edwards, P., xxiv, 71
Eisler, R., 165
Elam, K., 104, 183, 195
Ellis, H. A., 198

Empson, W., 178, 190
Endymion, 61
Erickson, E., xxiv
Espy, W. R., 124

Faber, M. D., xxiv, 173
Falk, F., 182
Farrell, K., 63, 91,
Fender, S., xxiii, xxvi
Ficino, M., 36, 40, 115, 173
Fisher, T., xiv
Fontanier, P., 207
fort/da, 2, 4, 6,14, 68, 74,161
Fox, R., 160
Franke, W., xvi, xxvi. 198
Fraser, R., 162
Freedman, B., xxiii, xxiv, 9, 99,
    162, 171, 173–5, 191
Freud, S., 1, 6, 124, 144, 160,
    187–8
Frye, N., xxv
Furness, H. H., 101
Fuseli, H., xxii

Gabo, N., 180
Ganymede, 55, 176
Garber, M. B., 74, 173, 182
Garner, S. N., xxiv,177
Garrett, S., 208
Garrick, D., xxi
Geertz, C., 172
Gilbert, W., 28–30
Girard, R., 168–9
Glass, J. M., 34–5
Goddard, H., xxii, xxiii, 114
Golding, A., 18, 92, 118–19, 121,
    184
Goldstein, M., 127,
Gombrich, E., 33
Granville–Barker, H., xxi
Graves, R., 81–2
Greenblatt, S., 162, 170–1

Greville, F., 31, 191
Griffin, A. V., 150, 197, 200
Grottanelli, V., 172
Guattari, F., 80, 183
Gui, W., xxiv, 127,

Hades, 186
Hall, J., 209
Hammelman, H. A., 154
Hamlet, 7, 28–9, 48, 68, 104, 134,
    139, 140, 193–4, 197–98
Hancock, J., 176
Hanson, N. R., 40
Hartman, V. S., 209
Hassel, R. C., xxiii, 114
Haydn, H., 209
Hazlitt, W., xxi, xxii, xxiv, 148–9,
    152–3
Hegel, 16, 35, 55, 101, 127, 144,
    169, 188
Henderson, K. U., 33
Henry IV, Part II, 195
Henry V, 122, 148, 195
Henry Vlll, 6
Henze, R., 209
Herbert, T. W., 209
Hercules, 186
hermaphrodites, 17, 166
Hermaphroditus, 17–18
Hermes, 18
Hinely, J. L., 127, 198
Hippolytus, 5, 58
Hodgdon, B., xv, 181
Hoffer, P. C., 209
Hofstadter, D., 112–13
Holbein, H., 49, 51, 66, 110,
    174, 184
Holland, N., xxiv, 173
Homan, S. R., xxiv, 120, 183
Hoskins, J., 192–3
Hull, N. E. H.,
Hunter, W. B.,

Huston, J. D., xxiv, 103, 115, 180, 186

incest, 12–13
Iser, W., xxiv

Jacobson, G. F., 210
Jacobson, R., 188, 193
James, E. O., 210
Jameson, F., 97–8, 164
James 1, King, 89, 191, 197
Julius Caesar, 37

Kafka, F., 22, 112, 191
Kant, I., 200
Keller, H., 188
Kermode, F., 210
King Lear, 82, 129, 150
Kittredge, G. L., 167
Knight, G. W., xxii
Kojève, A., 101, 169, 188
Kott, J., xxii, xxv, 55, 59, 64, 97, 176, 178–9, 186
Kramer, H. and Sprenger, J., 30, 185
Krieger, E., xxiv, 52, 137, 175, 198
Krieger, M., 196
Kristeller, P. O., 25

Lacan, J., xxiv, 1–2, 8, 10, 83, 124, 161, 164, 166, 167, 175, 189
castration, 12
demand, 55, 161
foreclosure, 80–4
gaze, 33–8, 147, 151, 153, 174
imaginary, 4, 6, 12, 14, 19–22, 27–47, 80, 136, 160–1, 165
mirror state, 21, 38, 115, 187, 196
name-of-the-father, 8, 12, 22, 68–9, 100–1, 178

paternal No, 6, 56, 163
phallus, 10, 11, 56–7, 173, 178
symbolic, 2–6, 8, 10, 19–22, 23–4, 79–80, 101, 125, 136, 160–6, 188
unconscious, 21
Lamb, M. E., 59
Landes, D. S., 28
Laqueur, T., 211
Leggett, A., 211
Leinwand, T., xxiv, 198
Lévi–Strauss, C., 7, 9–10, 14, 106, 166, 188
Lewis, C. S., xxv
Lewis, N., 179
Lewis, A., 176
Lily, W., 130
liminality, 72–6, 88, 103, 117, 136, 187
lodestar, 27–8, 30, 169
Love's Labour's Lost, 45, 108, 187
Lucian, 154
Lukacher, N., 174
Luna, 61
Lykaon, 184
Lyly, J., 78, 148
Lyons, C. R., 63
Lyotard, J., 196

Macbeth, 26
MacCannell, J. F., 162, 163
MacCary, W. T., xxiv, 54, 55, 176
MacFarland, T., 178
Maclean, 1., 212
Magritte, R., 40, 173
malaphor, 112–13, 191–2
Malcolmson, R. W.,
Manwood, J., 88–90
Marcus, M., 178
Marienstras, R., 85, 88–91, 185
Marshall, D., xxiv, 143, 166, 178, 181, 191, 194

Martindale, C. and M., xviii,
   121,
Mary, Queen, 6
Mary, Virgin, 6, 30–1
Matchett, W. H., 198
Mauss, M., 166
May, S. W., xvi
McFarland, T., 186
McClaren, A., 164
McGuire, P. C., xv, 181
McManus, B. F., 31
Mebane, J. S., 213
Mehl, D., 213
Merchant of Venice, 55
Merchant, W. M., 213
Meres, F., xv, xvii,
Merleau–Ponty, M., 33, 171, 172
Merry Wives of Windsor, 130
metadrama, 22, 117–45, 150
metamorphosis, 75, 113, 119, 136,
   169, 192
metaphor, 63, 82–4, 87, 97, 102,
   107, 111–16, 130, 140,
   157, 175, 188, 189, 191–2
metonymy, 20, 82–4, 104, 108,
   111–16, 124, 130, 140,
   141, 188, 189
Metz, C., 188
Miller, J. H., 198
Miller, R. F., xxiii, 114
Mitchell, J., 161, 162
Mitchell, W. J. T., 213
Montaigne, M., 188–9
Montrose, L. A., xxiv, 6, 150, 166,
   177, 190, 200
Morris, H., 89
Moser, D., 112–13
Moshinsky, E., xxii, 175, 182
mothers and stepdames, 2–5
Mowat, B. A., xvii, 191
Much Ado About Nothing, 134
Muir, K., xix,

Muller, J. P., 162, 165, 178

names, 100–6
navigation, 27–8, 169
Needham, J., 164
Neely, C. T., 166
Nelson, R. J., 214
Nemerov, H., 214
Nevo, R., 214
New Comedy, xxv, 21
Newton, T., 167

oedipal crisis, 1–2, 5–14, 56,
   162–3, 178
Olson, P. A., xvi,
Ong, W. J., 6
Opie, 1., 214
Orgel, S., 214
Ormerod, D., 59
Orwell, G., 34
Othello, 69, 171
Ovid, 17–18, 29, 30, 92, 99, 105,
   117–21, 182, 183, 184

Pagel, W., 183
Palombo, S., 214
Panofsky, I., 25
Paolucci, A., 77
Paracelsus, 104, 156, 167, 184
Paré, A., 156
Parker, P., 214
partition, 119, 117–20, 123,
   126–34, 196
Pascal, B., 67
patriarchy, 7, 13–14, 22, 66–71,
   135–6, 164–5, 181,
   186–7, 190, 200
Patterson, A., xxiv, xxv, xxvi, 159,
   192, 198
Pearson, D. W., 5, 163–64
Pechter, E., 215
Pepys, S., xx, xxi, 149, 196

Pericles, 13, 78, 163–64
Perkins, W., 195
Petrarch, F., 45
Phaedra, 5
pharmakos, 157
Phillips, R., xxii, 50, 175
Plato, 25, 28, 86, 96, 9, 131,
   Cratylus, 189
   Ion, 107
   Phaedrus, 36
   Sophist, 90
   Symposium, 17, 47, 48, 166
Plutarch, xvii, 3, 4, 9, 53, 105,
   166
Poole, R., 180
Preus, A., 164
Purdon, N., 78
Puttenham, G., 131
Pye, C., 174
Ragland–Sullivan, E., 162, 166
Randall, J. H., 189
Ransom, J. C., 196
Reformation, 6, 56, 165, 177, 185,
   195
Reik, T., 39
Rhoads, D. A., xxiv, 114
Richard II, 150, 164
Richardson, W. J., 162, 165, 178
Richman, D., 215
Richmond, H., 215
Ricoeur, P., 191–2
ritual, xix, xxv, 74–5, 93–4, 131,
   149, 187
Robbe–Grillet, A., 180
Roberts, J. A., 215
Robinson, J. W., 197
Romeo and Juliet, 107, 127, 142,
   148
Rose, J. R., 161
Rose, M., 173
Roustang, F., 162
Rowland, B., 77, 85

Rubinstein, F., 131, 197, 198
Rudd, N., 121

Sadler, J., 86
Salgado, G., xxi,
Sartre, J. P., 33–5, 49, 55, 90, 104,
   147, 172
Saussure, F., 140
Scarry, E., 143,
Schanzer, E., 216
Schlegel, A. W., 112
Schneider, M., xxiv, 159
Schwartz, R. B., 216
Scot, R., xviii, 81–2, 84, 86, 190
Scragg, L., xviii
Scrots, W., 174
self–centredness, 168
Seneca, 164
Serres, M., 156–7, 201
Sewell, E., xxiii, 104, 183
Shepherd, S., 53, 166
shifters, 103–4
Shylock, 13
Sidney, P. 21, 137
Siegel, P. N., 216
Silverman, K., 162
Simon, B., 217
Socrates, 47, 48
Southern, R., 196
Smith, J. H., 217
Snodgrass, W. D., 111
Snow, C. P., 156
Spenser, E., 53, 149–50
Sprague, A. C., 177, 182
Stallybras, P., 132
Stewart, S., 32
Stone, L., 162–63, 165, 166, 180
Strutt, J., 185
Stubbes, P., 130, 149, 156, 200
Studley, J., 164
Swander, H., 59, 179
synecdoche, 124, 133

Taming of the Shrew, 171
Taylor, A. B., 121,
Taylor, E. G. R., 27, 30, 169
Taylor, G. C., 217
Taylor, M. C., 16
Tempest, 65, 155
Tennenhouse, L., xxiv, 160
Testi, G., 184
Thiébaux, M., 90
Thomas, K., 177, 190
Thompson, A., 218
Thompson, A. and J. O., 7
Tieck, L., xxi
Tobin, J. J. M., 179
Toliver, H. E., 182
Topsell, E., 85–6, 91, 128, 173
translation, 121
Trewin, J. C., 177, 182
Troilus and Cressida, 37–8
tropes, 99, 107–8, 111–16, 191–3
Turbervile, G., 91
Turkle, S., 162, 183
Turner, V., xxv, 75, 198
Tuve, R., 192
Twelfth Night, 92

Van Gennep, A., xxv, 74–5, 94, 99, 198
Vergote, A., 218

Vlasopolos, A., xix
yvyan, J., xxiii

Walpole, H., 53
Warner, W., 181
Warren, R., 59, 175, 182
Welsford, E., 43, 173
Westlund, J. E., 16
Whatley, W., 180
White, T. H., 173
Wilden, A., 12, 129, 162
Willbern, D., 129, 195
Wind, E., 25
Winnicott, D. W., xxiv
witches, 30
woman, and seeing, 29
Wright, A. R., 183
Wright, C. T., 57
Wright, E., 173
Wyrick, D. B., 179

Yates, F. A., 170
Young, D. P., xix, xxii, xxiv, 43

Zilsel, E., 30
Zimbardo, R., xxii
Zitner, S. P., 120
Zukovsky, L., 168